ACROSS THE LINES

ACROSS THE LINES

Axis Intelligence and Sabotage Operations in Italy 1943-1945

DONALD GURREY

'Sent to spy out the land'

Foreword by
Lt-Gen Sir Edward Burgess KCB OBE

PARAPRESS LTD
Tunbridge Wells · Kent

In the same INTO BATTLE series:

Came the Dawn – 50 Years an Army Officer by Brigadier Paul Cook
Dual Allegiance – From the Punjab to the Jordan (WW2) by Monty Green
Haul, Taut & Belay – Memoirs of a Flying Sailor by Rear Admiral Sir Donald Gibson
Keep Your Head Down – Falklands Notes by Comdr Bernie Bruen
Let Go Aft – The Indiscretions of a Salthorse Commander by Cmdr H.G. de Chair
Letters from the Front – Letters of Lt Brian Lawrence, Grenadier Guards (WW1) by Ian Fletcher
Ordinary Naval Airmen by Jim Spencer
The Perilous Road to Rome Via Tunis (WW2) by Edward Grace
Soldier On! by Brigadier Joe Starling
Some Letters from Burma by Tom Grounds
They Gave me a Seafire by Cmdr Mike Crosley
Triumph and Disaster – The Autobiography of a Naval Officer by Cmdr Victor Clark
Wren's Eye View – The Adventures of a Visual Signaller (WW2) by Stephanie Batstone

© Donald Gurrey 1994
ISBN 1-898594-14-7

First published in the UK in 1994 by
PARAPRESS LTD
12 Dene Way
Speldhurst
Tunbridge Wells
Kent TN3 0NX

British Library Cataloguing-in-Publication Data:
A catalogue record for this book is available
from the British Library

Typeset by Vitaset, Paddock Wood, Kent
Printed and bound by The Ipswich Book Co Ltd, Suffolk

Contents

Foreword

This book deals with that little known aspect of war, the relentless struggle between Intelligence and Counter-Intelligence Agencies.

Before embarking on the detailed history of such operations in the Italian campaign, the author outlines the Commander's need for information, the methods of acquisition open to him and the opposition's actions to frustrate the gleaning of such intelligence.

This is then set in the context of Axis operations and Allied Counter-Intelligence in Italy between 1943-45. I can find no other definitive work where these threads are woven together.

The author is well qualified for his task having served on a Brigade Intelligence Staff in Tunisia, as an Air Liaison Officer and finally in Army Counter-Intelligence throughout the Italian campaign. As a German speaker he was well placed to examine Axis operations in depth and now analyse and describe them.

Although these events happened 50 years ago this book is invaluable to those involved with service intelligence and indeed to military historians in general.

17 June 1994   Lt-Gen. Sir Edward Burgess KCB OBE

Author's preface

While happily serving as an Air Liaison Officer in Italy in 1944 (having earlier been Brigade Intelligence Officer in the Tunisian campaign of 1942-43) I saw an Army circular calling for volunteers who could speak German and Italian. As I was due to return to Cambridge to read Modern Languages once the war was over, I reckoned it would help if I got a post which involved using these languages (which I spoke), so I put my name forward – in some trepidation, as the circular gave no indication of the nature of the work for which one was volunteering, and I was not a little worried that I might find myself being parachuted into Austria; not that I was averse to a bit of adventure, but I had been married just before going overseas, and was therefore a little reluctant to stick my neck out too far.

However, the reality was more mundane, and I found myself, after a language test, working in GSI(b) – the Army's Counter-Intelligence Branch, initially at HQ Allied Armies in Italy, located in the magnificent Palace of Caserta, and later at HQ 15th Army Group in Florence. This was a fascinating new field, involving tracking down and arresting the flood of espionage and sabotage agents – almost all of them, for obvious reasons, Italians – which the German Intelligence services were sending across into Allied-held territory. In the latter half of the Italian campaign we were catching something like 50 a month, few of whom managed to collect any useful intelligence for their German masters.

It is only in recent years that I have realised how little of all this intense effort by the Axis has been described and recorded, in spite of the intrinsic interest of the subject and the fact that many hundreds of books have been written about the many different aspects of World War II. Using material available in the Public Record Office and US Archives, and drawing on the recollections of a number of British officers involved in Counter-Intelligence work in Italy, I have tried to put together a cohesive account of these Axis activities, and of the Allied counter-measures, before the story sinks out of sight as we all die off.

The account would obviously have been much enriched if I had been able to track down former German intelligence officers who had served in Italy and were able to provide their side of the story. Sadly, in this I have had no success. There may be two factors which contributed to this failure. Many ex-members of the German Sicherheitsdienst were probably reluctant, in view of the not very savoury record of this organisation, to admit their past and prefer to keep a low profile; while a high proportion of Abwehr officers were, in 1939–45, middle-aged Reserve officers (chosen for their language abilities, usually acquired abroad as businessmen etc pre-war) who by now have either passed on or are in their eighties. I suspect that, even if I had been able to locate them, many would have had only failing memories of the events in question. It was typical of my luck – and something similar happened on several occasions – that SS General Wolff, the senior Sicherheitsdienst commander in Italy, actually died two days after I had posted a letter to him soliciting his help. The German side of the story has therefore had to be based largely on wartime documents, mainly the interrogations of GIS officers shortly after their final surrender in May 1945.

I would point out that much of the background material I have given on, for example, the OVRA, the X Flotilla MAS, the SID, the Black Brigades etc, described what the Allied Counter-Intelligence services knew, or deduced *at that time*; detailed post-war research may well have given subsequently a different slant to some of this data. So, lest any professional historian rise up in indignation as he reads it, I must quickly emphasise that these were simply the facts that we were using as our vade-mecum during the final period of the war, and in no way claim to provide a definitive history of them.

I should like to express my appreciation for the help and encouragement given to me by David Stewart (my wartime CO at GSI(b) 15th Army Group) and, at the Washington end, by Peter Tompkins, who has been most generous of his time and trouble; to Lt-Colonel Mike Jackson MBE for digging out some very useful documents at the Intelligence Corps HQ at Ashford; to Oberst Hans Krug a.D. for interesting documentation on the historical background and organisation of Wehrmacht intelligence, and other material; and to a number of former wartime colleagues who have been able to add their personal recollections of various aspects of counter-intelligence work during the Italian campaign.

I am grateful for willing help from the Imperial War Museum, Public Records Office and from several departments of the Ministry of Defence; and finally I should like to thank Mr Henry Mayer of National Archives Washington (Military Archives Division) for the trouble he has taken in making their records available to me.

1
Battlefield Intelligence

Many books have been written over the years on the subject of Intelligence, Counter-Intelligence and the exploits of secret agents. The field is a vast one; but it has tended to concentrate, no doubt to keep the reader's interest, on a selection of Causes Célèbres, although there have been occasional attempts to broaden the coverage of the subject in more professional detail.

Not a lot seems, however, to have been written on the sort of low level intelligence operations carried out by armies in the field, during times of war, aimed at providing immediate tactical information which could help the commanders on the spot to plan the next battle, indicate enemy weaknesses and targets, or give warning of what the enemy is up to.

The extent to which intelligence operations by armies in the field have been carried out has depended on a variety of factors. In classical times, and indeed right up to the early part of the present century, the commanders of such armies had relatively limited intelligence requirements, which basically boiled down to:

1. Where is the enemy?
2. What is his strength in numbers?
3. What are his intentions?
4. Where do his weaknesses lie?

– plus a certain amount of topographical information (is such-and-such a bridge still standing? Is there a ford over that river? Is the ground suitable for cavalry?).

Clearly, such overall subject-headings embrace other matters of keen interest to the commander in the field: for example, 'the enemy' may consist of several different bodies of troops, located in different places, sometimes considerable distances apart and even operating fairly independently (cf. Blucher and Wellington at Waterloo). As far as strength in numbers is concerned, he will want, if possible, a breakdown of the overall figure into cavalry, infantry and artillery, (or e.g. archers, elephants, tanks etc, depending on the historical period).

Both these categories of information would, historically, be obtained mainly by scouting troops of cavalry, and to a lesser extent by friendly (or cowed) tribesmen, by renegades, defectors and deserters, by prisoners taken, and to some extent by civilians who had arrived from enemy-held areas. At certain periods, and especially under certain enlightened commanders, there were also specially-trained intelligence-collecting units, such as the Corps of Guides, or scouts working directly to an officially-appointed Scoutmaster (at one time the third most senior appointment in the British Army).

Frequently, also, there would be the despatch of spies (often working direct to the Commander-in-Chief, as in the case of both Marlborough and Wellington) to collect such details, but the more important rôle for these was to attempt to cover the subjects described in 3 and 4 above, which could not easily be obtained from visual observation by cavalry or scouts. The heading 'enemy weaknesses' includes, of course, not only logistics deficiencies (shortages of food, fodder, petrol, ammunition and so on) but also, where the force is not homogenous, differences in nationality, character, motivation, allegiance, courage and discipline between the various groupings. Examples abound through history – tribes or regiments defecting from one side to the other, sometimes at the height of the battle; Scottish clans fighting against the English, but also at times against each other, or refusing to fall in with a battle plan devised by the leader of a rival clan. Eighth Army commanders in the Western Desert in 1941-42 frequently sought out those sectors of the front held by Italian units, rather than German troops, as the point of attack. Precise knowledge of the boundaries between different units, or the exact time when one division was being relieved by another, could all be usefully exploited if the information was available.

Additionally, in more recent wars, more technically-based intelligence can become, in the shorter time-span, of considerable importance to the commander in the field – where has the enemy laid his minefields? How will my own anti-tank guns cope with an attack by this new tank which the enemy is alleged to have on my front (i.e. is its armour so thick that our shells will simply bounce off it, and what steps must I take now in case this happens?) Has he got equipment which will enable him to cross that river, which at present protects my flank? Has he enough landing-craft to make a surprise attack from the sea well behind the front line?

Since the early part of the present century, moreover, two totally new means of gathering tactical intelligence have greatly expanded the range of options in this field: the aeroplane and the radio. Each has had a major impact, presenting both immense opportunities and (in so far as they are also available to the enemy) immense dangers.

The aeroplane took over, to a large extent (though not completely) the job previously done by cavalry and scouts; but it did a great deal more besides, since it could roam (the defences permitting) much deeper over enemy territory than the boldest cavalry patrol could usually hope to do. Its coming-of-age was on 22 August 1914, when a French airman spotted a German outflanking movement during the Battle of Mons. During the subsequent years of the Great War, air reconnaissance became a critical factor in military planning (not least because the trenchworks stretched from one extreme flank to the other and made any cavalry patrols impossible). Aircraft could not only locate (mainly by air photos) the positions of enemy guns and strong-points, so that these could be shelled, but more importantly, search for the vital physical indications that a major attack might be impending – the amassing of ammunition dumps, the movement towards the front of extra divisions, the laying of light railways to facilitate the resupply of ammunition once the attack had begun, and so on. Although the fighter 'aces' of the German and Allied air forces were the ones who attracted all the fame and glory, almost their sole rôle – at any rate until the final months of the war, when ground-attack aircraft were brought into play – was to protect the reconnaissance two-seaters from enemy attack (so that they could return safely to base with their photographs) and to prevent enemy observation aircraft from penetrating over their own lines. These rôles were expanded in the Second World War, when fast bombers themselves became a threat to operational planning, both by their ability to destroy vital bridges, blow up essential ammunition and fuel dumps, sink ships and block roads and convoys bringing up supplies. All these tasks were, however, largely dependent on prior intelligence to show where the targets were. In the future, of course, much of this type of intelligence will doubtless be provided by space satellites (provided these do not get destroyed by the enemy at an early stage, which would undoubtedly be his intention) and/or by 'drone' (pilotless) aircraft, carrying either cameras or TV transmitters.

The other new branch of intelligence-gathering which has blossomed since the First World War is that opened up by the use of radio communications by armed forces. The initial intelligence exploitation of this facility was made by the Allied and German navies during 1914-1918, mainly by the British, in order to locate the German U-Boats which threatened to strangle vital supply-lines; it proved to be an art of increasing subtlety, involving not only (where possible) breaking the enemy's codes, but also of becoming familiar with the patterns and habits of even individual morse signallers, so that a particular vessel could be identified merely by the manner and rhythm in which Signaller A or B used his morse key when transmitting, quite independent of the content of the message itself, which, even if the code was successfully broken, might give nothing away. The German Wehrmacht was quick to exploit this field in the Second World War, especially in respect of air intelligence. The Allies became aware of the need for tight radio security, and fighting units were trained to use codenames, coded unit identifications and map references to make things more difficult for the German Abhorchdienst (Listening Service).

Nevertheless, both inexperienced units (and the US forces were particularly weak in the early stages), and even experienced units in the heat of battle, could give a lot away.[1] In the latter situation it was of course of less importance, since events were usually moving too fast for the listeners to sort out the intelligence and pass it to fighting units who might be in a position to profit from it. Nevertheless it took a long time for the lessons to sink in, as Allied intelligence officers gradually became aware, from Enigma and from prisoners, just how much could be given away.[2] By the end of the war the standards were high. A document captured in August 1944 in Italy from a German unit commented favourably on Allied radio and telephone security, which was stated to have shown 'a degree of discipline never before attained'.

The Allies, too, were before long active in the same sector. Quite apart from the astonishing Enigma/Ultra operation, which had immense value, both strategically and, often, tactically, a lot of work was carried on by the 'Y' Service, covering the enemy's tactical signals. This not only enabled firm identifications of German units to be made, but on many occasions gave early warning of impending attacks, especially in the case of air attacks. On one occasion, in Tunisia in 1943, my divisional artillery received an urgent call from Corps HQ (which obviously originated in a Y Service interception of the Luftwaffe radio) to say that a Stuka squadron was just taking off and was to bomb our lines in the Bou Arada area, using as an 'aiming point' a round of mortar smoke shell, which the German troops opposite us were to fire onto our positions as the aircraft arrived overhead. Our gunners just had time to fire a round of 25-pounder smoke shell (much more visible than a mortar round) onto the German lines, so that the Stukas bombed their own troops as a result. The incident was very minor: but to hard-pressed troops crouching in wet and cramped fox-holes, the boost to morale was immense.

Probably the most important source of tactical intelligence to be mentioned is Prisoners of War (invariably abbreviated to 'POWs' in services usage). An army study paper dated 22 June 1942 on the subject of the interrogation of prisoners stated: 'It is estimated that at least 40% of our intelligence has been obtained from the examination of POWs.'

1. I recall my own Brigadier, during an attack towards Tunis a few weeks before the German defeat there, pressing the 'transmit' switch on his radio handset and calling 'Hullo . . . er . . .' – and then turning to me and asking urgently, with his radio still transmitting into the ether, 'What's the codename for the Ayrshire Yeomanry today?'
2. Almost worse was the damage done by an American Military Attaché in Cairo in 1941-42, whose nickname was 'Garrulous': he sent back to Washington a stream of signals, read by the Germans, giving details not only of military actions, of arms, aircraft and armour strengths, but also of operations which were impending.

It went on to add that the primary difficulty in examining POWs was to determine when and if they were telling the truth. By and large, however, the average POW from the armed service will, if he talks at all, tend to tell the truth as he knows it. Often he may not know accurate answers to the questions put to him, or will only be repeating 'scuttle-butt' that he has heard from his comrades. The average fighting Landser or Tommy or GI usually knows little, in the midst of a campaign, beyond what has been going on in his own unit and immediate vicinity; nevertheless even these limited facts can be of great help to the opposing interrogator, especially where personality information about the man's NCOs and officers is concerned, since if any of these latter are captured subsequently, it will enable the interrogator to find chinks in their armour and to give the impression that he knows everything about the unit concerned.*

Allied interrogators were often helped by the quantity of photographs – of their mates, their weapons or their homes – carried by German soldiers. In the British Army the possession of cameras by front-line troops was strictly forbidden, so that the only photos to be found on them, if captured, would be of their wives or sweethearts (or both). Our first detailed knowledge of the dangerous 'Tiger' tank came from photographs of it carried by an officer POW: on the other hand, he kept strictly to the 'Name, Rank and Number' formula, the maximum that a prisoner was obliged to reveal under the Geneva Convention, and refused to give any further information. At precisely the same period soldiers from a crack Wehrmacht parachutist unit were talking, to a skilled Canadian interrogator, both volubly and valuably.

POWs may be reticent on certain subjects, but will only rarely try to feed in false answers under interrogation, unless they have something to hide personally, such as SS atrocities, or incidents which reflect badly on them as individuals. This is, of course, not the case when enemy agents are interrogated; the latter will usually have every intention of concealing the truth as to why they were at the particular spot where they were captured, and how they have spent the previous days and weeks. As civilians, they cannot have recourse to the safety of the 'Name, Rank and Number' formula: they have to explain themselves, and it is here that they can be induced to make a full confession, once it has been shown that they have been lying. The innocent seldom have any reason to lie (though if they are deserters, criminals or black marketeers there may be certain aspects of their story they will wish to 'fudge'); but a captured agent, forced to tell a

*See illustration overleaf . . ., a photograph of an actual page from the author's notebook used when interrogating POWs in Tunisia in 1943. The details shown have all come from previous interrogations.

succession of lies (his 'cover story') has to be a very cool, very resourceful man if he is not to show his inner nervousness, especially once he has been caught out in his first falsehood.

Whether the POWs of one nation or another proved more secure under interrogation is difficult to assess. No POW who has 'spilled the beans' will wish to admit it afterwards, and statistics on the matter do not exist. Certainly on the Allied side enormous effort was put into subjecting worthwhile Axis POWs to skilled interrogation, and the results obtained were very great and very valuable. On the other hand, the author has spoken to British officers who were captured (one of them an Intelligence Officer, and therefore of potentially considerable interest to the enemy) who were only subjected to a very limited attempt at interrogation shortly after capture, and thereafter not at all.

An 'Order of the Day', issued by the Italian General Navarrini in 1943, read:

> When subjected to interrogation by our Intelligence Branch, all enemy prisoners refused firmly and categorically to give any military information whatsoever. They confined themselves to providing personal particulars and army numbers.
>
> More energetic demands and indirect questions intended to obtain certain details had no better success. The prisoners remained firm in their dutiful decision to obey the order not to talk, conscious of the fact that any other line of conduct would amount to treachery.
>
> I wish these facts to be brought to the notice of all units. Military honour demands that the spirit of dignity and pride of race should always be alive and present in the minds of our troops.

Against this, a former Wehrmacht officer who carried out a number of interrogations of Allied POWs in Italy has stated that many of them talked freely, especially air force crews. The reason in the latter case may be that the average aircrew, unlike the average soldier, did not basically envisage a scenario where he finished up as prisoner; it is unlikely that aircrews had the 'Name, Rank and Number' formula drummed into them quite as hard and frequently as fighting units of the Army. Moreover, it is much easier to get technically-minded prisoners (which is what most aircrews were) talking on non-sensitive technical matters, common to pilots and aircrew everywhere; once you have got a prisoner chatting, it is usually relatively simple to divert him to more interesting matters.

In their interesting book 'MI 9 – Escape and Evasion 1939-45', M.R.D. Foot and J.M. Langley (Bodley Head, 1979) quote a captured German intelligence officer in August 1944, who claimed that 'more than 85% of American POWs would give only their name, rank and number.

About 10% were responsive to the extent of giving orally their unit, and about 5% carried documents – mostly letters, notes and diaries – which gave valuable information.'

Nevertheless there can be no doubt that a number of Allied army prisoners did in fact talk fairly freely when interrogated; this is shown by an Intelligence coup in Italy shortly after the fall of Rome in June 1944, when the Allies captured the greater part of the Intelligence files of the German 14th Army Headquarters in one fell swoop. An analysis of the material in these files, which was written at the time, is quoted below in its entirety, since it illustrates not only the above aspect, but also shows what information the GIS was obtaining from radio intercepts, from agent reports and from prisoners, and at the same time the success which the Allies had achieved, both in security and in deception material, when planning the major attack which broke through the Cassino line and resulted in the capture of Rome. It will be seen that the GIS had 'identified' several Allied divisions which did not in fact exist – for example, '18th British Infantry Division', '6th Indian Division' and '31st Indian Armoured Division'.

The most significant item is a map showing our order of battle as known to the enemy on 12th May, i.e. the day after our attack began. This reveals serious gaps in the enemy's knowledge. He had on the whole a fairly accurate knowledge of the dispositions of those troops who had been for some time in the front line and which he had identified from prisoners. Thus he had correctly placed 85 and 88 US Divs, though he does not know under whose command they were. 4 and 78 British Divs are also correctly shown, though here again their subordination is not known (13 Corps HQ is shown at TERMOLI); 8 Indian Div is unlocated at rear of Army. 5 Corps and 10 Corps sectors are shown correctly though Corps HQs are wrongly located by a matter of a few miles, showing the limitations of location by D/F[1] (the same is true of 8 Army HQ, which is over twelve miles out and on the wrong side of the MATESE mountains; HQ Allied Armies Italy is shown in Naples).[2]

The mistakes are more surprising. In the French Corps sector only one French division had been identified; one other was unlocated in the rear and 3 DIA was shown at Salerno. In the Polish Corps sector only 5 Polish Div is shown forward, and 3 and 7 Polish Infantry and 2 Polish Armoured Divs are shown in reserve unlocated. The Canadian picture is very confused: 5 Cdn Armoured Div is shown at AQUAFONDATA

---

1. D/F = radio direction-finding (taking a bearing, from several different points, of a radio transmission).
2. Whereas it was in fact at CASERTA, 30 kilometres away.

under command Polish Corps, 1 Cdn Corps HQ is unlocated and 1 Cdn Div is shown at NOCERA. Some Canadian elements had, however, been identified by radio interception in the correct area, around MIGNANO. 6 South African Armd Div is shown by agents' reports as landing at TARANTO. At POZZUOLI large scale landing practices are shown as taking place on 7 May, involving an American division – according to agents the 36 Inf Division – and armoured formations. Finally the enemy carries on his map at PESCOPENNATARO (H 2564) the 18th British Inf Division, apparently identified by radio interception.

It will be seen that the picture presented to the enemy command was very faulty and corresponded exactly to what the Allied command wanted him to believe. He underestimated our strength in the area of our main attack by no less than seven divisions. As a result he credited us with having much larger reserves in the back areas and in view of this, and the fact that he believed at least three of these divisions to be on or near the coast, where landing exercises were going on, his appreciation was that our frontal attack was only a diversion and that we intended to carry out another landing in his rear. His dispositions on 11 May were clearly based on this belief; he had the minimum of troops in the line and his reserve divisions were disposed along the west coast to meet the landing which he confidently expected. As a result our attack was made in much greater strength then he expected (in the FEC sector, for instance, in more than four times the strength he expected) which greatly assisted our initial success. All German divisions in reserve were either grouped round the Anzio beach-head or strung out along the Western coast, and by the time the enemy had decided his fears of a landing were groundless, these reserves were so slow in reaching the scene of battle that they were drawn in and destroyed piecemeal.

This is a most impressive example of the advantages to be gained from thorough observance of security and counter-intelligence measures. All troops should be informed, now that this stage of the battle is ended, of the facts revealed by the above and it should be stressed that this success, which is due to our security measures and to the way in which they have collaborated by strictly observing them, has undoubtedly saved thousands of lives and been of the utmost assistance towards the victory that has been gained. It is recommended that unit security officers should use the facts given above in talks to the troops on the necessity of security; such a demonstration of its importance will go very far to remove any feelings of annoyance which may from time to time arise over individual security regulations.

The Situation Traces from subsequent dates show a gradual correction of the enemy's original false appreciation. For instance by 17 May the enemy had identified all four divisions of the FEC as being in action. By 23 May all formations on the Southern front had been identified in roughly their correct positions and in order to reduce this original underestimate the enemy has produced a 6 Ind Div and a 31st Ind Armoured Division, still retaining in the centre of the front his imaginary 18th British Div. It is natural enough that in the course of a battle the enemy should gradually find out what units are opposing him by taking prisoners, but it is unfortunately clear that Allied prisoners have been guilty of giving away a great deal of information. Interrogation reports have been captured giving the names of three officers and nineteen Other Ranks who were taken prisoner by 4 Parachute Division on 29 and 30 May. From interrogation the Germans were able to gain a considerable amount of information on the tactical situation and even on such subjects as Allied convoys. On the tactical situation prisoners gave away the strength and organisation of their own unit, with the names of their officers, the previous history and present intentions of their unit and their neighbouring units and the password for the day. One man revealed the name of an Allied division which had moved from this theatre to another. It is obvious what a danger to the Allied cause and to the lives of comrades such complete disobedience of security instructions entails. It is clear too that when the German interrogator is met by the proper refusal to give away information there is no attempt to apply pressure; in the case of four men the same interrogator who had obtained so much information from the others merely noted that he was unable to obtain any important information at all. However, some fairly important documents were captured with these men which should not have been exposed to the danger of falling into enemy hands.

In conclusion, the evidence made available by the capture of the intelligence documents of the German 14th Army shows that the Allies went into battle on 11 May 44 against an enemy almost entirely blinded by the fog of war. Misled as to where the main weight of our attack was to fall, he had placed his reserves where we wanted them, far away from the point of attack. From these mistakes he was never to recover and from then on he always found himself a move behind his opponent.

In the Italian campaign, the importance to the Wehrmacht of POW interrogation increased as time went on, due to the unsatisfactory situation in respect of other sources of intelligence. During the final months, when air reconnaissance had faded out almost completely and occasional periods of enhanced radio discipline baffled the German Listening Service, POW statements provided the best intelligence, with reliability assessed at 90%.

The following account of interrogation methods used at German 10th Army HQ was provided by the senior Ic officer himself:

1. *Direct Methods*

The most proven method of interrogation was comradely and decent treatment, giving the POW the impression: 'We are all soldiers together'. The interrogator acquainted himself with all known facts about the POW's formation and made liberal use of these during informal conversation. Everything was done to deny the POW getting the impression that he was being interrogated and wherever possible he was left to take the initiative in divulging information. It was attempted to make the POW feel at home in his natural milieu, so a sharp difference was made from a language point of view between the interrogation of British and American prisoners. The interrogator was obliged to be familiar with all topical slang expressions of the Army or formation concerned, and on principle no note-taking took place in the sight of the POW. Notes were either made by another interrogator, who overheard the conversation from an adjoining room, or else the interrogator himself reconstructed the results of the talk from memory.

If the POW was still strongly under the influence of his experiences at the front no time was lost in capitalising on his state of mind. In such cases it usually paid to ask direct questions until he answered them.

In many cases alcohol proved of invaluable assistance. Several interrogations proved to be much easier because the POW had been told by his officers that he would be shot by the Germans. This was particularly the case with some Italian troops and American negro troops, though in a few cases this applied to white troops as well. The most helpful subjects of interrogation – if they talked – were corporals and sergeants with long service, who often had a surprisingly wide knowledge of military details outside their own unit or field of activity. They could volunteer for example information on reserves, other units in the Mediterranean theatre, chain of command, reorganisation, new weapons etc. Private soldiers, though in many cases talkative, were seldom of much use because of their restricted knowledge. Officers were only of use if they fell for indirect methods (see below) or if, during protracted and friendly conversations over the lunch or dinner table, they could be induced to commit indiscretions.

2. *Indirect Methods*

The use of stool-pigeons often produced good results. The fact that Allied troops in the Italian theatre consisted of so many different nationalities made this type of indirect interrogation much easier, as it was possible for example for a versatile German to pass himself off as a

Canadian when talking to a New Zealander, and as a New Zealander when talking to an American. Interest in the other man's unit became in such circumstances much less suspicious.

In a few cases war-wearied Allied soldiers were found who would act as stool-pigeons. In one case an embittered and degraded British corporal brought good results for the Germans, for which he was rewarded with liquor.

For identification purposes questionnaires which included the name of the POW's unit proved very satisfactory. POWs were told that the filling up of these forms was a necessary preliminary to the announcing of the man's capture and the informing of his family that he was safe.

The use of concealed microphones was tried on several occasions by the interrogation team, but results did not compensate for the trouble involved. The microphones themselves were merely the normal field telephones and produced very bad results inside buildings. At a location near Avezzano the microphone was concealed in an electric light socket, and later it was hidden in the telephone. The members of the interrogation team acted as operators, but proved very unenthusiastic; owing to bad acoustics and unsuitable microphones the results obtained were of very slight value. The experiment was eventually discontinued.

The post-surrender interrogation of the Interrogations officer of 1 Para Corps (a Lutheran Pastor, operating far from the normal sphere of activity of his calling) gave further comments on the interrogation methods in use, in this case at a formation closer to the battle front: 'The first objective of 1 Para Corps interrogators was to obtain the POW for interrogation as soon as possible after capture i.e. while he was still suffering from the direct moral effect of it. The paratroops tended in the later stages of the war to fraternise with captured POWs, and the result was often to allow POWs to regain their presence of mind and thus make the task of the interrogator more difficult. In some cases, however, this was not of great account, because general war-weariness tended to make the majority of POWs more talkative.'

In some cases – e.g. at Corps Tactical HQ during a battle – no attempt was made to use subtlety on prisoners who were reluctant to talk; it was attempted by a brusque military-style interrogation, consisting of rapid staccato questions, to get the chief facts out at once, calling into play the psychological mechanism of the parade ground and military training. No use was made, on principle, of any form of vituperation or of language damaging to the soldier's personal 'dignity'.

In other circumstances the interrogation took the form of a conversation, in neutral tones, on 'well-known military facts', or of a 'free-running comradely chat' in which the psychological skill of the interrogator was often helped out by alcohol. The weak point for many British soldiers was an unwillingness to be 'rude' by giving a flat negative answer to a courteously-framed question. The ideal was to keep the POW unaware for as long as possible that he was in fact being interrogated; to this end he was often made to think he was merely at a POW Collecting or Transit Post. Among other tricks was the technique of asking the prisoner for his impressions of the Germans and the German military situation, thus allowing the conversation scope to move gently over to the Allied side by means of a series of comparisons.

Theoretically there was no limit to intelligence which could be obtained from POWs and deserters. On the Russian front at least, German experience was that, in practice, restraints were imposed by:

(a) insufficient numbers of POWs and deserters – both quantitively and qualitively
(b) limited willingness to talk
(c) limited knowledge
(d) poor interrogation facilities (time, place)

It was found that, in Stalin's Russia almost everything was classified as 'secret', so that even prisoners who were intelligent, of a high social level and were willing to talk, knew in fact very little about events, other than information of a most general kind.

There was another problem, more specific to Russia than anywhere else (except perhaps China). Of a population of some 200 million Russians, only some 120 million spoke and wrote Russian; the balance spoke at least 20 different other languages (not just dialects). If one includes the vast number of dialects, so different that a White Russian can hardly understand a South Russian, it can be seen that there were great problems in fully exploiting the POW potential.* The main weight of interrogation of 'front line' prisoners was carried out at German divisional level, often perforce using interpreters – something which invariably weakens the effectiveness of the intelligence officer putting the questions.

It does appear that, at least in the early years of the war, the British were ahead in the art of interrogation. Fritz von Werra was a Luftwaffe pilot who was shot down over Britain, interrogated and interned; shipped over to Canada, he escaped in 1941 and got back to Germany via South America – the only German POW to achieve this. He was able as a result to give

*In the early days of the war the author had, in his troop, a lad from Glasgow whose accent was so strong that he had to use the troop sergeant as an interpreter. If taken prisoner, he would certainly have totally baffled any German interrogator.

German Intelligence valuable information of British interrogation techniques, which were at once passed down to Luftwaffe aircrew in a booklet entitled 'How to Behave if taken Prisoner'. It advised that 'complete and persistent silence is the only defence against enemy interrogators'.

Von Werra was taken to 'sit in' on interrogations at Dulag Luft – the German interrogation centre where Allied aircrews were taken when captured. According to the authors of his biography[1] interrogation there had up till then been of a superficial, almost farcical, nature. He is said to have reported to Goering, Head of the Luftwaffe, 'I would rather be interrogated by half a dozen German inquisitors than by one RAF expert'.

NAME, RANK AND NUMBER

While the Dulag Luft interrogators seem to have accepted that 'Name, rank and number' was in reality all that a prisoner was obliged to divulge (however hard they might try to persuade the prisoner otherwise), this whole subject seems to be fraught with extraordinary confusion. German troops themselves, in their security training, were told that they not only were obliged to give name, rank[2] and number, but also home address, date and place of birth.

Major Pat Read, the Colditz escaper, in his book *Prisoner of War*[3] states that the POW's name, number *and unit* had to be reported to his country through the Protecting Power or the Red Cross. But in a later chapter, quoting the regulations on the treatment of POWs, it is stated that 'no form of coercion may be inflicted on prisoners to induce them to provide information other than surname, *date of birth* and army number'.

The most authoritative ruling seems however to come from the book *MI 9 – Escape and Evasion*, quoted above, p.11. The authors quote the actual wording of the relevant Geneva Convention paragraph, dated 27 July 1929, which lays down: 'Prisoners are to be treated humanely; no constraint is to be applied to those who refuse to give any information beyond their own rank, *or* their service number' (one must surely understand that they would have to provide their name as well). The authors go on to comment that 'the tag familiar to British and American servicemen, "Name, rank and number", was convenient to remember, and useful for administrators; it went beyond the letter of the law'.

Highly relevant in this context is the fact that every soldier wore permanently round his neck a string carrying his identity disc, stamped with his name, rank and army number. It is hardly realistic, therefore, to maintain that any of these details might be denied to the enemy, even if the Geneva Convention gave legal justification for so doing.

1. 'The One that Got Away', by Kendal Burt and James Leasor (Elmfield Press, 1973).
2. 'Deutsches Handbuch der Streitkräfte', 1944.
3. Hamlyn, 1984.

(a) *Line-crossers*

Once however a front line of some kind has stabilised for more than a few days, and especially where the terrain is broken, mountainous or only sparsely inhabited, the role of the 'line-crossing' informant assumes greater importance. His operation is made that much easier if there is plausible 'cover' available in the shape of a flow of genuine refugees, among whom he can conceal himself. Such a flow was readily available in Italy in 1943–45 – mainly from north to south – Italians who had been forced to move to the North earlier to work in the northern industrial cities, former members of the Italian armed forces who had deserted and sought to join their families in the south, girls separated from their fiancés, wives from their husbands etc. The same was true of large sectors of the Russian front, especially where the front line consisted only of a series of widely-spaced strong-points. In fluid battle situations, on the other hand, a large number of prisoners were often captured, the total sum of whose intelligence was better than that of a more limited number of line-crosser agents; in many cases they might also have documents on them, which were usually of appreciable value in contributing to the intelligence picture.

According to one German study, the Wehrmacht in 1942–44 had an average of 500–800 agents active on the Eastern Front, the Russians four times as many behind the German lines – a figure which does not include partisans.

(b) *'Stay-behind' agents*

Where an army is conducting a fighting retreat, or evacuating a region or country, there is almost always scope for its intelligence organisation to train, and install in suitable premises, together with long-term funds and, usually, W/T communications, agents whose intelligence tasks will begin once the enemy have occupied the area in question. Such agents, if reliable and secure, may be able to operate for considerable periods of time without being identified by the opposing counter-intelligence forces.

Agents dropped in by parachute, or landed from the sea, fall somewhere between the categories of Line-crosser and Stay-behind. Unlike Line-crossers, they can carry a W/T set with them with which to set up a reporting channel; but they still have the problem (unless they have reliable friends with whom they can take refuge) of finding somewhere secure to stay and from which they can operate.

A German analysis of sources of intelligence on the Russian front gave the following breakdown of the respective contributions of the main categories listed above:

POWS: 50%
Deserters: 17%
Captured documents: 12%
Radio intercepts: 16.5%
Agents: 4.5%

A similar analysis made by the German forces in Italy will be found in Chapter 17.

2
Factors Affecting the Collection of Intelligence

It follows from all the preceding paragraphs that a commander's intelligence requirements could, at least in theory, be fulfilled in a number of different ways, none of which would probably provide the whole story, but which, collated together, could expand and confirm each other. Nevertheless, one of the major problems for Intelligence staffs is that they may well be getting a mass of conflicting evidence, and have therefore to take great care in weighing the reliability of each item, bearing in mind that the enemy may well be 'feeding in' false information over one channel or another in order to mislead.

Moreover, not all these sources of intelligence may be open to the commander, or be sufficiently effective in terms of quantity or quality of the material, depending on a variety of external factors over which he may have little control. If one or more of these intelligence-collecting methods is unable to make sufficient contribution, he will need to attempt to increase activity in other sectors to make good the shortfall, in order to fill in, as it were, the gaps on the intelligence map.

Some of the external factors are as follows:

GEOGRAPHICAL

In the empty spaces and severe heat/sand conditions of the Western Desert, for example, the use of Line-crossing agents was almost impossible. Occasional use might be made of wandering Arab nomads, but their allegiance to one side or the other was highly unreliable and they were not much used (except of course to be questioned about the enemy if they appeared to have come from his direction). The German Abwehr did mount an operation in 1941 to get two English-speaking agents (Klein and Mühlenbruch) into Cairo, planning to land an aircraft in the desert and unload a motorcycle and sidecar, in which they would drive into the city; but the aircraft crashed and Mühlenbruch was killed. A second attempt was made by Count Almaszy, an Abwehr officer who was a desert specialist, using a special commando to escort two other agents, Eppler and Sandstede, far down to the south by truck, depositing them close to Assiut – a trip of some 1700 miles; from there they made their way to Cairo by train.* But apart

*Due to the distance and time involved (12 days) the operation can hardly be said to fall into the normal 'line-crossing' category.

from infiltrating agents into Egypt among refugees arriving from Greece and Turkey, these two operations seem to have been the only ones attempted. In such a situation the 'cavalry' solution offered the best scope, and both the Long Range Desert Group and, on the German side, the Brandenburg Regiment, carried out effective reconnaissance well behind the front line, over long periods of time. Such sorties had the advantage over air reconnaissance that they could also watch main supply routes by night, when most convoys would be moving because of the danger of air attack by day. They could also, if lucky, bring back prisoners with them for interrogation.

WEATHER

Weather can play a critical rôle in intelligence-gathering, in so far as mist and fog can ground reconnaissance aircraft, or else, over the target, prevent them from seeing what is going on below them (and preventing photography). The same may perhaps apply to some types of satellite observation in the future. The classic example was the Ardennes 'Battle of the Bulge' in December 1944, when fog hindered both observation of the preparations for the attack, and identification of its scope, size and direction once it had been launched. The stringent ban on the use of radio by the German units forming up for the attack provides yet another example of the important part which radio intercept intelligence can play – or rather, how the lack of it, especially linked to foggy weather, can leave a commander blind to his opponent's intentions. Line-crossing agents, had they been employed, could of course have given away the German plan and indeed, given the size of the forces involved, would have had little difficulty in realising, and reporting, that something big was afoot; but at that stage of the war, where the Allies had been moving fast across France and the Low Countries and were just reaching the German frontier, and where Enigma and air reconnaissance appeared to be providing satisfactory coverage of Wehrmacht activities, it is doubtful whether Allied intelligence agencies would have been under much pressure to provide line-crossing agents, or indeed whether they would have had time to find and train agents for such missions. In fact, it would have been hard to convince Allied commanders that such a need might arise; the idea of Hitler being able to scrape together a striking force of this size was not one which, at this late stage of the campaign, had crossed anybody's mind.

There are two other aspects of the effects of weather on intelligence operations – one of them adverse, one positive. Clearly, stormy weather at sea can make operations to land agents by boat almost impossible, just as deep snow, especially when coupled with icy weather, can render line-crossing on foot an exhausting, often hazardous, undertaking.

22

On the other hand, any snowfall over a few inches in depth can make the task of the photographic interpreter very much easier. While, under normal conditions, it is possible to camouflage to a reasonable extent (depending on the amount of time available and the amount of trouble one is prepared to take) gun positions, command posts, ammunition dumps, foxholes etc, using camouflage netting, brushwood, hay or whatever blends with the local landscape, a fresh layer of snow reveals at once every pattern of human activity. The snow around gun positions becomes trampled; tracks run between command posts and units; tank tracks show where a tank has been hidden under a haystack; barbed wire entanglements stand out against the white background. It is useless to shovel snow over tracks that have been made, hoping to conceal them: such shovelled snow in no way has the appearance of virgin snow, and would not deceive a trained photo interpreter for a moment. An attacking force has thus the best possible intelligence about the physical defences it is faced with.

THE TACTICAL SITUATION

A retreating army has few opportunities to take prisoners. Its cavalry (or armoured reconnaissance) units can stay around just long enough to identify the routes by which the enemy are moving up, and may possibly have a chance to identify the enemy units concerned before they, too, have to pull out. On the other hand such situations do provide an ideal opportunity, in inhabited areas (i.e. other than deserts or deserted steppes) to train and install what are termed 'stay-behind' or 'post-occupational' agents, who are deliberately left to be over-run by the advancing enemy. The aim will be to provide them with a sufficiently good cover story and funds to enable them to survive and report tactical intelligence – usually by radio in modern times, although pigeons, mail or personal contact (going back through the front lines once this has stabilised further on) have all been used. It goes without saying that the stay-behind agent needs to be totally fluent in the local language if he is to survive; usually he is a native of the country concerned, or the offspring of indigenous parents. Sometimes he may be able to pose as a national of a third country not directly involved in the conflict.

Another aspect of the tactical situation is that where the front line stabilises for longish periods, armies prefer, both for security reasons and because it is more reliable, to use 'line' communications (i.e. field telephones, with cable laid by their own signallers; or sometimes making use of existing telephone networks) between units and headquarters. Thus the Y Service (or the Abhorchdienst as the case may be) have little radio traffic to intercept and exploit. The history of Enigma confirms that German army keys used in Italy were not very productive once fighting had stabilised at the Gothic Line, because of the use of line communications.

23

This is perhaps a slight misuse of the term 'political': what is meant is a situation such as that in Occupied France in 1940–45, and in Northern (Nazi-occupied) Italy, where Allied intelligence units could make use of the existence of a potential, or actual, pool of indigenous intelligence-gatherers, who could be recruited by (or in many cases, linked up with) Allied agents or military personnel infiltrated or dropped into the regions concerned. The Allied agents (usually in teams of one Head of Network plus one or more radio operators) would then act as two-way channels to the intelligence staffs in the UK (or at secure locations overseas), briefing the local networks on what intelligence was required and sending the answers back to base. Such agents would not a priori always need to be able to pass as natives; sometimes they could be given protection by their local groups, or might operate from within reasonably safe country areas loosely held by the Resistance or Maquis. By the end of the war in Italy some 35 such radio links in North Italy were being 'worked' from the Allied agent W/T base at Bari.

A single agent, such as the OSS agent Peter Tompkins in Rome at the time of the Anzio landings, could play a vital rôle in reporting by radio a broad range of tactical intelligence collected by a wide network of local Italian helpers – from the identity and movements of German units passing through the city, bombing targets suitable for attack by Allied aircraft, the results of such bombing, lists of addresses in Rome which were of counter-intelligence interest, down to indications of German military intentions (e.g. to defend the city, or make a fast retreat northwards). In a highly fraught situation such as existed at the time, with frequent German *razzias* (see Glossary), critical food shortages, and very numerous Fascist informers, such operations call for the highest degree of courage and quick-thinking by the individual agent.

THE AIR SITUATION

As has been shown, air observation plays a critical rôle in the ability of the commander to find out what his opponent is up to on the battlefield. The value of Allied air supremacy by the final year of the Second World War lay not merely in the advantage of being able to attack targets inside enemy-held territory more or less at will, but also in its denial to the Wehrmacht of any direct observation inside Allied-held areas. An astonishing report from Oberbefehlshaber Südwest★ (i.e. the German Command HQ in Italy), dated 3 February 1944, discussing the German failure to foresee the

★See Appendix A for full text in English.

DOLMANN, capo della Gestapo, Pensione Pfister, Pzza della Trinità dei Montil.

SCOTTI, spia delle S.S., Albergo Dragoni, p° IV° stanza No 73, Largo Chigi.

SEMPREBENE Achille, di Vittorio n. Roma 27/9/906, lavora per la Gestapo; Vle Parioli 95.

STERN Gottardo di Gustavo n. Vienna 13/12/893, maggiore dei bersaglieri, spia al servizio dei tedeschi; V. Mondovì 38 p° II° int. 5.

TEDESCHINI Cleto fu Francesco n. Vignarello 28/10/898, squadrista, spia pericolosa. Pzza S. Giovanni in Latera no 48.

KUNST Elisa fu Francesco n. Ganulscho (Austria) 18/11/889, la sua trattoria in V. Tre Cannelle 26 é frequentata da molti soldati tedeschi e dalla Gestapo. AB. in Vicolo Paganica 23.

NISTRI Pierfrancesco di Angelo n. Santacroce sull'Arno (Pisa) 4/4/909, spia de le S.S.V. delle Tre Madonne 12, tel. 874883.

NOVIELLO Antonio di Angelo n. Roma 1/10/921, é nei Battgl. 'M'; pericoloso. V. Sabotino 2A.

PALOZZI Giuseppe di Benedetto n. Roma 6/8/926, é nei Battgl. 'M', ha ucciso il magistrato socialista, Mario Fioretti. V. Guerrazzi 6, tel. 582890.

RICCI Renzo fu Giulio n. Savona 30/11/912, segretario di GRAZIANI. V. Felice Cavallotti 4 int. 10.

SACCHI Romeo fu Giuseppe n. Milano 5/2/882, spia dei tedeschi, ha fatto arrestare inglesi ed ebrei. V. Palestro 13.

ANDREI Carlo, spia pericolosissima dei tedeschi, Pzza Gentile da Fabriano 3.

ANNIBALI Renato fu Umberto n. Roma 20/9/902, capo squadra milizia fascista pericoloso. Ha il negozio di materassa io in Pzza S. Eustacchio 51.

BERTE' Enrico Rodolfo di Giorgio N. Aldobiadine (Treviso) 1/7/894, col., spia dei tedeschi.

KOLMAR Olga (Von), tedesca, vive da 4 anni in Italia, denunciatrice di ebrei al servizio della Gestapo. Albergo Imperiale, V. Veneto 24.

LIMONGELLI Luigi, giorna lista, spia. V.E. Stewenson 24, tel. 850246.

NARDI Ga stone di Luigi n. Firenze 21/10/897, a ddetto a ll'ufficio recluta mento del P.F.R., spia al comando tedesco; il figlio Luigi é volontario nei Battgl. 'M'; il Nardi é in subaffitto presso Lucia Bagli in Corsenengo. Corso Trieste 165 int. 5.

CHIARISSI Lucci, spia delle S.S., V.S. Alessio II, tel. 581006. Ufficio F.I.N.F. A.V. Bocca di Leone 25, tel. 64964.

CRISMAN Nino, spia. V. Lunigia na 15, tel. 866604.

FONZI Marta, spia pericolosa delle S.S., é bruna, ondula ta, con una frezza binca. Ha una rosticceria in V. Cavour 289. Ab. in Via del Boccaccio 25, tel. 45962.

Anzio landings on 22 January, stated that 'they had had no intelligence either before or after the landings', and admitted that there had been no air reconnaissance of the Naples area since 11 December 1943 – i.e. a gap of no less than six weeks in coverage of the Allies' main supply port. Nor had they installed sufficient (or sufficiently effective) stay-behind agents in Naples to ensure that at least one network was reporting. On other occasions, sabotage agents were sent in to AOT with missions to destroy aircraft on airfields which were not, in fact, being used by the Allies – something which even a high-level air reconnaissance would have established beyond any doubt.

In fact, according to German intelligence sources interrogated immediately after the campaign, the only occasion when air photography played an appreciable part in Italy in completing the intelligence picture was at the Anzio Beachhead, when by concentrating the whole of the available aircraft resources on this comparatively small area it was possible to obtain regular coverage of the front by air photography. The photos proved invaluable for the selection of artillery targets, for establishing exact locations during POW interrogations and for the correction of battle maps.

CONCLUSION

General Frido von Senger und Etterlin, Commander of the German XIV Panzer Corps, has written in a book about the battles of Cassino:

> The German leaders were almost always caught by surprise, as their intelligence lacked some essential factors. The Air Force was practically done for. While being pushed back, enemy prisoners are rarely brought in. Italian agents worked for both sides, but most of them hoped for an early victory of the Allies and therefore probably put in sincerer zeal for the Allied side.

In spite of the latter factor, agent-running was one of the few ways left open to the Germans to try to improve the supply of intelligence to their battlefield commanders. It will be the object of this book to describe how the German Intelligence Services in Italy, with some help from Italian Fascist units, sought to organise intelligence-gathering and sabotage operations, and to show how such operations were parried and frustrated by the Allied Counter-Intelligence services.

3
Military Security – The Whys and the Wherefores

Security can never be absolute, only relative; it is not an end in itself, but only a means to an end. There can thus be no absolute standards, principles or measures of security which can or should be applied to every situation: they should be applied only in relation to other factors in the situation and as far as other, possibly over-riding, considerations may permit.

Military security consists of two main strands, a warp and a woof, each knitting together to form as waterproof a fabric as possible. One of these strands is the existence of trained counter-intelligence personnel who can direct specific measures aimed at identifying and catching enemy agents, and, when they are caught, utilising to the maximum such information as can be obtained from them about the enemy's existing and future intelligence and sabotage operations. The other is the setting up of physical military and civilian controls on travel, movement, access to sensitive areas, dumps and ports, postal censorship etc, aimed at making it more difficult for enemy agents to achieve their objects. Each of these two aspects will be studied in more detail below.

To become more effective, security of necessity has to become more oppressive. If the civilian population in the country in question (either in one's own country, in occupied territory or in battle areas) can be treated as unreliable or hostile and be subjected to harsh measures (for example, no one is allowed to move out of his own town or village; or curfews are imposed, limiting movement to a few hours a day) then security is easier to attain. Against this, harsh measures may well result in active resistance by the population in question, leading to partisan or sabotage activity, and thus to an increase in the security problem rather than an improvement. In Italy, the German forces were caught in a cleft stick over just such a problem. The Italians were originally their allies, but then mainly defected to the other side. Of those located in German-occupied Italy, a number were pro-Fascist, but many more were, by 1944, anti-Fascist and anti-Nazi – or merely wanted the war to end. The terrain in North Italy was admirably suited to partisan resistance, and the latter tied down very considerable German and Fascist forces, and was a factor which German commanders always had to bear in mind when moving troops or supplies. They were thus faced with the difficult problem of whether to treat the population as friend or foe.

There were several notorious cases of the execution of innocent hostages by German forces (mainly the SS) as a result of attacks on German troops by the Resistance. Even disregarding these, however, there was a general deterioration in the German attitude towards the Italian civilian communities in Northern Italy as the war progressed, not helped by the deportation of Italian males for forced labour in Germany. At Appendix B is the text of a letter from Mussolini to the German Ambassador to Italy, which shows all too clearly the oppression that was being imposed. In that part of Italy occupied by the Allies, in contrast, their armies were by and large welcomed as liberators, and while small nuclei of Fascist supporters were to be found in various places, there was never any sign of an effective resistance movement (or even of small bands of partisans) taking root, even though parts of the terrain, for example in the wild Aspromonte mountains* of Calabria, would have been admirably suitable. Allied security measures had, therefore, to bear in mind the need, wherever possible, to avoid spoiling this atmosphere. There was indeed, among Allied troops, and dating from quite early days of fighting in the Western Desert, an awareness that the Italians as a whole were not exactly keen on the war and were happy to be rid of the Germans, so that there was a not unsympathetic feeling towards the ordinary Italian civilian and a readiness to let bygones be bygones. From the security point of view, therefore, there were in Italy daily situations in which the requirements of security conflicted with the demands of operations or administrative expediency, or with the needs of the civilian population and the efforts of Allied Military Government to enable an effective and friendly Italian administration to run the liberated areas.

A classic example, in the purely military sphere, of the conflict of interest which could arise was the controversy, which had in fact raged for years, over the wearing of divisional emblems on the sleeve of the individual soldier's battledress (and the marking of similar emblems on the unit's vehicles). There was possibly no single measure which would have contributed more handsomely to security than the total abolition of such signs: and they remained one of the basic items of intelligence which every German agent was instructed to note and report – moreover one which he could observe without risk to himself. But the advantages of these signs, from the point of view of morale, esprit de corps, traffic control and discipline generally were considered to outweigh their detrimental effect on security – so the signs remained in use.

Other conflicts could arise in the imposition of postal censorship, and in the enforcement of civilian movement regulations, the issue of curfew

*Nowadays the principal area used by Mafia and Camorra kidnap gangs for hiding their victims while ransom negotiations are under way.

passes and, especially, the internment of civilian officials whose administrative efficiency might be as high as their political and security rating was low. It was essential to distinguish between the needs, and the convenience, of the civilian population. While the demands of military security could not give way to civilian convenience, they had occasionally to be modified to meet the real needs of the people, especially in respect of food, health and the restoration of essential industries. A specific example of the problems which could arise was one in which the author was himself directly involved, when Italian saboteurs landed from the sea near Rimini and blew up four RAF vehicles. The area was one of closely-packed holiday villas, all of which were now crammed with civilian refugees, even to the extent of two married couples sharing one tiny garage, with a blanket hung between them. It was, moreover, a bitterly cold winter. Within hours of the explosions, and before it was found that the attack had in fact come in from the sea, the Security Officer of the RAF unit was adamant that the entire civilian occupants of the area must be cleared out, since he considered that it was from among these that the attack had come. The bitterness and hardship which such an evacuation would have engendered can be imagined and the author argued strongly against it, both on humanitarian and practical grounds. Fortunately the sabotage party was captured a few hours later, so that the issue did not come to the crunch.

There were also not only conflicts between security and other interests, but also occasional cases where security was divided against itself. For example, the banning of civilian mail services in the forward areas, which was primarily a security measure designed to prevent leakages of information, tended to increase the amount of illicit travel between the rear and forward areas, since many people in these areas were determined, for family, romantic or business reasons, to make contact with each other in any way they could, regulations notwithstanding. The problem of priorities had to be solved by a consideration of the relative dangers which might result from the measure itself, on the one hand, and from its repercussions on the other. Those engaged in security work needed therefore not just tenacity of purpose and imagination, but flexibility of method and approach. The immediate objective was security: but the purpose of security was to assist in the defeat of the German Army, so that this latter was the real and ultimate aim of all security measures and all security personnel. The latter could (or should) not allow security to clog the machine which was designed for, and engaged in, the defeat of the enemy. They had to judge when to insist on security requirements as a first priority, i.e. when these would make for greater efficiency of the machine, or when to modify such requirements in the light of other factors of equal or greater significance, when insistence on the security measure could cause a breakdown or loss of efficiency in the working of the machine as a whole.

4

Military Security: the Allied Counter-Intelligence set-up in Italy

The basic manpower of military security in the British Army was (and is) provided by Field Security Sections (FSS). The US equivalent was the CIC (Counter-Intelligence Corps). The French Securité Militaire also lent expert assistance in Naples and Rome, as well as carrying out its normal duties with the French Expeditionary Corps. Since the Allies in Italy were almost fully integrated at higher levels, senior Counter-Intelligence officers at Army Group level and above might be British, American or occasionally French, all working together in the same sections. At lower levels, the CIC mainly operated in the US 5th Army zone, the FSS in Eighth Army areas: but further behind the lines both CIC and FSS would operate together, with whatever allocation of towns, areas or duties appeared most convenient or effective.

Each fighting division had its own FSS/CIC section; these would be the first people to deal with any suspect persons found in the divisional area. Behind them, at Corps and Army levels, there were further FSS and CIC sections, sometimes allocated to specific towns, sometimes to specific duties. (No. 300 FS Section, for example, was responsible for the handling of British agents, both on their outward journeys to enemy territory, and after they 'clocked in' with front line troops on return; they handled the administration, transport and general 'nursemaiding' of such individuals, and manned suitably-located reception points close behind the forward areas of the fighting front.)

The work of FSS and CIC was directed by GSI(b) officers (G-2 in US parlance) at Corps, Army and Army Group levels. GSI(b) officers were generally, but not invariably, members of the Intelligence Corps; a number of other officers were seconded to such work from other arms or regiments as the work-load increased – an ability to speak German and/or Italian being one of the main requirements. The collation of information about enemy agents, its analysis and the passing of guidance material, 'Wanted' lists etc to lower formations was mainly carried out at 15th Army Group, where the GSI(b) section numbered some eight officers, both British and American. Behind 15th Army Group was HQ Allied Armies in Italy (AAI), located, from early 1944 onwards, in the palace of Caserta. The latter too had its own GSI(b) section, which covered security events in areas outside the forward areas (for which 15th Army Group was responsible) and issued further counter-intelligence or security guidance papers, usually of a wider nature.

To give some idea of the number of units involved, the following was the allocation of Field Security and CIC detachments to the front line areas in Italy in May 1945, excluding those which operated in the rear areas (Rome, Naples etc):

5th Army: 3 CIC detachments, 2 Italian Security units
IV Corps: 4 CIC detachments, 1 Brazilian CIC (with the Brazilian Division), 7 FS sections (of which one was South African, one Polish)
8th Army: 2 CIC detachments, 18 Field Security Sections (of which one New Zealand, one Polish)

It will be seen that the counter-intelligence scene was a highly international one, which however worked together surprisingly well.

Working alongside the above organisations were other units of considerable importance in the counter-intelligence battle:

(a) the SCI units (Special Counter-Intelligence Units), of which there were four – three British (SCIs 1, 2 and 3) and one American (SCI/Z)
(b) CSDIC – the Combined Services Detailed Interrogation Centres
(c) SIM/CS – Italian Army Counter-Intelligence on the Allied side
(d) No 1 ICU (Intelligence Collecting Unit), also known as 'S' Force

Details of the above units are given in the following paragraphs.

THE SCI UNITS

These were specialist and relatively secret counter-intelligence units, each numbering five or six officers, whose task was to seek suitable openings for the exploitation of captured enemy agents. This included not merely the 'turning' of the agents themselves (if they agreed to cooperate), but also the use of their W/T sets and codes, their code-names and other essential details – that is to say, the agent himself could sometimes be dispensed with in running a 'play-back' or deception operation if it was felt that this could be done with sufficient verisimilitude to convince his German 'control' that all was in order.

SCI officers were usually experienced interrogators and were brought in at an early stage after an agent's arrest; this was essential, since if the case appeared a promising one, his signals link back to the Germans had to be activated without delay in order to avoid arousing suspicion.

SCI units came under direct command of AFHQ in Algiers, but were instructed to work in close conjunction with HQ, Allied Armies in Italy and with 5th and 6th Armies. They had access to especially sensitive intelligence (including Enigma) concerning the GIS, which could not, for security reasons, be distributed and acted upon in the normal way, for risk of compromise. They were specifically responsible for the penetration of enemy intelligence services, but had no rôle in the enforcement or supervision of more routine military and civilian security measures.

CSDIC: THE COMBINED SERVICES DETAILED INTERROGATION CENTRES

These centres, manned by Army, Navy and Air Force linguists, provided the essential skilled interrogation personnel who dealt with both enemy armed services prisoners, and with captured agents.

The successful interrogation of POWs requires certain conditions which can be satisfied only in some organisation operating solely for that purpose; in particular, it requires that the interrogator should have the very latest information in detail so that (a) he can be enabled to break down the mental resistance of the prisoner, and (b) he may recognise important information when it is alluded to by the prisoner during his examination. This entailed having different sections of CSDIC to specialise in each of the three services, and another section to deal with enemy agents, since the interrogator, to be successful, had to be at least as knowledgeable as his prisoner on the specialist aspects of the individual's activities, on the specialist terms he would use as a matter of course in his work, and wherever possible on the names of the man's comrades and superior officers.

The first CSDIC was set up at Maadi, six miles from Cairo, in December 1940, where some 60 prisoners could be 'processed' at any one time. From mid-1941 CSDIC also supplied interrogators for 'forward interrogation' close behind the front, so that tactical intelligence could be obtained from prisoners during the course of a battle, in time for it to be exploited tactically on the spot.

'Stool pigeons' were used by the Navy and Air Force, but almost not at all by the Army. They were of great value in security/counter intelligence interrogations; two of the most successful, used by CSDIC in Egypt, were former enemy agents, who became first-class interrogators.

CSDIC HQ in Italy was set up at Portici, near Naples. Another unit worked at Bari, on the east coast, called SILO, which screened the thousands of refugees reaching Italy from the Balkans and interrogated suspects or identified GIS agents; they held extensive records on the Balkans in general and on Yugoslavia in particular. By early autumn 1944 a Counter-Intelligence section of CSDIC had been set up in Rome, consisting of approximately six officers, whose function was the detailed interrogation of enemy agents, suspects and 'persons of special security interest' (the CSDIC unit in Florence, for example, found itself, soon after the German surrender, interrogating Frau Himmler and her daughter). Given the limited size of the section, and the very large number of enemy agents being arrested, it was not possible for each and every arrested GIS agent or suspect to be given a full CSDIC interrogation; the following categories were soon laid down for those who were to be processed in this way:

(a) important enemy agents who were thought to have much useful information to reveal
(b) enemy agents who appeared to have valuable information, but who were unwilling to talk
(c) persons who were strongly suspected of being enemy agents, but would not admit it
(d) other persons of exceptional security interest, from whom important CI information was to be extracted – e.g. senior OVRA officials, Fascist Republican Ministers etc.

Agents of no special significance were only to be given a tactical interrogation by SCI, CIC/FSS or SIM(CS) (see below).

An Italian CSDIC was also formed from SIM staff, under the control of Lt-Colonel Revetria, Head of the Ufficio 'I' of SIM, initially to help deal with the acute problem of screening the flood of civilian refugees. Lt-Col Revetria selected a few Italian officers whom he considered suitable for CSDIC work, and these were trained by one of the British members of CSDIC in the arts of detailed interrogation, eventually becoming the nucleus of SIM/CSDIC. By November 1943 they were issuing their first reports, and were especially useful in the interrogation of the numbers of Italian services personnel who were coming south after deserting from Fascist Republican units in the North. Before long SIM/CSDIC officers were appointed to be attached to the Refugee Interrogation Points (RIPs) operated by both 5th and 8th Armies in forward areas close behind the front lines.

SIM/CS (CONTRO-SPIONAGGIO)

That part of the Italian Army Intelligence Service which remained with the Badoglio Government was originally part of the Comando Supremo of the Italian Army. Collaboration with the various Allied security and Counter-Intelligence agencies in Italy, though slow to develop, became by degrees both close and sincere, and proved to be of considerable value to Allied Intelligence. By mid-summer 1944 it had been gradually expanded and entrusted with progressively increasing responsibilities. In order to place it on a more satisfactory footing it was reorganised in August 1944 as an entity separate from the Comando Supremo and became the Italian CS Battalion, with its own separate establishment. Its strength was set at 1000 all ranks, headed by Major Dotti, who had given full cooperation to the Allies and was held in high esteem by them. SIM/CS set up centres in Milan, Bologna, Turin and Trieste as soon as these were liberated.

The unit also established a coast-watching service to look out for landings by enemy agents, and for suspicious activities by residents of coastal areas.

NO.1 ICU ('S FORCE')

The Intelligence Exploitation Force, or 'S Force' (later to be formalised as No 1 Intelligence Collection Unit) was defined as 'a force embodying representatives of recognised Intelligence Agencies, designed to deal with the confused period, both military and political, which normally follows the capture or liberation of a large centre of population by combat troops.'

During this 'confused period' S Force was to carry out the exploitation of intelligence objectives, such as the seizure and safe-guarding of documents, archives etc and the arrest of enemy agents and major sympathisers. It was recommended that the organisation of the force should be flexible, but based on a permanent nucleus of trained and experienced personnel to which the necessary protective troops, transport etc would be assigned in the planning stages of an operation. It had also to be able to sub-divide itself in order to be able to deal with multiple targets at the same time.

After the capture of Tunis and Naples, where only ad hoc arrangements had been made, two main defects were demonstrated: inadequate detailed planning and preparation of intelligence target information, and lack of any continuity of command and staff. Accordingly, more detailed arrangements were put in hand in preparation for the capture of Rome, and a considerable body of specialists – mainly intelligence and counter-intelligence officers and NCOs – was assembled some months in advance. Targets were not, of course, purely GIS unit premises and agents; the Italian Armed Services minstries, major banks and other governmental establishments all had to be seized at the earliest possible moment to prevent possible destruction or pillaging, and to enable important intelligence documents to be safeguarded. In consequence, the 'S Force' for Rome included considerable numbers of RAF, RN and Army intelligence officers on temporary loan. The OC of the force was an American, Colonel George Smith, GS(Int) of 15 Army Group.

The Rome 'drill' was worked out well in advance and was so successful that it was decided to retain the essential elements of the Force as a permanent body, to be called No.1 ICU, which was used subsequently in Florence and in all the main cities of the Po Valley.

5

Military Security: the Practice

Military security disciplines, as exercised in individual units, had an important rôle to play in neutralising enemy espionage and sabotage activities: they could not only prevent the agent from effectively carrying out his mission, but could also facilitate his detection. Civil and military security were complementary in this; each presented a considerable obstacle to the enemy agent, while both together, if working properly, could make the obstacle almost insuperable.

Military security, where it applied to information (as opposed to material), aimed at preventing the soldier's own words or actions from providing the enemy with intelligence, so that nothing was handed out to him 'on a plate': as one contemporary security instruction put it, he must be made to 'come and get it' i.e. to emerge from his obscurity and risk making himself conspicuous.

The force of this distinction can be seen by comparing the chances of survival of two agents, A and B, one operating in an area or among troops where security was weak, and one where it was good. A could sit and listen; B had to ask questions. A could find documents in rubbish heaps or cloak-rooms, B had to attempt to steal them from offices. A could enter a military area or HQ through the main gate unchecked; B had to climb over a wall. A gets driven through military road-checks in a military truck in which he has cadged a lift; B has to make detours round them on foot. Examples were legion. An officer in one British unit in Italy, in 1945, reported that he thought an Italian girl employed by one Army unit was worth investigating as, although she claimed to be Italian, she spoke with what seemed to be a German accent and had from time to time asked questions on military subjects; she had also, on one occasion, asked an Italian acquaintance where she could obtain certain radio parts.

On checking records, the local Field Security Section found that, although an army application for the 'vetting' of the lady had been submitted, it had not yet received security clearance pending further routine enquiries. It was later found that the unit had in fact already been employing her for two months before they had applied for clearance to do so.

Acting on these two leads, the FSS decided to search the flat in which she was living. This was done while she was out one evening at an Allied officers' dance. Positive evidence was found to justify her immediate arrest as an enemy agent on her return – an arrest which would never have taken place if the officer in question had not been alert.

The effective security control of the civilian population, both in movement and communications, the supervision of hotel registrations, the internment of doubtful elements, and the 'vetting' of applicants for Allied employment – was an important element in apprehending enemy agents. These measures were routine and humdrum, and of all the leads that needed to be followed up, only one in twenty turned out to be of real interest. Much painstaking and apparently unrewarding work had therefore to be constantly undertaken, and not allowed to become casual in its implementation.

To effect control of civilian movement, Allied Occupied Territory (AOT) was divided into three different sectors:

(a) Army and Corps areas. Here civilians were forbidden to travel more than 10 km from their homes without an Allied Military Government pass. These areas lay between the front line and what was designated the Rear Army Security Control Line (RASCL), usually some 25-40 km to the rear. The defining of this line was the responsibility of GSI(b) at 15th Army Group, and it was of course advanced at intervals as the front line itself moved up the peninsular.

(b) territory under Allied Military Government administration. This lay to the rear of the RASCL and stretched for a considerable distance southwards. Here civilians were forbidden to travel from one province to another within the area, or into this area from what was designated 'King's Italy' – that is, the rest of Southern Italy not falling under the above two categories.

(c) Within 'King's Italy' there was no restriction of movement, nor within Sicily and Sardinia. A pass was, however, required for moving between Southern Italy, Sicily and Sardinia.

In addition to the above restrictions, the main security weapon was the establishment of a widespread system of 'snap' check posts in the Army and AMG areas, established for a few hours daily at irregular times and varying points. Similar check points were set up in the Italian Government areas by the Carabinieri and Guardia di Finanza. Such control points provided a real hazard, not only to those (relatively innocent) persons moving without the necessary documentation, but also to GIS agents, who could suddenly find themselves, round a bend in the road, obliged to produce identity papers and a valid reason for their presence at that spot.

One GIS agent who had travelled fairly widely in AOT admitted under interrogation that after a previous mission he had made the following recommendations to the GIS on how to pass through road blocks without a permit:

36

(a) Carry no luggage. You can then pass as a local inhabitant.
(b) The average Carabiniere is obstinate and ignorant. Speak to him with a Northern accent. If he is a Southerner, he will be impressed. If he is himself a Northerner, you will establish a bond of sympathy with him.
(c) Use long and complicated words when talking to a Carabiniere. This will confuse the issue and further impress him. His usual answer will be: 'All right, you can pass this time, but don't let it happen again.'
(d) The best form of civilian transport is a lorry carrying foodstuffs or other goods. You can say you belong with the lorry and are responsible for loading and unloading it.

Anyone staying in a hotel overnight had to give full personal details to the hotel owner, who had to send these details in a 'Scheda di Notificazione' to the local police station within 24 hours. FSS/CIC carried out periodic checks of these lists at police stations in their area. Three agents were arrested in a single month as a result of such routine checks; names would be compared with the 'wanted' list held by FSS, compiled largely from the interrogation of arrested agents.

There were other, less direct, ways in which these hotel registers could prove useful. A girl called Lea Pacini was arrested north of Florence and refused to admit any connection with the GIS. She was finally taken to a skilled Canadian interrogator working at 5th Army HQ. She proved equally obdurate under his interrogation, but he was convinced that her name was *not* Lea Pacini, and that she was not Italian. He noticed that she had with her some quite nice personal possessions with the initials 'LP' marked on them. Aware that the Abwehr and SD had used a number of the Florence pensions and hotels to lodge their agents and officials, on a hunch he asked all the counter-intelligence units in Florence to check the hotel registers for a girl with these initials. After a long search an FS section came up with the particulars of an Austrian girl named Liselot Pickel, found in the register of a pensione which had been bombed and where the records had had to be dug out of piles of rubble. It was clearly the same girl. Copies of the Preliminary Arrest and Interrogation Report on Lea Pacini/Liselot Pickel, her Statement and List of Property are reproduced on pages 29-42. Her Identity Photographs can be seen in the plate section.

The value of routine security measures and controls on civilian movements may not result merely in the direct detection of enemy agents, but may have secondary effects, summed up in a document on security matters issued in October 1944 by GSI(b) at HQ Allied Forces in Italy:

Firstly, they tend to make the agent (a man with a guilty conscience) adjust his movements and actions in such a way as to evade the security measures which he knows to be in force, or which he believes *may* be in force. In this way he is liable to make himself conspicuous: his evasive actions, his use of roundabout routes, his cautious manner, his uncertain behaviour – these will tend to pick him out from the crowd and facilitate his detection. If he has no security measures to fear, none to complicate his normal way of life, he will behave normally and merge into the mass.

Secondly, his first contacts with our security measures, his ignorance of exactly what measures are in force and where he may encounter them, may well make him lose his nerve and abandon his mission: he may give himself up or simply 'go to ground': whichever he does, he will no longer be a danger. We have already met with many such cases, of agents who accepted an espionage mission in good faith, who crossed the lines with the firm intention of carrying it out but who then threw in their hand on realising the unforeseen difficulties they were up against and the various pitfalls that might entrap them. We can well understand such action on the part of an agent if we imagine ourselves in a similar situation; the mere sight of an SS uniform might shake us: consider your reactions to SS police checks, to applying for a pass at the Kommandatur and to the possibility of being interrogated by the SD . . .

The *fear* of what may happen, if based on reasonable evidence that such things *do* happen, can have a considerable influence on one's actions. All control measures, whether applied on a 100% or a spot-check basis, will help keep the agent guessing, so that he can never feel safe: he will not know what he may meet round the next corner or where he can safely spend the next night. If he goes to a house he may be questioned about his identity: if he spends it in the open he may be arrested for being out after curfew: if he moves without a pass he may be questioned; if he is questioned he may make a slip, or he may be searched (and that wad of money be discovered) or his identity card be recognised as false. But if he encounters or notices no security measures, no dangers or hazards, he will quickly gain confidence and behave just like the next man.'

To: A.C.of S, G-2 5th Army.
From: 427 Field Security Section.

Subject:- Preliminary Arrest and Interrogation Report on Enemy
          Agent

1) Personal Particulars of Agent.
   PACINI Lea di Mario e di Angela ROSSI
Born: 27 Aug '17 at UDINE
   Nationality - Italian
   Id. Card. 487394 issued Florence

2) Circumstances of Arrest
    PACINI Lea was arrested by Sgt J.H.Flowerdew 427 FSS at
    0200 hours 14 Jan '45. She was detected as a result of the
    following circumstances:-

   a) Lt R.S.Eldridge, O.C. Entertainments Section 1 Div, reported
      to FSS office that subject's actions were suspicious.
      Lt Edridge stated that PACINI was either Austrian or German,
      that she spoke Italian, German and English, & was working
      for the Allies; he said that subject went to a music school
      & had asked the proprietor's daughter where she could
      obtain certain radio accessories; PACINI had also insisted
      that no-one should divulge her address.

   b) this information was followed up, & on13 January '45 a
      perquisition was made of PACINI's apartment in her absence.
      In the apartment were found a transmitting and receiving
      radio set, crystals, spare valves, wire etc, also a revolver
      with a shot in the barrel.

   c) A guard was placed on the apartment and on the street door
      of the address. At 0200 hours 14 January PACINI Lea was
      brought tothe street door in a car which immediately drove
      off. When she entered, Sgt. Flowerdew asked her whether her
      name was PACINI Lea. She replied that it was, then she led
      the way upstairs. At the door of the apartment she insisted
      on taking out her key, rather than knocking, as she said she
      did not wish to disturb the landlady. She entered - saw that
      a perquisition had been made, & was immediately questioned
      by Major M. Smith, 3 S.C,I.

3) Employers
   No information.

4) Method of Entry into Allied Territory.
   PACINI Lea has been at the address in Viale Massini 13 since
   before the Allied arrival in Florence.

5) Mission
Subject says that she will say nothing of her mission. She admits
however that after the electric current was cut off in August '44
she made efforts to buy an accumulator in various shops; she was
unable to do so, & was almost in despair when she asked Sig.IORIO
of the music shop Via Dante Rossi 19, if it were possible to
procure one. This was a few days before the current was
restored in September '44. When asked directly "Have you ever
transmitted on your radio?" PACINI replied "I came in and saw
that you had found the radio. It is of no use trying to hide
anything. What do you think the radio is for?"

6) Means of Communication

  Standard ABWEHR Transmitting and Receiving radio.

7) Possessions

  Transmitting and Receiving set, complete with crystals, spare
  valves, wire, aerial and suspected code. Walther revolver
  No. 183054 W. with one round in the barrel, spare magazine and
  box of approx 100 cartridges; these were found in a bedside
  cupboard.In a drawer in adjoining room a few German notes were
  found. In addition 2000 lire in A.M.Currency was found. The
  frequency plug in the set was 5173 kHz. There were three
  spares 6350,3 kHZ, 4340,7 kHZ 6394,1 kHZ

8)Other Agents and Contacts

  No information. PACINI states repeatdely that she has always
  been quite alone

9) Other points of interest.
   Own story

PACINI Lea says that she came to Florence in July or August '43.
She has always been well-to-do and has had no financial worries.
She first went to various hotels and later to the PiazzaDelle Cure
7, c/oDott.SCHULER, who went north with the Germans. About July
'44 she found this apartment in Viale Mazzini 13 through an
agency in Via Della Condotta.
When asked whether she had been away from Florence since August
'43 she said that she went to Trieste, possibly about Sept!43
Prior to the Allied arrival in Florence, she took part in many
sports, horse-riding, tennis, swimming etc and her hobby is
singing. On 18 October '44 she went to the Civil Labour Office,
was standing outside considering a notice that interpreters were
needed, when a sergeant came out, asked whether she was inter-
-ested in the job, & invited her in. She was questioned by an
officer. Asked whether she objected to working outside Florence,
she replied that she only wished to take music lessons here,
otherwise she was willing to go to any camp. She started work
the following day at 15 S&T Column RAF. She attended dances at
this and neighbouring camps about twice weekly.
Questioned about her money PACINI states that for a long time
she has had 'no communication' & has had to sell some property
including a bicycle.

10) Interrogator's Comments.
PACINI Lea is very intelligent. She says freely that she expects
to be shot & welcomes dying "For her Fatherland". She insists
that "Her Fatherland" is Italy though her accent gives the
impression that she is German.

11) Present Status

  Imprisoned at S.Verdiana gaol, Florence, at disposition of
  3 S.C.I. Action proposed- Further interrogation.

15 January '44
                          (signed)
                          6411350 Sgt. J.H. Flowerdew
Copy to: G.S.I.(b) 15 Army Group
         3 S.C.I.

40

STATEMENT BY PICKEL Liselot

The following statement is made of my own free will and I clearly understand that anything I state may be used in evidence against me.

I state that I was known as PACINI Lea but that my real name is PICKEL Liselot.
In about July '43 I volunteered for service with the Abwehr.
I was trained at Trieste as a W/T operator, and sent on a mission by Doctor WEBER and MEYER. The mission was to obtain information, especially military information, in Florence. I received 10,000 lire a month until the end of October '44 and 15,000 lire a month from Nov '44 until Jan '45, in addition to about 700 to 900 Swiss francs.

I arrived in Florence in Oct. '43 and installed the W/T set at Piazza delle CURE 7. From Oct. '43 until Feb '44 I stayed in Florence and had daily contacts with my Control Station at Vienna, sending at first practice messages and later, local information.

In Feb '44 I transferred to ANCONA and returned to Florence in May '44.

About July '44 I moved to another apartment in Viale Mazzini 13 in Florence.
After the Allied arrival in Florence I was unable to transmit until the end of Sept '44 owing to lack of electric current. When the current was restored I contacted my control station by means of the W/T set. From that date until a few days before my arrest I transmitted about forty (40) messages a month. These messages gave military information. I made notes in German shorthand about Allied convoys, troop movements, and details of Allied units.

I have read this statement. I understand it fully and sign my name willingly.

s/s Liselot Pickel

We, the undersigned, state that the above statement was given voluntarily and signed in our presence.

	7689347 unintelligible, 16 FSS
2 Apr '45	6411350 J.H. Flowerdew Sgt. 427 FSS

LIST OF PROPERTY OF PACINI Lea

(a)   1 standard Abwehr transmitting and receiving
      radio set marked SO 19, together with four
      frequency plugs Kcs:
          5175khz
          43407khz
          63503khz
          63941khz
      The whole in a portable case.

(b)   Package 1.
          Small insulators
          Spare fuses, lead plugs etc.

(c)   Package 2.
          Spare cables – wire – aerial wire with
          insulators.

(d)   Valves.
          1 Telefunken 945   AZ11
          2 Telefunken – unmarked except for 'fo h' on base
          1 Telefunken 030
          1 Telefunken 6I66
          1 Telefunken AZ 11   014
          1 Telefunken AZ   027
          1 Telefunken marked 163
          1 Telefunken unmarked.

(e)   1 pair headphones marked SAFAR R 2000 with flex
      and plug.

6

The German Intelligence Services (GIS)

In order for the lay reader to comprehend the variety and intricacies of the various intelligence operations which were launched by the Axis in Italy during 1943–45, a brief overall outline will be necessary of the organisations involved and of their relationship to each other, hopefully described in relatively basic form without going into an excess of detail.

There were two main components involved, each an offshoot of the two power centres of the Nazi Reich under Hitler:

(a) The Abwehr ('Defence') – the espionage and security organisation of the Wehrmacht (Armed Services), headed by Admiral Canaris.
(b) The Sicherheitsdienst (SD Security Service) – originally the security unit of the SS, but which became the political intelligence service of the Reich. It was thus a Nazi party organisation, quite separate from the Armed Services.

It should be borne in mind that, throughout the rise of Hitler and indeed throughout the whole history of the Nazi régime until its final collapse, there was constant tension between the German officer class, especially the older and more senior officers, and the Nazi party leaders. The German generals, many of them from 'Junker' families with high social standing and ethics, were largely appalled by the coarseness and brutality of many of the Nazi leaders (one has only to look at photographs of Roehm, Strasser, Himmler, Heydrich and others to share this aversion). That Himmler, a former chicken farmer, should become the most powerful man in Germany after Hitler (himself a mere ex-Corporal) was anathema to most of them: but, as other historical accounts have shown, they were forced down a slippery path where they largely surrendered their consciences to avoid any accusation of treason to their country, after being compelled to sign an oath of allegiance to Hitler himself.

This clash of character and ethics also mirrored itself within the two German intelligence services, especially at the top. Initially their spheres of operation did not seriously overlap, since the Abwehr was involved purely in military intelligence; but as the war situation deteriorated friction grew, and finally Himmler was able to achieve the downfall of Canaris in June 1944, and the Abwehr came directly under Himmler's control (although this did not greatly affect its operations at the fighting fronts). The situation might be compared with that existing in the USSR up till

1990, where the Army ran its own military intelligence organisation, the GRU, while the Communist Party had its own, much larger and more powerful, set-up in the KGB.

THE ABWEHR

The Head of the Abwehr was Admiral Canaris, who had held the position since before the war. Of Greek origin, Canaris was a notorious right-wing intriguer, politically associated with traditionalist Army circles and not a Nazi Party man. Much has been written of his apparent attempts to pass important intelligence to the Allies, and to mislead Hitler with false (or the absence of) intelligence in circumstances where this could assist Allied military operations. Such matters are outside the scope of this book. The senior officers of the Abwehr were all drawn from the Armed Services, mainly from the Army itself.

REGIONAL ORGANISATION

Each military area of Germany (Wehrkreis) had a corresponding Abwehr unit – an 'Abwehrstelle', usually abbreviated to AST. In occupied territories AST were set up in principal cities – for example in France there were ASTs in Paris, Lyons, Dijon and Angers. In neutral, or in Satellite countries the Abwehr station was called the KO (Kriegsorganisation) and was given diplomatic cover in the German embassy or legation.

Many ASTs had subordinate stations under them, called Nebenstellen, or NESTS, and these in turn might have substations, called Aussenstellen, or AUSTs. The smallest Abwehr cell of all, possibly consisting of only one or two people, was called a Meldekopf (MK).

In important countries allied to Germany, such as Italy before July 1943, and Hungary, the Abwehr was represented by a liaison officer (VO) at that country's indigenous intelligence service.

FUNCTIONAL ORGANISATION

Functionally the Abwehr was divided into three main operations sections (Abteilungen) plus an Administration section, numbered as follows:

Abteilung I: collection of operational intelligence
Abteilung II: sabotage and subversion in enemy territory
Abteilung III: security and counter-espionage
Abteilung Z (for Zentralabterlung): Administration

These designations ran downwards through all subordinate formations and indicated the primary function of the unit.

The following gives a more detailed breakdown of the work and organisation of the four Abteilungen.

This, in effect the most important section, was subdivided into several departments (Gruppen) of which the following were the main ones:

I/H (for Heer, or Army: espionage against foreign armies)
I/M (for Marine, or Navy): espionage against foreign navies
I/Luft (for Luftwaffe): espionage against foreign air forces
I/Wi (for Wirtschaft, or industry): economic espionage
I/G (for Geheimsache, or secret materials): forged documents, secret inks, photo equipment etc

The first three of these departments were the most important; all ASTs and nearly all smaller units had officers representing each of them on the strength. The individual officers of these departments had a large measure of independence; they selected their agents, and except for reference to Abteilung Z (see below) for checking and registration, they ran them at their pleasure. The agent 'belonged' to the officer running him, and if recruited and employed by e.g. a Gruppe I/H officer in Paris he would be an I/H spy, although additional assignments from other Gruppen might be passed to him if it appeared that he might be well placed to bring back intelligence in such fields. He would however report exclusively to his 'owner', the Gruppe I officer.

With such loose control, secret intelligence work, especially in neutral countries, afforded considerable opportunities to the unscrupulous or lazy. As the war went on, and faced with the prospect of being 'weeded out' and sent off to fight on the Eastern Front, more and more Abwehr officers began to turn in reports which they must have known to be wholly or largely invented by their agents: or even to descend to invention themselves. They were encouraged in this by lax treatment at Berlin HQ, which rarely meted out the criticism they deserved. Moreover, HQ was far too prone to allow Abwehr officers and head agents to keep details of their networks entirely to themselves, on the excuse of 'security'. In Portugal especially the manufacture of false intelligence became something of a national industry during the later years of the war.

Vested interests also played their part. Abwehr officers who discovered that their agents were inventing intelligence did not like to admit their mistake in recruiting the man in the first place, and HQ often found itself obliged, for face-saving reasons, to support incompetent subordinates. So the Abwehr snowball of corruption and inefficiency grew, with, eventually, disastrous effects on its existence.

All this does not mean that Abteilung I performed no useful service. In many ways it was well organised, many of the officers were honest and industrious, and in technical matters such as radio it was very efficient. But in the obtaining of genuinely secret intelligence through well-placed agents, Abwehr output was small compared to the money and effort expended.

ABTEILUNG II

Here the division of work fell under two headings:

S-Work: Sabotage
J-Work: Subversion (Insurgierung)

Abteilung II was the active, positive arm of the Abwehr. It was concerned with both material and moral sabotage, the latter function including Fifth-column operations of every kind. Penetration of enemy territory by agents equipped to destroy aircraft on the ground, sink ships in harbour or blow up ammunition dumps was the job of Abteilung II on the material side, just as fomenting dissidence within enemy or enemy-occupied territory was its job on the moral side.

Abteilung II also had a defensive rôle in preventive anti-sabotage and anti-guerrilla work in the field, although in practice most of this aspect appears to have been handled by Abteilung III (see below).

Abteilung II officers were attached to almost all Abwehrstellen, and ALST Paris had a special out-station at Nantes for Abteilung II purposes only. In France, Abteilung II agents were trained in parachute jumping and sabotage, and were despatched to the UK and even to the USA. Efforts were also made by Abteilung II to create a Fifth-column out of Breton, Welsh and Irish nationalists. In Spain, sabotage attacks were made by Abteilung II agents on British shipping in Gibraltar and Spanish ports, and efforts were made to excite disaffection among the tribesmen of North Africa.

ABTEILUNG III

Abteilung III was the security and counter-espionage section of the Abwehr, responsible both for the security of the Abwehr itself and of the Armed Forces as a whole. For the latter purpose it worked in close collaboration with the Geheime Feldpolizei, the security police of the Wehrmacht. The GFP consisted of regular policemen seconded for army duties, and was responsible to the senior Wehrmacht officer of the district. Local detachments of the GFP might be responsible to a local Wehrmacht intelligence officer, or to the local Abwehr station (usually in the person of the Abteilung II officer at that station). There were also, inevitably, close connections 'on the ground' with the corresponding section of the Sicherheitsdienst; these were more satisfactory in occupied countries than in neutral countries, but even in occupied countries there were ambiguous cases and disputes over responsibility which had to be settled either by pragmatic arrangements or by reference back to HQ.

Abteilung III was, like Abteilung I, divided into separate sections covering army, navy and air force security; these three were grouped together under the symbol III W (i.e. Wehrmacht), which formed the section responsible for co-ordinating general security and counter-espionage work in the armed forces. Another department of particular interest was III F (= Fremde, or Foreign). This directed work beyond the frontiers of Germany, and in wartime, was the largest and most important section, responsible (inter alia) for the penetration of enemy espionage services. Neutral countries provided the happiest hunting grounds for this purpose, with Spain and Turkey high on the list.

ABTEILUNG Z (ZENTRALABTEILUNG)

This was the administrative department. Its most important section was ZO (Organisation) which, apart from being responsible for general organisation and planning of the whole Abwehr, kept the Central Card Index (ZK) to which reference had to be made for identity checks, and also kept the ZKV (Zentralkartei Vertrauensmänner), which was the central card index of agents employed by the Abwehr. This was a vital part of the machine: there could be complications if one section of the Abwehr tried to recruit an agent who was already working for someone else, and the potential 'pool' of likely agents could well, in a given area, be relatively restricted.*

There was a Z-officer at every Abwehrstelle – not generally a Services officer, but a civilian holding officer status; the rank was known as Sonderführer.

Where fighting was taking place, or seemed likely to do so, each Army Group had an Abwehr Group attached to it, divided into 'functional' FAKs, each of which had a number of Trupps (FATs) under its command. The initial figure of their numbering corresponded to their parent Abteilung in Berlin. Thus in Italy (an Army Group area) Abteilung I of the Abwehr – engaged in offensive intelligence-gathering – was represented principally by FAK 150, with its subordinate Trupps numbered 150, 151, 152 and

---

*I have not been able to establish whether there was any cross-checking beween the Abwehr ZKV and its SD equivalent. This would appear to be a necessary corollary.

153; Abteilung II had FAK 212, controlling FATs 253, 254, 256, 257 and 258; while FAK 309, representing Abteilung III, which by the nature of its duties needed to have a wide geographical spread over the whole of German-controlled territory, had nine Trupps under it, numbered 347, 348 and 368 to 374. Apart from counter-espionage work, the Abteilung III Kommandos also did postal censorship and W/T security. Abteilung II Kommandos, in addition to their normal function of launching offensive sabotage missions against enemy territory, were also often used for counter-partisan work.

FAKs had no fixed strength of officers and men: this depended on the work they were engaged in. An Abteilung I Troop might consist merely of a Lieutenant and a few 'Other Ranks' ('Enlisted Men', in US terminology). Abteilung II Troops were generally much larger. The average Abteilung I FAK might have 3-4 Trupps subordinate to it, whereas an Abteilung III FAK might have as many as ten to twelve.

Abteilung I and Abteilung II FAKs would principally be occupied in two specific fields:

(a) During a German retreat, in setting up 'stay-behind' agents, who would allow themselves to be overrun by the enemy's advance and would then, under some suitable 'cover' for their residence, start operating on behalf of their German controllers. Abteilung I agents would collect operational and tactical intelligence, which was usually reported back by radio in code; it was common practice, therefore, for the stay-behind team to consist of at least two persons, one of whom would be the W/T operator. Abteilung II agents would be provided with hidden dumps of explosives and equipment, laid down before the Germans retreated, and would be expected to dig them up and go into action against suitable targets once the security situation allowed it. They, too, would wherever possible have a W/T link back to base, both in order to make reports and to receive instructions, and also so as to call for fresh supplies and money (to be dropped to them by parachute) should the need arise.

Such stay-behind agents worked under great psychological disadvantage, since by 1943 there seemed little prospect that any German retreat would later be reversed. Agents prepared to remain loyal to their German masters when retreat followed retreat proved extremely few, and most stay-behind (S/B) networks were failures. Such agents were not normally Germans: in France they would be Frenchmen, in Italy, Italians – although a few Italian-speaking Austrians from the South Tyrol region were used in this rôle.

Stay-behind agents worked their W/T links not to the location of the

FAT or FAK which was running them, since this might have to change from time to time and not always be ideal for radio reception: they worked instead to fixed radio stations well behind the front.

(b) Sending agents into enemy territory. The method whereby such agents were sent would depend on their rôle, personal quality and the availability of aircraft, submarines etc. A number were dropped by parachute behind the lines, or landed from the sea by submarine or small boat, or sent in with a party of genuine refugees arriving in fishing craft: such agents, who usually took a W/T set with them, represented a considerable investment in training time and resources, and tended to be higher grade agents, recruited and run by the FAK itself. Lower grade agents, recruited by the FATs, were in the main 'line-crossers' on short-term missions to bring back *de visu** reports on enemy unit identifications etc., with orders to re-cross the lines back into German-held territory after a couple of weeks. Some, however, had longer-term missions to carry out specific rôles well behind the front line areas.

Line-crossing agents would seldom carry W/T sets with them; the risk of interception by enemy troops, or by movement controls immediately behind the front, was much too high – especially since W/T sets in those days had none of the miniaturisation with which we are familiar today, and were the size of a small suitcase. On rare occasions, if they were high-grade agents and other means of despatch (e.g. by parachute) were not available, they might be instructed to make contact with an existing W/T network, to which they would deliver their intelligence reports for encoding and despatch by radio. In a few cases they were given secret inks for use in messages to be sent back by a line-crossing courier.

If longer-term agents (S/B or otherwise) found themselves running short of money or supplies, it could occasionally become necessary to re-supply them by an air drop well away from the front line areas, the money often being carried in by a new agent arrival.

In the majority of such cases the drops were in fact 'engineered' by Allied counter-intelligence, who had captured a W/T agent and, to use the professional jargon, 'played him back' by using his radio messages to indicate that he was still free and operating, and in need of funds. The Germans themselves had of course great success with similar 'play-backs' in Belgium against SOE.

---

*Standard expression in Intelligence circles meaning 'seen by an Agent with his own eyes'.

Before the outbreak of the 1939-45 war the Wehrmacht had no equivalent intelligence organisation, at the level of lower fighting formations, to that in the British Army: Intelligence appointments began only at divisional level. There was no 'School of Army Intelligence' where specialist training was given in such work. At the outbreak of war regular General Staff officers on Ic appointments were only in service at Corps and Army level; even here, intelligence about 'the enemy' only played a very limited rôle in the training of such officers. In the German General Staff (OKH) there was indeed a department entitled 'Foreign Armies' (Fremde Heere) which studied the organisation of potential foes, but their work was limited to the writing of strategic studies. Little attention was paid to tactical intelligence, and intelligence work in combat units has been described by one German officer as 'like it was at the end of World War I'.

Indeed the 'I' side of the German Army had a status very different to that enjoyed by their equivalents in the British and US Armies. Since German Army doctrine was opposed in general to the creation of specialists, the Intelligence side developed, not into an independent branch of the service, but into an auxiliary department of the tactical command. This conception of the 'I' side found its expression both in the limited training undergone by Ic officers and in the position occupied by many Ics within their formations. This depended to a considerable extent on the opinion of intelligence work held by the Commander and his Ia (i.e. Operations Officer) as well as on the personality of the Ic himself.

The post of Ic in a division had, in peacetime, originally been a Captain's appointment, later up-graded to Major. It had been anticipated that in war, as in peace, the Ic posts in army formations would be filled by young General Staff officers (with rank at least of Captain) who had been through the 'Kriegsakadamie'. The Ic would in such a case be, as his title suggests, the third General Staff officer of the formation.

As a result of the vast expansion of the German Army, however, both before and during the war, it was found no longer possible to provide for all formations the requisite trained Staff Officers for the Ic appointments, and increasing use had to be made of Reserve officers (wherever possible, of those who had professional experience abroad as businessmen, diplomats etc, and who spoke foreign languages) – initially at Divisional level, and then for Corps and Army HQs. The campaign against Poland revealed the lack of an effective intelligence organisation, and steps were taken to rectify the situation.*

---

*But the first ever Intelligence Handbook – 'Vorschrift für das Nachrichtenwesen' – was only issued in 1941.

The fact that most Ic posts were filled before long by Reserve Officers was a measure of necessity, due to the lack of sufficient fully-trained Staff officers. One of the results of this was that Reserve officers were entrusted with all the duties of an Ic but were denied any corresponding rise in rank (the system of promoting to an 'Acting' rank was unknown in the German Army and was, in such cases, a considerable disadvantage). Needless to say, an Ic working under these circumstances often had great difficulty in putting over his point of view to the Ia, because the experienced 'senior' General Staff officer did not like being argued with by his 'junior' Reserve officer.

The Ic at Divisional level had in fact no real independent function. According to the military manuals he was 'assistant to the Ia' in everything to do with the enemy, and was bound in every case by the Ia's decision. All important intelligence messages were signed by the Ia himself. In some divisions the Ia even reserved for himself access to the GOC where intelligence matters were concerned, or at least laid down what could or could not be alluded to.

Intelligence training proper only began in the German Army in 1943, when Ic courses began at Posen (Poznan). The fact that such courses were not started until 3½ years after the start of the war speaks eloquently for the status enjoyed by intelligence work in the German Army. Even then, officers sent to Posen were often those on whose services the division did not lay much store, or else those to whom the division believed it was doing a favour because of their age or health. Experienced or useful officers were seldom selected. The results of this 'hit or miss' policy were not conducive to an efficiently working 'I' machine. In the final two years of the war the Ics, espcially at divisional level, possessed the most varied antecedents, qualifications, ages and ranks. Invested with the doubtful authority described above, they were often in little position to contribute much to the German war effort although, as already mentioned, much depended on the personal relations between the Ic and his Ia, and the interest (or lack of it) shown by the Division's commander. At 65 Infantry Division, for example, the GOC displayed a keen interest in all intelligence coming in*, whereas the Ic of 48 Infantry Division described the attitude of his Operations officers by quoting a typical greeting from them: "So what have the Brothers Grimm to tell us today?"

In spite of these generic disadvantages, it cannot be said that, overall, the intelligence capabilities of the Wehrmacht's fighting formations were particularly weak at battlefield level (as distinct from Higher Command

*65 Infantry Division, which included in its ranks a considerable proportion of Russian Asiatics, had some unusual components in its Ic staff: not only a Russian interpreter, but also one 'Obermullah' and one 'Mullah', responsible for the religious welfare of the divisional Muslims.

levels), especially in the field of their Abhorchdienst, interrogation of POWs and their tactical reconnaissance. In Italy many divisions ran a 'Nahaufklärungstrupp' (Close Recce Troop) under control of the Ic, which utilised the rugged terrain to send in teams for 1-3 days at a time, which would lie up under cover and observe Allied troop movements, HQ and gun locations, supply routes and timings etc. The Russian campaign brought about a big expansion of the whole Ic organisation, which by the end of the war, on the basis of continuous experience in battle conditions, had reached a very effective level. In more static fighting, as in Italy for much of the time, the Ic product was however considerably more restricted, and the lack of air reconnaissance gave a disproportionate value to seemingly very low-grade de visu reports, which frequently were their only source of information. This no doubt accounts to some extent for the profligacy with which both Ic and Abwehr poured untrained and untested youths and peasants across the lines.

Ic at divisional levels and above, in fact, had the right to employ agents and line-crossers, although generally speaking this right was in the main only exercised at Army level. In this they differed from the British Army, where agent-running formed no part of the duties of GSI or Field Security personnel. Although, as mentioned above, the German word 'Abwehr' was normally used to describe this aspect of Ic work (literally meaning 'defence' but more specifically 'counter-intelligence') the concept also included reconnaissance in the sense of the gathering of operational intelligence, and thus espionage also. However, the Wehrmacht made a fine distinction on this point, although this was more a mental attitude than something codified – nor, in international law, would the distinction be accepted as having any validity. 'Aufklärung', i.e. 'reconnaissance' was one thing (even if carried out by civilians), but 'Spionage', i.e. espionage, was something different. 'Aufklärung' was aimed at collecting de visu intelligence about the enemy in the line facing the German troops, and would normally only cover territory stretching back say 20-30 kilometres behind the front; it embraced the on-the-spot recruitment, not only of local inhabitants and 'line-crosser' civilians, but also, especially in the Russion campaign, the use of deserters from the enemy side, who were sent back across the lines to collect military intelligence. The emphasis was always on the locations and identities of the opposing troops.

'Espionage' was, to the Wehrmacht, another kettle of fish, involving sneaky methods and professional training – the infiltration of agents into enemy organisations, such as Officers' Clubs, supply services, ports and so on, with the aim of obtaining intelligence well beyond mere de visu reporting. This was the job of 'the' Abwehr, that is to say of Canaris's organisation, although each Army Command was supposed to be aware of, and to a certain extent control, what operations the latter was engaged in on the Army Front. FAKs were in fact supposed to be, to use British army terminology, 'under command', but were, in reality, only 'in support' of the relevant Army in the field.

The differentiation between these two methods of intelligence-collection can be seen more clearly in the staff duties laid down for different sections of the Ic part of an Army Command HQ in the Wehrmacht:

Sachgebiet 3 (area of duties) covered the following activities:

> running of informants of the Secret Intelligence Service (here the term used is 'des Geheimen Meldedienstes') together with the responsible Abwehrstellen.

Sachgebiet 4 dealt with:

(a) Defence ('Abwehr' in its generic sense) against enemy espionage and sabotage.

(b) Liaison with Abwehrstellen (i.e. the ASTs of the Canaris outfit).

(c) Operational direction of the Geheime Feldpolizei.

The Ic at Army Command thus had a more direct responsibility for the operations of those small ASTs which were working as outposts of those homeland Abwehrstellen which, in peacetime, had been responsible for intelligence work in the geographical area in which the Army now found itself.

It can be seen that the situation was already more than a little complicated. It was confused still more by the fact that some Army commanders (especially those of the old Prussian school) regarded espionage with a highly jaundiced eye and wanted nothing to do with it; in consequence liaison with the FAKs in their area was little more than nominal. At lower levels, the FAK officers sometimes established a working relationship with Ic officers at Corps or Divison HQs, and used their facilities (such as help in infilitrating agents through the front lines) – sometimes in exhange for specialised equipment, such as radio sets, or indeed for anything which was in short supply in the forward areas. In many cases Ic agents and FAK agents would go off together across the lines, and it was not unknown for Ic agents to be recruited 'on the side' by a FAK, without the relevant Ic officer being aware of it.

Even where the link between an Abwehr FAK and its Army HQ was working as it was supposed to, extraordinary complications could arise. While the FAK had its own direct line of communication back to its parent organisation in Berlin, it was also supposed to (and usually did) pass to the local Army HQ Ic a copy of the intelligence which its agents had obtained, where this was relevant to the battle area in the widest sense of the term.

However, agent reports are seldom passed up to higher echelons in their original form: they are assessed, discarded or accepted, commented on or (not unusually, especially in units where a little embroidery seems useful, or the discarding of possibly unwelcome aspects of the intelligence has become a habit) rewritten. A report sent back over Abwehr channels would, if it was important enough, be shown to Hitler; it was not unusual for the same intelligence to be included, somewhat later, in OKW assessments, where it might have quite a different slant to that given it by the Abwehr, with the result that Hitler would pull the rug from under his generals' feet by saying that 'he had sources of his own who had given him quite a different picture' to that which the Army High Command was presenting. As can be imagined, such incidents could make life very difficult for the OKW generals.

THE SICHERHEITSPOLIZEI AND SICHERHEITSDIENST:
POLITICAL AND HISTORICAL BACKGROUND

Heinrich Himmler held three major offices which together gave him, through the Nazi Party, unlimited control of the German people (and of the peoples of all occupied territories). He was:

1. Minister of the Interior
2. Chief of the German Police
3. 'Reichsführer SS', that is, the National Leader of the SS, the élite of the Nazi Party, – and thus controller of its Security and Intelligence Service.

In addition to the rank and file of the SS itself, the following representative organisations were thus subordinate to Himmler through their respective chiefs:

1. The Uniformed Police (Ordnungspolizei, or ORPO) whose functions were the normal ones of law and order, directing traffic, quelling riots etc. (But not dealing with crime as such.)
2. The Security Police (Sicherheitspolizei, or SIPO), subdivided into:
    (a) the Criminal Police (Kriminalpolizei, or KRIPO)
    (b) the Secret State Police (Geheime Staatspolizei, or GESTAPO).
3. The Party Security and Intelligence Service (Sicherheitsdienst des Reichsführer SS, or SD).

The SIPO and SD were jointly controlled by Dr Ernst Kaltenbrunner, and their combination under Himmler's aegis made them together the Nazi Party's strongest weapon for the maintenance of National Socialism in Germany and the imposing of Nazi methods, and the Nazi creed, in countries seized by Germany.

54

THE SIPO

In June 1936 Himmler was appointed Chief of the German Police under Frick, the Minister of the Interior, but with the right of direct access to Hitler on police maters. The years before the war were spent in a thorough re-organisation of the German police into an efficient instrument of repression in the intrerests of National Socialism, with a regional organisation (see below) under miniature Himmlers, designed to secure the same coordination of repressive force at regional level which Himmler himself could ensure at the top, breaking down the former federal allegiance of the police forces. The police themselves were divided into ORPO and SIPO, the latter headed by Heinrick Heydrich.

THE GESTAPO

The GESTAPO grew from the Prussian Secret Police to be a national force outside the normal control of law, and was directed centrally from the Gestapoamt in Berlin. The KRIPO already had a long tradition of centralism. Heydrick, with the title of 'Chef de Sicherheitspolizei und des SD' was able to begin a process of penetration and re-shuffling which culminated in the direction of GESTAPO, KRIPO and SD by a single office, which after September 1939 was called the Reich Security Head Office (Reichssicherheitshauptamt, or RSHA) and the formation of a largely joint service in which the individuality of the constituent parts was partly lost, especially when they followed the German armies into occupied Europe.

THE RSHA: CENTRAL CONTROL

The RSHA, responsible under Kaltenbrunner for the control of all three police services, consisted of seven departments which were numbered Amt I, Amt II, Amt III and so on. Only three of these – Amt III, Amt IV and Amt VI are of direct relevance to the subject matter of this book.

Amt III directed the main functions of the SD inside Germany and in occupied territory, i.e. the collection by secret methods of information about all forces, events and facts of importance for the supremacy of the Nazi movement and the supervision of all spheres of life for opposition or subversive activities. Personnel were drawn mainly from the pre-war SD Hauptamt rather than from members of the GESTAPO or KRIPO.

Amt IV was the logical descendant of the original Gestapoamt and was concerned with the investigation and combating of political opposition to the Nazi state in all its forms, both at home and abroad – political opposition being construed in the widest possible sense. It included espionage by foreign powers, underground movements both inside Germany and in

Occupied Europe, Communists, Jews and all other non-military manifestations of unfriendliness towards Hitler and the Nazi state. Amt IV ran numerous agents, including those for the penetration of enemy espionage services.

It was not concerned with the gathering of intelligence on, or the assessment of trends of thought among, the German people, but with the collection of information, and executive action thereafter, against specific persons, organisations, parties, and groups.

Amt VI was a largely autonomous section, controlling the SD foreign political intelligence service; as such, it was the section of principal interest in the context of SD espionage operations in Italy, and is therefore treated more fully below.

Below the level of the RSHA the three services – KRIPO, GESTAPO and SD – remained separate, although they worked closely together. Regional co-ordination, in the pattern of the RSHA, was achieved through 'Senior SS and Police Chiefs' (Höhere SS-und Polizeiführer, abbreviated to HSSuPF) whose powers were a replica of those of Himmler, but at regional level: such senior officers were directly responsible to Himmler and were men of immense authority in their own territories. The HSSuPF controlled an area roughly corresponding to that of an Army Wehrkreis, and was generally as SS Gruppenführer (a rank roughly equivalent to General). In his area he was the supreme police executive authority, and in time of emergency could become its virtual dictator. He commanded the services of all SS personnel in his area, and in an emergency (such as occurred after the attempted assassination of Hitler) those of the Waffen-SS as well.

Under the HSSuPF came an 'Inspekteur der Orpo' (IdO) and an 'Inspekteur der Sipo und des SD" (IdS). In an emergency the IdS was replaced by a 'Befehlshaber der Sipo und des SD' (BdS), i.e. a Commander in name as well as in function. The IdS was superior to the IdO and co-ordinated the whole range of GESTAPO, KRIPO and SD activities in line with general instructions from Berlin.

The 'executive arms' of the organisation were these three latter branches. The KRIPO can be quickly dealt with: it concerned itself with 'common' crime in all its forms – provided it was not political crime, in which case the GESTAPO took over. The latter's task was to detect political crime and to take preventive measures against treasonable acts and plans against the nation, a formula which covered almost any kind of activity by individuals and parties alike. By a law of 1936 its doings were specifically freed from any review by courts of law, and it had, therefore, complete power to carry out executions or to order 'preventive arrest' or 'protective custody'. Inside Germany, its personnel acted as the executive, on counter-espionage matters, of the Abwehr. One of its most notorious rôles was of course the supervision of the concentration camps.

THE SICHERHEITSDIENST

In 1925 the SS (Schutzstaffel, or Protection Squad) was established, virtually for the personal protection of Hitler and other leading Nazis. In 1929 Himmler became its head, the 'Reichsführer SS'. It set up its own political intelligence organisation, the 'Sicherheitsdienst des Reichsführer SS', or SD, the official task of which was to support the SIPO as 'an information service both of Party and State', and 'to keep watch on the endangered spheres of life of the people'.

In descriptions of the police state run by the Nazi despots the SD has tended to get little mention, swamped to some extent by the notoriety of the GESTAPO. It maintained an extremely secret information network both inside and outside Germany, with its sphere of interest ranging from the highest political matters to the sympathies of individual citizens. Its personnel were for the most part unknown to the average Party member, let alone to the general public. SD agents in factories, Government departments and elsewhere frequently had, to outward appearances, no party connections, and Amt VI representatives abroad, except in occupied countries, were generally provided with some kind of diplomatic cover. Himmler, as its head, had direct access to Hitler and on questions affecting the morale of the home front the SD, via the RSHA, was the chief source of appreciation and information.

COLLABORATION BETWEEN GESTAPO AND SD

The work of GESTAPO and SD was closely integrated at all levels. Regionally, both of them were directed in their work by the IdS; since the SD's work was 'advisory' and the GESTAPO's 'executive', the SD would usually place its product at the disposal of the GESTAPO. The regional offices of the two organisations were however distinct.

Co-operation between the two was close and for practical purposes they could be considered an individual whole, working for the same ends and staffed with the same kind of personnel.

Whereas inside Germany itself the KRIPO, GESTAPO and SD, although under a common HQ, remained almost entirely separate entities, when abroad their identity was much less distinct, although Amt VI, as will be seen later, maintained in many ways a separate existence. The organisations by which the SIPO and SD carried out their repressive functions in the interests of German security was in general as follows:

1. *The HSSuPF and his Befehlshaber (Commanders)*
In occupied countries such as France and Norway the HSSuPF represented the supreme police authority; he was in command of all SS (except the Waffen-SS, which in the course of the war became crack SS fighting divisions, raised to fight as part of the German army) and German police forces. He delegated his police functions to a BdS and a BdO, whose functions corresponded to those of the Inspekteurs in Germany; their executive powers were however much greater, since the BdS, in addition to commanding the German police forces in his area, was responsible for controlling and motivating the indigenous security police. Furthermore, he shared with Abwehr II the responsibility for the detection and arrest of enemy agents and for the penetration of underground or subversive organisations (including partisans, Resistance fighters, etc.).

2. *The BdS's Headquarters*
Under the BdS's command was an HQ office which contained sections (Abteilungen) corresponding to the RSHA Aemter in Berlin. The responsibilities of these, and their methods of operation through their executives in the SIPO and SD Kommandos, followed closely those of their parent offices. Abt IV in particular directed the main counterespionage policy in the occupied territory; its subsection IV E was responsible for penetrating Allied organisations and detecting espionage, and ran large numbers of agents of all nationalities, many of whom were of poor quality. Communists, Jews and Freemasons were, as usual, the subjects of special attention.

Abt VI maintained a largely separate existence and might even be unknown to some members of the rest of the BdS's HQ. It maintained close direct touch with Berlin and conducted many of its operations, which were mainly directed beyond the frontiers of the country in which it was located, on instructions received direct from the RSHA.

3. *Kommandos[1] and Einsatzkommandos (Mobile Operational Commands)*

The BdS in occupied countries delegated his command to regional Kommandeure der Sipo und des SD (KdS) who, according to conditions in the area in which they were operating, were in charge of either static regional 'Dienststellen', or posts, in the main centres of the region, with Aussenstellen (Out-stations) in places of lesser importance, and/or of mobile operational Kommandos, the latter especially to be found in operational or semi-operational areas such as Italy or Yugoslavia.[2]

Einsatzkommandos were sometimes grouped together in a larger 'Einsatzgruppe', which was generally under direct command of the BdS. Einsatzkommandos of SIP and SD varied in size, the average being around 70 men; they were mixed bodies, consisting of officers and men drawn from the SIPO, the SD and (for guard and arrest duties) the Waffen-SS and SCHUPO. The SD members appeared to watch closely the morale and efficiency of their comrades, and to be disliked and mistrusted on that account.

AMT VI

Amt VI's active espionage outside the Reich was the most secret of all the RSHA's activities, and much less information about it was available to the Allies than information about Abwehr espionage. During the course of the war it gradually expanded in competition with the Abwehr, especially when Abwehr results, in terms of productive and correct intelligence, proved lacking. We shall hear more of this later. Amt VI controlled espionage centres in every capital city in Europe, both occupied and unoccupied, and through South America. Its personnel were almost exclusively SD members, working exclusively for the interests of the SD as the Party intelligence organ.

AIMS AND METHODS

The principal and original assignment of Amt VI abroad was secret political intelligence. Its more important reports were shown to Himmler himself after evaluation; others were passed to the German Foreign Office or to the

---

1. The word Kommando in German is closer to the English term 'Command' (in the sense of a military entity) than to the 'Commandos' as a specialised raiding group or unit. Nevertheless it does refer to individual units, not to larger groupings.

   After June 1944, as will be related later, these were re-titled Frontaufklärungs-Kommandos and -Trupps (FAKs and FATs), meaning Front Reconnaissance Commands. To avoid confusion, the latter term will be used throughout.
2. The static Dienststellen and their Aussenstellen were in fact often referred to loosely, but inaccurately, as Kommandos as well.

OKW as appropriate. As a natural development of this purely intelligence function, the SD also promoted 'Fifth Column' activities among Fascist and pro-German groups abroad. The Amt VI representative might play an active part in the politics of a foreign country, acting as a direct intermediary between the German Government and its supporters or sympathisers abroad. In a neutral country the Amt VI officer might in this respect supplement the work of the official German mission (and in an occupied country, of the Reichskommissar).

Thirdly, Amt VI duplicated the work of Abeteilung II of the Abwehr, in training and despatching saboteurs and, if possible, fomenting insurrection in countries where this could make a contribution. It ran agents of this kind in North Africa, Syria, Persia, Italy, Russia, England and South America; generally they proved however to be no better trained or selected

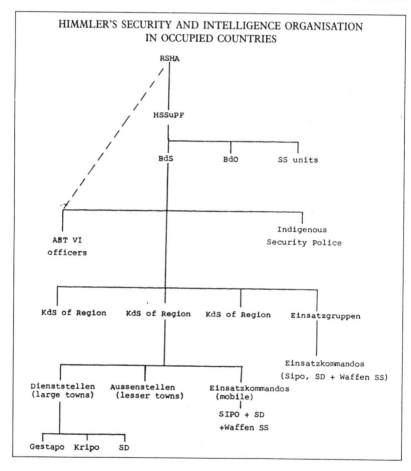

than Abwehr agents in the same category. In Southern Russia Amt VI devoted a lot of effort into fomenting disorder among national minorities, by dropping groups of trained saboteurs or agitators by parachute near vulnerable communications or supply centres.

IN OCCUPIED COUNTRIES

In occupied countries Amt VI officers were subordinated to the HSSuPF, and under him to the BdS. Despite this formal channel of command, Amt VI officers in occupied countries are known to have reported direct to Berlin in some cases, and to have received their orders from there without these passing through the HSSuPF or BdS. Their work might not even be known to other SIPO and SD officers in that particular country; the political intelligence they provided depended more on personal contacts than on paid agents. A couple of examples will illustrate their modus operandi:

(a) Until the Allied landings in North Africa in November 1942, the intricacies of Vichy politics were of the greatest importance to the Germans. Amt VI was kept informed of every plot and counter-plot by their representative in Vichy, who enjoyed close personal relations with Laval and other prominent collaborators. During the crisis of 1942 Himmler was kept au courant with every development. The officer in question, Dr Reiche, whose work was kept separate from that of the GESTAPO or other SD personnel in France, was known to the initiated as 'Himmler's political observer'.

(b) The same phrase, or its variant, 'Himmler's personal representative', was applied to Eugen Dollman, who occupied a position in Italian politics precisely analogous to that of Reiche in Vichy; he enjoyed the confidence of most of the prominent Fascist personalities in Rome, loved art, music and good living – in short, was thoroughly 'salonfähig' (in contrast to Kappler, the Head of the SD in Rome, a brutal officer who typified the worst aspects of the Sicherhcitsdienst). Dollman, in consequence, was better informed about political trends than the German Ambassador. He played a leading part in the re-constitution of Mussolini's puppet government, knowing exactly who was reliable from the German point of view and who was not. Later he played a leading part in the negotiations with the Allies, resulting in the German surrender in Italy.

In mid-February 1944 Admiral Canaris was dismissed as head of the Abwehr, after a series of intelligence disasters abroad; later he was imprisoned, and then hastily executed shortly before the end of the war. Amtsgruppe Ausland was detached from the sinking Abwehr and, initially, came under the top staff section of the OKW, the Wehrmachtsführungsstab. But by June the RSHA had gained complete control (something they had been trying to achieve for a considerable time) and had introduced the following changes:

(a) Abt I and II of the Abwehr were removed from OKW control and became a new section of the RSHA, known as the Militärisches Amt.
(b) Abt III was split up in several ways, mainly under Amt IV (GESTAPO) but with some parts (i.e. III/F) under Amt VI.
(c) Abwehrkommandos and Abwehrtrupps became Frontaufklärungs-kommandos and -trupps (FAK and FAT), and remained under the command of the senior intelligence officer (Ic) of the local military formation.
(d) The terms AST and KO dropped out, and were replaced by KdM, standing for Kommando des Meldegebietes, or 'HQ of the Reporting Area'.

From August 1944 onwards most of the senior Abwehr offices in Berlin disappeared and the Militärisches Amt was taken over by Walter Schellenberg. Abwehr II was placed under Otto Skorzeny, now head of VI/S (Sabotage) after his successful rescue of Mussolini from mountain-top internment by Badoglio.

While these changes did not greatly impinge on the lower levels of intelligence operations in the field, they did (as we shall see) eventually raise the quality of agents and of the conduct of missions to some degree, not least in the determination and improved security of those sent across the lines, and without doubt Abwehr officers at the front will have felt some pressure to smarten up their operational output and efficiency with the sinister overlords of the SD breathing down their necks.

A good example of the ruthless nature of Amt VI work, even at an early stage of the war, is shown by a File Note, issued by Amt VI E 12 on 14 May 1940 and passed upwards without comment to the Head of Amt VI E; in translation it reads as follows:

Re: *People in Italy working against Germany*
Agent I/H 6841 reports by W/T transmission of 7.5/14.5., Message Number 223:
I should like to bring to Germany persons who are clearly working for the enemy, where you confirm this fact. This could be done, I think, by

concealing them behind Oedhofer's crates of fish. Naturally you yourselves could also indicate to me anyone you would wish to have transported in this manner, or to have bumped off.

Suitable helpers are available, whereby one would not have to nail one's colours to the mast or run any great danger. In order to carry out tasks of this nature we should need the appropriate knock-out substances:

(a) something which one puts in food or drink and which produces unconsciousness for a short period (1-2 hours)

(b) something which when injected can produce a doze of about 4-8 hours.

It is worth noting that this message was sent before Italy had come into the war on the German side, and was still (theoretically at least) a neutral country, with British and American embassies still in situ.

7

Other Axis Organisations

Before we move on to study the actual course of the intelligence battle in Italy, this is perhaps a convenient moment to look briefly at various other organisations, both German and Italian, which played some rôle in the matter, and mention of which will occur in subsequent chapters. These are:

(a) the KdK (Kommando der Kleinkampfverbände, or Small Battle Units Command)
(b) the X Fotilla MAS
(c) the Servizio Informazione Difesa (SID)
(d) The OVRA
(e) the KOCH outfit
(f) the Corpo delle CCNN (Blackshirt Corps)
(g) the Movimento dei Giovanni Italiani Repubblicani
(h) the Centuria del Fascio Crociato
(i) the Brandenburg Regiment
(j) KdM Munich (AST Munich)

These organisations are described in more detail below.

Note: The histories of the KdK operations in the Mediterranean theatre, and of the X Flotilla MAS, overlap and integrate to a very considerable degree. The account of the KdK story is based on the interrogation of the German officers involved, while that of the X Flotilla MAS comes from the interrogation of Italian members of the unit; the two accounts are thus inevitably coloured by the national viewpoint of each camp, and in some cases therefore differ in emphasis or detail – the picture being additionally complicated by the repeated series of reorganisation and re-allocation which different portions of the X Flotilla MAS were subjected to. There is probably little to be gained by striving to homogenise the two histories in order to make every detail match exactly: they correspond sufficiently accurately for our purposes. Injustices may occur where specific attacks appear to be attributed, possibly wrongly, to German or to Italian personnel: the truth is that the degree of integration often makes it difficult to decide, on the basis of unspecific accounts, which nationality was involved, or whether the attack teams were mixed.

Up to the time of the Italian surrender in September 1943 the only 'small boat' operations carried out by the Axis powers had been those of the Italian X Flotilla MAS in the Mediterranean, using two-man submarines, frogmen etc. Admiral Doenitz, commanding the German Navy, had been much impressed by these achievements and by the Royal Navy attack on the *Tirpitz* with mini-submarines, and in September 1943 he appointed Rear-Admiral Heye and a small staff to plan the production, organisation and operational use of a number of such units.

On 18 November 1943 a naval Special Operations Section was set up, the Marine Einsatz Abteilung (MEA): this was a purely naval unit for commando-type operations, the initial plan being for six commandos of 12 men each; these were to be based mainly in N Germany, but a branch was to be started in Italy at La Spezia, the main base of the Italian Navy. Establishments were initially for training purposes only; actual operations were to be controlled by the local Commander-in-Chief.

Discussions and proposals for the improvement and reorganisation of the MEA took place over the next few months, and its relations with the Brandenburg Division and X Flotilla MAS (see p.67) were gradually adjusted. On 18 January, 1944 Hitler approved the immediate construction of 50 midget U-boats and of a considerable number of one-man torpedoes, with the intention of their being used against the Allied invasion of North Europe when it came.

On 20 April, 1944 it was decided to abolish the MEA and to create the KdK, or Small Battle Units Command, controlled by a new section in the Naval War Staff entitled SKL/S. The basis of its work would be as follows:

(a) Close co-operation with the Abwehr, with the Intelligence Section of the Naval War Staff, and with all other similar Army, Luftwaffe and SS organisations.

(b) Operations prepared by the SKL/S would normally be carried out by ordinary naval units and commands, working in close co-operation with the KdK.

The KdK was composed of Small Battle Flotillas (K-Flotillen), each divided into Marine-Einsatzkommandos (MEKs). Flotillas would consist of 50-60 boats, divided into MEKs of 10-12 boats each.

Operations were to be directed by SKL/S through special Einsatz-Stäbe (Operational Staffs) formed in each operational area. There were three such areas –

> the west coast of Italy
> Northern Italy
> The Adriatic

A gradual process of integration with the X Flotilla MAS began, and when necessary, X Flotilla MAS crews were brought up to strength with German naval personnel.

Operations were launched in early 1944 against the Anzio bridgehead, but results were not striking, although on the night of 20/21 February one assault boat claimed to have sunk a destroyer and possibly a corvette as well.

Responding to pressure by the German Naval Command in Italy, Berlin then approved the allocation of 1,765 officers and men from the Navy to X Flotilla MAS, which was re-organised into the following units:

(a) Assault Boat unit, comprising two-man and one-man boats and the so-called 'pigs' (maiali), the original Italian two-man 'human torpedoes'.
(b) A frogman unit, (Gamma men).
(c) An S-Boat unit.
(d) A saboteur unit (remaining under control of the Abwehr).

Quarrels over the allocation of new assault boats, torpedoes etc. arose: Berlin had initially insisted on a proportion of 1:3 in favour of the Germans, but finally a formula of 2:3 was accepted. Nevertheless on 15 April Italian officers of X Flotilla MAS seized the whole of a recent delivery of two-man Assault Boats, and the Germans had to call in the police and security forces to recover their own share. An entry in the War Diary of the German Naval Command for that day records that 'the Italians were doing everything possible to distract German efforts to reanimate the Assault Boat units'.

Thereafter various sorties were made by assault boats, but only minor successess were scored.

Meanwhile the KdK units on the east coast of Italy had been equally trying to achieve results, working from a KdK base at Cigale: these were mainly MEKs 20, 71 and 90, and by frogmen working in co-operation with S-boats and Assault boats.

Abortive attacks were made on Ancona on the nights of 15/16 September, 1944 and 18/19 September. On the night of 9/10 January, 1945 MEK launched a commando raid behind the Allied lines on the east coast south of Ancona, and claimed two road bridges and a railway bridge destroyed. Allied reports of this attack merely mention the railway bridge, which was on a little-used line and caused few problems to the flow of supplies to the forward areas.

During the early months of 1945, assault boats were used for landing agents on the French Riviera. The first attempt appears to have been made on 21/22 February, when two two-man boats failed to get their agents ashore; by 25 April however it was claimed that 28 agents had been landed.

The next big operation to be mounted on the Adriatic coast was on 15/16 March, once again against Ancona, using seven S-boats, two two-man and

Kapitän Hermann Baltzer
Abwehr I(M)

Dr Otto Begus
Head of Amt VI/S, Verono

Prince Valerie Borghese
Commander of the X Flotilla Mas

Lieut-Colonel David

Colonel Hans Engelmann:
C.O., Führungsstelle Italien

Colonel Wilhelm Harster, BdS

Colonel Hans Helfferich
Head of the Abwehr in Italy

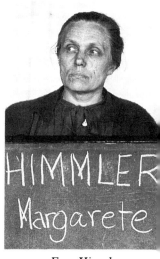

Frau Himmler

Obersturmführer Alois Holzget.
At BdS Italien

SS Major Herbert Kappler,
Head of the SD in Rome

Sturmbannführer Dr Fritz Kranebitter:
Head of Abteilung IV (Counter-
Espionage) at BdS Italien.

Lt. Lossen, alias Erico Se
2 i/c, FAT 150

*Captain Ludwig Mohr:
dministration, FAK 150*

*SS Captain Erich Priebke, Assistant
to Kappler at SD office in Rome*
COPYRIGHT DONALD GURREY

*Georg Plaaten, alias Guido Polino
CO, FAT 150*

*SS Colonel Rauff, Head of the SD
for Lombardy, Piedmont and Liguria*

Nazi war criminal Walter Rauff in Chile

Lt. Ernst Schmidt-Burch

Leutnant zur See Georg Ses
Abwehr I(M), Florence

Untersturmführer Walter Segna:
Liaison officer between BdS and
the Fascist Party

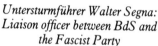

Elisabeth Tabbo, alias 'Annabella'
and 'Countess von Hodenburg':
FAK 150

Lieut-Colonel Joachim Steinberg
CO of FAK 309

Sturmbannführer Rudolf Wiha
Head of Personnel Branch,
BdS Italien

*Obergruppenführer Karl Wolff: Supreme
Police and SS Commander in Italy*
COURTESY OF THE IMPERIAL WAR MUSUEM

Cognome *Del Giudice*
Nome *Teresa*
Padre *di Rodolfo —*
Madre *Barra Amelia*
nato il *8. 7. 1920 —*
a *Firenze*
Stato civile *nubile*
Nazionalità *Italiana*
Professione *A. C.*
Residenza *Firenze*
Via *B. San Lorenzo 17*

CONNOTATI E CONTRASSEGNI SALIENTI

Altezza	*1. 65*
Corporatura	*regolare*
Capelli	*biondi*
Occhi	*castani*
Naso	*regolare*
Segni pari	

FIRMA DEL TITOLARE *del Giudice Tere*

FIRENZE li *6 LUG 1943*

IMPRONTA DEL DITO
INDICE SINISTRO

IL PODESTÀ
d'ordine del Pode
Il V.ce Segretario

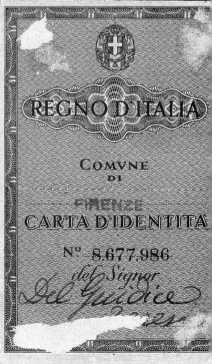

REGNO D'ITALIA

COMVNE
DI
FIMENZE

CARTA D'IDENTITA

N° 8.677.986

del Signor

Del Giudice

Del Giudice, Maria Teresa

Fosca, Viola

Bianchini, Floriana

Ferida, Luisa

Antonini, Bruna

Anzioso, Anna

Ciappei, Ida

Stacciola, Maria

Pacek or Pocek, Fea

six one-man Assault boats, manned by personnel of MEK 71; the objectives were to sabotage fuel and stores dumps and to attack a bridge and an airfield. While these attacks were in progress, the one-man boats were to attack shipping in the harbour, and eight Italian agents were to be landed by collapsible dinghy 20 miles south of the port. Fog however prevented the Assault boats from reaching their objectives and the commando operations had to be abandoned. The eight agents were however landed by dinghy near Ancona; even this part of the operation was a failure, since they were all captured shortly afterwards.

During April, the last month before the German surrender, Assault boat operations were confined to the landing of agents on the coast north of Ancona, except for a single raid on the night of 18/19 April, when Commando troops landed north of Ancona and successfully blew up an Allied fuel pipe line. Given that the German forces in Italy surrendered two weeks later, this served little purpose. As can be seen, a very considerable effort was put in to the KdK concept by the German Navy. By the end of the war the KdK was some 17,000 strong, half of them operating in the Mediterranean, half in N Europe (mainly along the Dutch and Belgian coastal estuaries). The final assessment by Royal Navy historians of its achievements ran: 'The German naval authorities attached an importance to the KdK which was out of all proportion to the results achieved: no disappointments or failures ever shook Doenitz's or Heye's faith in their new weapons, but were logged as "valuable experience gained for the future"'. Unfortunately for them the future never arrived.

The exact relationship between the MEA, the KdK and the MEKs was in the main not fully clear to Allied Counter-Intelligence at the time, although it was appreciated that some Abwehr operations were being run in conjunction with parts of them. In allocating 'unit of origin' to a number of agents who were arrested, all three of the above titles were used somewhat indiscriminately.

THE X FLOTILLA MAS

This was a crack Italian naval unit, comparable perhaps in some ways with the Royal Marines and their Special Boat Section (SBS). MAS stands for Motoscafi Anti-Sommergibili, or Anti-Submarine Motor-Boats – a quite misleading description of their rôle. Prior to the Italian armistice in 1943 the X Flotilla MAS, with HQ at La Spezia, was divided into three groups:

(a) the 'BDS' group, employing slow manoeuvrable two-man torpedoes

(b) the 'Cotrau' group, using midget submarines and explosive motorboats known as MTSM

(c) the 'Gamma' group, consisting of first-class swimmers, i.e. 'frogmen', who proceeded underwater to their targets, on which they fixed limpet mines.

The Flotilla was responsible for attacks on Allied shipping in French North Africa, Gibraltar and Alexandretta, and in some of these operations a high degree of success was achieved. Under German control it carried out similar attacks at Anzio. It never formed part of the Italian Intelligence Service, although it received certain assistance from the latter; nor, prior to the 1943 armistice, had it collaborated with the German Intelligence Services: it was in fact an élite unit which jealously guarded its secrets.

On 3 September, 1943, the comander of the Flotilla, Prince Valerio Borghese (see plate section), had talks with an Abwehr representative, and in October he met Admiral Doenitz, Head of the German Navy, in Berlin, when arrangements were made for putting the Flotilla, or at least a major part of its formations, under the joint direction of the German Navy and the Abwehr. For the next two months there was considerable bickering as to the respective rôles of these two authorities; but early in 1944 an understanding was reached, and thenceforward recruitment, training and expansion were rapid.

The naval side of the Flotilla was taken over by the KdK; most of the Gamma units were placed at the disposal of Abwehr II for sabotage work. The only part of the Flotilla which was still under Italian control was the San Marco Regiment, a non-specialist part of the Flotilla consisting of ordinary fighting men used mainly in an infantry rôle; this was however used as a pool by the Germans from which to recruit for Abwehr II operations.

Expansion resulted in the X Flotilla MAS reaching a total of 50-60,000 men by the end of 1944, comprising whole divisions of infantry, artillery and engineer battalions, plus a number of special formations such as 'assault units' (still known as 'X Flotilla MAS', but now only a small part of the whole), sabotage units, battalions of swimmers, parachutists etc. During the last few months of 1944 all the land units of the San Marco Regiment were amalgamated to form what was then designated 'X Division MAS', and the whole organisation, under Prince Borghese, was given the shortened title 'X MAS'. The San Marco Regiment disappeared in this process, but became the San Marco Division (also known as 1 Marine Infantry Division), existing as a component part of X Mas.

Personnel consisted mainly of young men who had volunteered for X Flotilla MAS in preference to being drafted to units trained in Germany and commanded by German officers. Apart from a few exceptions, none of the men were excessively pro-Fascist or pro-German; 90% of them were under 25 and many had come from the former 10 Arditi Regiment and from the Folgore and Nembo Parachute Division. Morale was high.

Apart from the special formations used for sabotage etc., the bulk of the X MAS land units finished up employed on anti-partisan duties, although at least two of the battalions fought at Anzio, another in Northern France and others on the Italian front.

Of the special formations linked with GIS operations – i.e. the 2 Battle Group MAS, the most important was the VEGA Battalion of swimmer-demolition troops, formed in October 1944 from three swimmer companies of the Folgore group and commanded by the Italian Naval Lieutenant Rossi. While much of the latter had been employed that summer in anti-Partisan operations, three sections were then placed under the command of Abwehr Kommando 212 and given the name of 'RUDI Group', from the name of its CO, Rodolfo Ceccacci. Meanwhile the sea assault units of X MAS Flotilla continued as before with surface craft and Gamma personnel.

While Spezia continued to be the main centre and base, the two following locations were of particular significance in the context of Abwehr work:

(a) Jesolo (40km from Venice): HQ of a Gamma school controlled by the MEA and run by Lieutenant Sowa. Suitable candidates were sent there from Spezia and were then recruited by FAK 212.

(b) Capena (25km north of Rome): up until the capture of Rome this was a centre for training in land sabotage operations, organised by FAK 212. Selected recruits from Jesolo received final instructions and assignments at Capena before being sent across the lines. Count Thun von Hohenstein, CO of FAK 212, made Capena his HQ in early 1944. Records show that in February 1944 between 35–40 men had arrived there for training that month and 25 more were expected in March. A number of agents who had passed through the centre had already been captured by that time.

It must be admitted that the confused re-organisation and expansion of the whole X MAS concept, with its large number of different units all calling themselves loosely 'X MAS' often made life difficult for Allied intelligence staffs trying to identify responsibility for specific sabotage operations.

THE SERVIZIO INFORMAZIONE DIFENSA (SID)

Until the time of the Armistice in 1943 the Italian Intelligence Service was formed by three independent bodies working for each of the service Ministries, and collaborating only to a minimum extent with each other. These were:

SIM: Military Intelligence
SIS: Naval Intelligence
SIA: Air Intelligence

The efficiency of these two organisations must be considered from two angles. In the field of offensive intelligence, very little was achieved by any of them, and their general record was one of poor organisation, insufficient funds, lack of attention to detail and want of enthusiasm. On the other hand counter-espionage, which was a branch of SIM, was extremely efficient, and defensive penetration operations against enemy networks were carried out with success.

Collaboration with the Germans was on the smallest possible scale. Except in the case of the SIS observation service in the Straits of Gibraltar, the Germans appear to have regarded the activities of their allies with contempt and, although prepared to use their reports, they gave nothing in return.

After the Italian Armistice the SID became totally split, with half joining the Allies (to become SID/CS) and half (often purely by force of circumstances and geographical location) supporting the Fascist cause. Late in September 1943 the Ministry of Defence of the Mussolini government proceeded to the creation of a new intelligence organisation, embodying the existing members of SIM to be found in its territory, personnel of the Naval SIS and Air Force SIA, together with the Carabinieri. The moving spirit behind this organisation was Marshal Graziani, by this time a staunch Republican. The officers of the new service, which was to abandon the Royalist and conservative policies of the old SIM, were required to sign a declaration of allegiance to the new Salò Republic and to promise their willingness to continue to fight alongside their German comrades. It should be said that this oath was in many cases not taken, or was given in bad faith since many of the SIM officers concerned, although apparently anxious to continue their specialised police and intelligence duties (and no doubt to avoid being sent to front-line fighting units or to Germany), scarcely approved the character and aims of the new regime.

Its initial chief was Dr Vittorio Foschini, but in late January 1944 Foschini's freely expressed anti-German attitudes led him to disaster; he was kidnapped by the SS as he left Graziani's villa on Lake Garda and disappeared to Germany.*

His successor was Lt-Colonel Candeloro De Leo, a Carabiniere officer described as 'capable and unscrupulous' (although it must be said in his favour that he was still prepared to sign passes for at least a couple of his officers so that they might go on 'indefinite leave' to avoid taking the oath of allegiance; both, in fact, made their way over to the Allies and gave a full report on events at SID). De Leo modified Foschini's plans, and while

---

* According to Kappler (interrogated at the end of hostilities) Foschini had made the mistake of rebuilding SIM with its former staff, most of whom were Badoglio supporters.

undoubtedly less anti-German than his predecessor, continued to carry within the organisation many senior officers of doubtful loyalty to Mussolini and his adherents.

In March 1944 the SID departments were briefly as follows:

(a) OMEGA (Offensive Intelligence: supposed to run offensive intelligence operations abroad, but the Germans disapproved of this and it existed in name only.

(b) DELTA (Defensive Intelligence): this was the most important branch of SID, with the majority of its officers seconded from the Carabinieri. The Rome office of the section was headed by Captain Colombini, probably one of the few fervent Republican Fascists in SID.

(c) SIGMA (Internal Political Intelligence): this collected information on civilian morale and the reactions of the various classes to the Mussolini regime and to the Germans, who were naturally keenly interested in its reports.

(d) the 'Centro Raccolta e Elaborazione Notizie', which was purely an HQ section concerned with evaluating intelligence received. It included however a section carrying out the breaking of Allied codes and cyphers, headed by Capitano Fregato Donnini – a very lukewarm Republican who had an English wife and was closely supervised by the GESTAPO. This section enjoyed constant and close German supervision at all levels.

(e) KAPPA (Communications): this installed W/T sets to enable Mussolini to keep in direct touch with SID HQ, and also similar facilities to the offices in Rome, Florence and other important centres, using codes supplied by the cryptographic branch. There was, however, a sad deficiency in radio sets, both in quantity and quality.

(f) ZETA: Postal Censorship throughout Republican Italy, using mainly retired Army officers.

An Allied Security Memorandum issued at the time advised: 'In dealing with members of SID, it should be remembered that, had many of them been stationed in territory under Allied control in the early days of the Italian campaign they might well be working now as SIM co-belligerents alongside Field Security and CIC . . . It seems apparent that the majority of SID is of dubious loyalty to the Republican cause, and that the extremists have by now declared themselves: the disposal of each SID officer [i.e. that Allied security personnel find themselves faced with – *Author's Note*] should therefore be treated very much on its merits.'

Nevertheless the SID continued to collaborate closely with the GIS, who made use of its personnel and contacts on very many occasions.

In 1926 Mussolini formed a secret political police force, the Ufficio Politico Investigativo (UPI) from the ranks of the MVSM to investigate an attempt on his life and against the regime. Two years later this amateurish organisation showed its incompetence when it failed to deal with a serious outbreak of 'Red' agitators in the northern cities. It was therefore decided to form a new Party-inspired body, created by the Ministry of the Interior and placed under De Stefano, Director of the Political Police Division and of the General Directorate, Public Security. De Stefano, who already controlled both the Questura (Police HQ) political agents and the Carabinieri Investigation Squads (both plain clothes organisations which carried out political investigations) formed this force from drafts of his professional policemen, from staff from the public Security organisation, supplemented by likely recruits from the party and the Armed Forces. The work to be undertaken was exclusively the investigation, penetration and unmasking of communist (or any other) political activity held to be subversive: the new organisation was called OVRA. HQ was set up initially in Milan with Italy divided into zones, each controlled by an OVRA office and employing a wide system of paid informants. By 1943 about 1800 OVRA staff were operating.

THE OVRA AT WORK

Provincial OVRA men worked in close collaboration with local police HQ officials, assisting them with arrests and searches of a political nature, but themselves concentrating almost exclusively on the anti-State activities of Italian citizens. Movements of foreigners as such did not interest them: these were the concern of SIM's counter-espionage branch. OVRA members were empowered to pursue their investigations freely from one province to another; their numbers might alter in each zone as subversive activity was thought to wax and wane.

The key position in OVRA was that of 'Zone Inspector', who received all the findings of his zonal organisation and sent them on to the head of the Political Police Division in Rome. If necessary the Head of OVRA was required to report direct to Mussolini, if urgency so demanded.

OVRA men were encouraged to spend a good deal of their time out of the office 'making contacts', their principal hunting-grounds being cafés and places of entertainment. Drawings from the Ministry for secret funds appear to have been heavy and frequent. One Zone Inspector, Ingrassia (OVRA chief for Tuscany) spent 60,000 lire a month in the spring of 1944 before the Allies took over his Florence HQ, though admittedly his cars were at the time operating on Black Market petrol, which doubtless increased his overheads. The seamy side of OVRA is reflected most obviously in its notorious development of the informer system. Originally it was intended to have a number of informers in every social and political milieu, acting voluntarily out of idealistic motives: soon, however, the system embraced a large collection of shady characters, including many ex-convicts, who were rewarded from time to time by their particular OVRA 'employer' with gifts of cash or by Party protection. It is a sorry fact that many a person saved himself from criminal or political penalty by turning OVRA informer. Agents were seldom briefed: they gathered what information they could in their own way. There was no obligation on the part of the individual OVRA official to disclose to his superiors the names of his informants, though it may be assumed that some check was made on the numbers used and the cash dispensed.

One OVRA Inspector, under Allied interrogation, claimed that 'third degree' methods of interrogation were never used (something for which the organisation had a very bad name with the general public) nor were false documents issued to agents and informants. His explanation for the sinister reputation of OVRA (which came second only to the GESTAPO in this respect) was that unscrupulous members of other police forces would often commit atrocities in OVRA's name. It must be borne in mind however that this source was no doubt using a certain amount of whitewash to save himself from Allied internment; the truth probably lies somewhere between the nasty picture drawn by anti-Fascist forces and this 'only a civil servant' pose of the trapped OVRA official.

OVRA also operated abroad, using Italian diplomatic cover. Records show that three OVRA agents operated in London from 1937 onwards, and received a series of monthly cheques, evidently on a graded scale, for about £100, £75 and £50 respectively, some of the money undoubtedly being used for maintaining some sort of informant system. In September 1939 these 'regulars' migrated to New York, where they stayed until the entry of Italy into the war. Another point of historical interest is that Quepo de Llano, one of Franco's leading generals during the Spanish Civil War, was 'on the books' as an admitted OVRA agent operating in Seville in 1941-42.

After the downfall of Mussolini and the formation of the Badoglio government the OVRA must have felt some trepidation; however, although its name and political orientation was changed, it continued to exist as an organisation and its purpose remained the same, viz: the protection of the régime (not now a Fascist one) against subversion. Senise, a former Chief of Police in Rome, assumed duty as Badoglio's Chief of Italian Police Services, and one of the few things he was able to accomplish before he was disposed of by the Germans was to summon together all the

OVRA top brass and order an investigation into illegally-amassed Fascist fortunes. Little work seems, however, to have been undertaken on this, due to the generally chaotic condition of all State and Party institutions and the lack of resolve of many OVRA officials.

After the Armistice OVRA reverted to its pro-Fascist orientation and by the end of 1943 its new chief, Tamburini, had moved with the Ministry of the Interior to Maderna, on Lake Garda. The OVRA HQ, now no longer smelling out the fortunes of Fascist millionaires, had the role of protecting the new régime and remained in Rome until March 1944, when it moved to Valdagno, near Verona.

Meanwhile the Ministry at Maderna was loud in its complaints about the dearth of reports. The Zone Inspectors (for the zones, that is, which had not been occupied by the Allies) had had a hard winter looking for informers and were often unable to produce anything but 'routine reports' on the reactions of the local populace to the UPI, the SS, rationing and the like. Stress was also felt at the centre of the organisation, as the Germans had peremptorily ordered the evacuation of both Maderna and Valdagno at short notice (it is not clear why this order was given or if it was in fact carried out).

By this time many of the OVRA personnel had become as elusive as the informers and were not appearing for duty. Further, as liaison between centres had not been developed by radio, the poor state of road and rail communications made it difficult to keep in touch. A few diehards continued to work, assisted at times by SID, which was permitted to exist, as described above, very much under German control (in practice if not in spirit). Just as they showed little confidence in SID, so the Germans seem also to have mistrusted OVRA agents as intriguers and opportunists, although the latter, as supporting pillars of a sagging Republican regime, should ostensibly have been numbered amongst their most valuable Italian allies.

Nevertheless lower-level OVRA officials were well placed to suggest to the GIS names of suitable people to act as agents for line-crossing and similar operations; as stated earlier, no record appears to have been kept of the names of OVRA informants, so that it is impossible to correlate these with the names of identified GIS agents, but it would seem likely that the GIS will have tapped this obvious pool of talent (if talent is the right word).

The following is an assessment, made in 1944, of the security threat represented by OVRA officials when new areas were occupied by the Allies:

Generally speaking, in view of their intimate association with the repressive (and corrupt) elements in the Fascist creed, OVRA officials, wherever encountered, should be regarded as potentially dangerous elements, well trained in police methods, almost universally disliked by the populace, with a flair for trickery and subterfuge. In some cases, doubtless,

OVRA officers and men merely 'followed their trade' without much conviction or undue malice, but most ranks, and of curse especially those who have continued to operate loyally for the Republic, are highly promising candidates for internment. Their informers, however, who so frequently find their way into Allied security Black Lists under such high-sounding titles as 'OVRA spy' etc are in general of meagre security significance.

THE KOCH OUTFIT

Pietro Koch, a 39-year old ex-wine merchant, was a Fascist fanatic who collaborated with Caruso, Chief of Police in Rome during the German occupation, and with the Gestapo; he had a squad of 67 people under his command, ten of them women, who specialised in tracking down anti-Fascists and Allied agents, and then torturing them. He operated from the former Pensione Oltramare, on the top floor of a yellow six-storey block at 2 Via Principe Amedeo, and later from the Pensione Jaccarino, Via Romagna, where the cellars were fitted out for torture. His girl friend Marcella Stoppani was described as 'a stenographer who laughed at the sight of blood, liked to kick men in the groin and wrote sadistic poetry'. In March 1944 he handed over a number of his prisoners for massacre by the SD at the Ardeatine Caves.

After the fall of Rome he went to Florence and then to the Villa Triste in Milan, by which time his methods of interrogation had achieved further refinements. For some reason he collected a number of people from the theatre world to act as his accomplices and informers. One of these was Luisa Ferida, a well-known Italian film star of the period.

After the war Koch was tried for war crimes and executed.

CORPO DELLE CCNN: THE BLACKSHIRT CORPS
(ALSO KNOWN AS THE BRIGATE NERE)

This organisation was one of several ugly growths which were not absorbed into the Guardia Nazionale Repubblicana. It was organised on provincial lines, and was composed of military-type 'action squads' whose aims were supposed to be 'the maintenance of order, the defence of the Italian Social Republic, action against bandits and outlaws and the liquidation of any groups of enemy parachutists who may be dropped' (Decree of 3 August 1944). Its chief was Alessandro Pavolini, Secretary of the Fascist Party, who sometimes handled in person the operations of its units – although he was a civilian minister and the Brigate seem to have formed part of the Italian army. In practice their duties seem to have been almost entirely of an aggressive type of police work, although elements did make an appearance in the battle for Florence; the Corps was in fact formed to help the Germans in fighting partisans and in rounding up labour for work in Germany. In both these functions they had considerable success. The Corps consisted in fact of several thousands of what were described (in security reports of the period) as 'the most unsavoury individuals in Europe', while their handling of Italian prisoners (from the partisans etc) was confirmed by many sources as being 'more hideously sadistic than is that of their German hunting-companions'.

The numerical strength per province being estimated at about one thousand, it would seem at first sight remarkable that such a large number of Fascist thugs should be available to be persuaded to leave their homes for long periods in order to accept the discomfort and danger of bitter guerrilla warfare, waged against their compatriots. An analysis of the records of the Paduan members of the Corps provides, however, some explanation, in that for the most part the list was made up of hooligans who had evacuated from the Southern Provinces of Italy – 'whose dregs were thus emptied onto the unfortunate Northerners', as a contemporary report put it.

Although nominally under the command of the Provincial Federal Commissioner of the Fascist Party, the latter had little influence on the planning of his Brigade's activities, the deciding factor being the will of the Sicherheitsdienst, who held power of veto over planned punitive expeditions. In any expedition of importance SD officers and NCOs usually participated, and important prisoners were handed over to them, with power to decide on their release, imprisonment or execution.

Although each Brigade – of which there were some 26* by the end of 1944 – had a permanent HQ organisation, the main body of its members served on a part-time basis and were selected from the more able-bodied and enthusiastic Fascists of the area who were not already in the armed forces. The Decree of September 1944 also laid down that officers and NCOs of the armed forces, the GNR and the police, including regular soldiers, might, if they were members of the Fascist Party, be compulsorily transferred to this new 'Auxiliary Corps', as it was termed.

Each Brigade was to 'assume the name of one who has given his life for the cause of Republican Fascism'. Soon afterwards each Brigade seems to have acquired a 'political office', consisting of a captain and about thirty members, the function of which appeared to be exclusively concerned with watching the anti-Fascist (especially the Communist) situation.

* By 9 April 1945 the Brigata Nera comprised 43 territorial Brigades located in the main towns and cities, plus 5 Mobile Brigades (each of approx. 3,000 men) stationed in Milan, Padua, Modena, Intra-Bergamo and Brescia.

According to a captured agent – an ardent Fascist and a godson of Pavolini, who had already completed two political espionage missions into AOT and was captured on the third – a scheme was drawn up in December 1944 whereby clandestine Black Brigades would be organised in AOT for disruptive and subversive purposes. The plan is said to have been sponsored by Pavolini and approved by Mussolini and the German Ambassador, Rahn. The ultimate objective was the re-establishment of Fascism in AOT, with an underground Brigade, to be known as 'Brigata Nera Italia Invasa' organised in every Department of AOT (excluding for some reason, Sicily and Sardinia – possibly because of the difficulty in getting there). These brigades were to consist of specially selected personnel drawn by Pavolini from the Black Brigades in North Italy and despatched to the South for the purpose, the target figure being 1,200-1,500 members for each brigade. As the Allied armies advanced, Brigades already in existence in the areas now overrun were to go to ground and continue their activities as underground Fascist resistance groups.

It is doubtful whether much progress was ever made in the implementation of this ambitious scheme; it stood little chance of success under the conditions existing at AOT at the time. Nevertheless, the Black Brigades organisation provided a ready-made and fertile recruiting ground for the GIS's post-occupational disruptive plans.

THE MOVIMENTO DEI GIOVANI ITALIANI REPUBBLICANI

This was founded in October 1941 by a group of young, ambitious and somewhat naïve enthusiasts, who visualised it as a movement for the regeneration and salvation of Fascism by a return to first principles, blaming the 'inept and corrupt Fascist Old Guard' for the Italian disasters in Greece and Africa. But inadequate funds, distrust by the established Republican Party and the lack of any solid backing, and of organising ability at the top, doomed the movement, after 2-3 years when it alternated between active recruiting and stagnation, to eventual failure.

By the end of June 1944 it had been virtually taken over by Abwehr II as a source of recruits for sabotage and intelligence operations. Though some members were trained and sent south, they were soon captured by the Allies and the story of the MGIR runs into the sand.

CENTURIA DEL FASCIO CROCIATO

This organisation was originally the brain-child of Colonel David, an Italian who became notorious as a recruiter for the Abwehr. Centred in Venice, it was founded in October or November 1943 and David was assisted in its formation by a certain Renato Pericone, who became its Second-in-Command. Pericone, however, sharply criticised various other organisations in which David was active because of the recruitment of women for solely sexual reasons and, as a result, David soon relinquished his position and Pericone took over sole control.

Under Pericone the CFC, in addition to serving as a central reservoir for the GIS, attempted to become an intra-party political police agency. Personnel were largely drawn from X Flotilla MAS. Members continued to serve in the units to which they were regularly attached or, if they were non-military, resided in private quarters elsewhere. The CFC provided no special agent or technical training; this was done by the GIS when the CFC individuals joined them.

By mid-April 1944 Pericone had gathered a group of some twenty followers. They were called together and told that each man was to be ready to cross the lines on either an espionage or sabotage mission for the Germans. Shortly after this a civilian, Corrado Slievo, was set up as liaison officer between the GIS and Pericone, and called forward a number of CFC members for this purpose.

At this point Pericone seems to have developed a violent mistrust of the Republican Fascist Party, to such an extent that he tried to break away from it altogether and to ally himself and his organisation more closely to the Germans. This plan, however, got no further, as Pericone was denounced to the Fascist Party Secretary, Pavolini, and arrested.

After various disputes, the Centuria was reorganised by the Prefect of Venice on Pavolini's orders. Pavolini had come to an agreement with Dr Bauer of the Abwehr that the CFC would continue to serve as a reservoir for GIS agents and that, while it would depend financially on the Fascist Party, the men drawn from it by the GIS would be paid by the Germans.

By the late summer of 1944 Centuria had over 100 members, a number of whom had by then crossed the lines and fallen into Allied hands. Thereafter it seems to have largely dropped out of sight, probably having lost momentum after Pericone disappeared from the scene.

THE BRANDENBURG REGIMENT

The Brandenburg Regiment (later expanded into a division) was a unique, constantly-changing organisation which had no equivalent in any of the Allied armies; the nearest description one can venture is that it was a mixture of the Commandos and SOE, but even this is far from the mark. It was essentially an offshoot of Abwehr II, and saw Admiral Canaris as being its chief; in its heyday it consisted of three battalions (18 companies) plus some extra units.

Its origins go back to September 1939, when AST Vienna assembled at Brück an der Leitha, Austria, a group of some 300 Sudeten Germans whom it was planned to use for sabotage attacks from Upper Silesia (which they knew well) across into the Polish rear areas – that is, the attacks being launched from the Slovakian half of what had been Czechoslovakia, not occupied by Germany. They were 'camouflaged' as members of a sports group on holiday. Due to the quick ending of the Polish campaign they were not in fact committed to this task operationally; but Dr von Hippel, of AST Vienna, had little difficulty in 'selling' to the Abwehr in Berlin the operational advantages of assault engineer units composed of men who knew the terrain and the languages of countries and regions likely to be attacked by Germany, and he obtained permission to recruit two companies, with the title Baulehrkompanie zbV 800 (Construction Training Company 800, for Special Duties), to be used both for the forthcoming attack against France and the Low Countries, and in the East and Southeast of Europe.

An HQ was set up in Brandenburg, on the River Havel not far from Berlin, where Abwehr II already had a training centre for saboteurs, agents, W/T operators etc. On 15 December a third company was added, consisting mainly of Czech and Sudeten Germans; later Germans from Roumania, the Baltic states, Palestine and SW Africa were pulled in, recruitment being on a very ad hoc 'old boy net' basis, not unlike that of SOE. Only ethnic Germans were accepted (unlike the Waffen-SS, for example, which finished up with more non-Germans than Germans in its ranks). By Christmas 1939 the title 'Brandenburg' was adopted for all members of the Baulehr Bataillon, as it had now become.

Unlike the British Commandos, the tasks allotted to it were not primarily destructive, but preventative, i.e. in a German attack their rôle was to go in ahead of their own troops and seize vital targets before the enemy could destroy them (usually using disguise and deception, with the Brandenburgers dressed in the enemy's uniform and speaking his language). These they would hold until the main German attacking force could catch up with them and exploit the situation. The normal size of the Brandenburg commando in battle tasks was the company, formed of two half-companies, each of two 'teams'; total strength of the company was some 300 men.

By the end of 1941 the Brandenburg group had expanded into a Regiment and was operating in these small units down the whole of the German fighting front, from the north of Finland, down through the USSR, in the Balkans and North Africa. Two teams had led the assault on Holland and Belgium in 1940, going in a few hours before Zero Hour, in Dutch uniforms, to seize two bridges essential for the advance. Very many similar operations were carried out in Russian uniforms on the Eastern front. In

Roumania, while it was still technically neutral, one Roumanian-speaking company went in, in civilian clothes, to safeguard the oil-supply routes from Ploesti. English-speaking commandos from I Battalion were to have been used in British uniforms for Operation Sealion, to land at Folkestone, Dungeness and Weymouth.

No 4 Company (I Battalion) were trained as parachutists. At the end of 1942 a 'sea-landing' company was formed, including a large element of German naval personnel, for use in seizing the Toman Penisular, east of the Crimea. By September of 1942 it was decided to expand this company into a 'Küstenjägerabteilung' or Coastal Rifleman Detachment, consisting of four companies and equipped with Assault Boats and 12 sabotage boats (Sprengboote). Their mission was to fight enemy partisans from the sea, and to carry out commando operations behind the enemy lines, including attacks on enemy ships and harbours. Most of the personnel came from the German Navy. This unit became operational in January 1943, and was mainly used along the Dalmation coast and among the Greek Islands in purely commando-type operations.

The Italian surrender in September 1943 resulted in Brandenburg units being rushed south. The 2nd Battalion was used in Central Italy to round up escaped British POWs (of which a considerable number had emerged from Italian POW camps and were roaming at large), against Italian partisans and along the east coast to counter Allied attempts to pick up escaping POWs and evacuate them by sea. 4 Company of the Küstenjägers hurried to Sardinia to protect the island against possible Allied landings; 14 Company of the Brandenburg Regiment proper was already there in this rôle, and on 9 September it seized the important naval port of Maddelena, on the north tip of the island, using the traditional techniques of bluff and deception. However, with the Allied landings at Salerno, it was decided by the German High Command that both Sardinia and Corsica could not be effectively defended, and by 5 October both elements had been evacuated to the Italian mainland. They were not thereafter used for offensive 'Brandenburg-type' operations in Italy, although one company was used in an infantry role at the Anzio Bridgehead.

Allied CI staffs in Italy were well aware of the security threat posed by these formations. By November 1943 they were already in possession of a list giving the full names and date of birth of 140 Brandenburgers who had been stationed in Sardinia, each name having paired with it an Italian alias. The men were said to speak fluent English and to have made at least five parachute jumps. The names of their officers – Captain Benesch, Captain Hettinger and Naval Kapitän-Leutnant Martiny – were also known. It seemed likely that these men, given the known history of the unit, would be used – either in Italian or British uniforms – to land in, or be dropped into, Southern Italy, and a general alert was issued. In the event this never happened, and the companies that had been in Sardinia were eventually sent to fight in Yugoslavia.

When the SS took over the Abwehr most of the Brandenburg Division finished up being used as ordinary PanzerGrenadiers, while the Coastal units were merged into the Navy's Kommando der Kleinkampfverbände. Only a 'rump' of some 900 linguists was left for special duties, which in August 1944 were listed as follows:

> Russian: 210
> English: 181
> Serbocroat: 185
> French: 189
> Italian: 344
> Various: 610

However, the original Brandenburger concept was basically only applicable in a scenario involving blitzkrieg advances by the German forces; with the Wehrmacht in permanent retreat from mid-1943 onwards there were relatively few opportunities thereafter for the use of their special talents. Doubtless also the Sicherheitsdienst was jealous of their renown and was keen to emasculate them, fearing perhaps their use as an Abwehr private army if a crunch situation should arise between Abwehr and SS.*

KDM MUNICH

There is one further unit to consider before proceeding to the description of operations carried out by organisations inside Italy. We have seen that where the Wehrmacht was in action, Frontaufklärungskommandos were allocated in support, and this was the case in Italy. At the same time, countries surrounding Germany were also the responsibility of Abwehrstellen inside Germany: in the case of Italy, this was AST Munich (later, after the RSHA re-organisation, re-designated KdM Munich-Kommando

*A number of errors seem to have arisen, in respect of the Brandenburg units, in various military histories. One of these states that the Regiment was developed in 1942-43 out of the success of the Küstenjäger companies. This is putting the chicken before the egg. At least one other writer ('Military Elites' by Roger A. Beaumont) claims that Otto Skorzeny was in command of detachments of Brandenburgers for the operation to rescue Mussolini and for the troops used in the Ardennes attack, dressed in Allied uniforms and aimed at sowing panic behind the Allied lines. Both these accounts are incorrect. The Mussolini rescue was carried out by men of the Fallschirmjäger Lehr-Bataillon, while the Ardennes unit (Einheit Stielau) was organised by Skorzeny with English-speaking 'volunteers' (most of them did not know what they were volunteering for) grouped under Panzer Brigade 150. There is no mention of either of these operations in the semi-official history of the Brandenburg Regiment ('Die Brandenburger – eine deutsche Kommandotruppe', by Helmuth Spaeter: Verlagsagentur Walther Angerer, 1978).

des Meldegebietes). In 1944 it was headed by Lt-Colonel Waag, later superseded by SS Obersturmbannführer Glitz when the RSHA took over. While its main activities were directed towards Italy, the KdM also dabbled in France, the Balkans, Russia, Greece and North Africa, as well as looking out for possible agents for despatch to the UK and USA. The main offices were on the second floor at 7 Theresenstrasse, Munich, with a small office on the central Stachusplatz to act as a 'check in' point for new arrivals and visitors.

Apart from sending agents to Italy to report on political matters, the KdM set up a radio training school in Verona for the training of post-occupational agents, under Leutnant von Ossenbach (a W/T expert) in February 1944. In the summer of the same year Oberstleutnant Waag took over the AST (as it then was) and started a policy of training W/T agents to be parachuted into Italy behind the Allied lines. Von Ossenbach moved from Verona to St Ulrich (Ortisei) and a combined W/T and espionage school was set up under command of Leutnant von Ach. The latter used the cover name of 'Zeno', while von Ossenbach called himself 'Don Pablo'. The unit assumed the title 'Meldekopf Zeno'.

Other Ast Munich personnel were sent in as recruiters for the school, operating mainly in Turin and Milan. In September the school moved once again, this time to Merano/Hafling. When trained, recruits were usually taken to the airfield at Bergamo (the Abwehr despatch point here being named Dienststelle Carmen) and despatched by parachute into Allied Occupied Territory. Records do not show where their parachute training* as such was carried out. Between 20 November 1944 and 7 March 1945 some seven missions were launched, the men usually going in pairs. Not one of these ever made contact with their radio base, according to a member of the Abwehr staff.

From January 1944 the AST was also involved in recruiting W/T agents for post-occupational missions and in setting up a post-occupational network for the Piedmont region. Agents were selected and trained as 'stay-behinds' for Venice, Bologna and Ancona, but all these missions were abandoned when it was decided at the last minute that none of the agents was clever enough to operate, once over-run, without arousing suspicion. A fresh collection of Italians, who had been operating as political informants for the AST on petty Fascist squabbles in towns of N. Italy, was selected in April and May 1944 to form a stay-behind network for Piedmont, but one of their number talked too openly about the plan and these recruits, too, were dropped. Further groups were subsequently chosen and trained for the task; records do not show the outcome.

*If any. In at least one case no such training was given before the agent was parachuted; possibly this was general practice.

Other agent missions were planned by the KdM against the South of France, to operate by fishing boat out of San Remo; these too came to nothing, with KdM Munich complaining, in messages to their representatives in Turin, that agents were being sent down to San Remo for despatch 'hopelessly equipped and without documents'.

8
The German Intelligence Services in Italy:
Phase I: 1940-September 1943

The operations of the GIS in Italy can conveniently be divided into four periods, each of which had its own special characteristics:

1. From 1940 to the Allied landings and the Italian armistice in September 1943.
2. From September 1943 until the fall of Rome on 4 June 1944. This included a long static period through the winter, embracing the battles for Cassino and the Anzio landings – but also covering the occasion, in early March 1944, when the RSHA took over control of the Abwehr after the ousting of Admiral Canaris.
3. From the fall of Rome to the capture of Florence and the manning of the German 'Gothic Line' in the mountains north and north-east of Florence (early August 1944) – a fluid period as the Wehrmacht fought a delaying action up the centre of Italy while the Gothic Line defences were being prepared.
4. The slow and bitter fighting through the winter of 1944-45 and the early spring, with the Allies seeking to pierce this final defence line and break out into the Po valley. This was achieved in mid-April, and was followed by the German surrender on 2 May.

PHASE I: 1940-SEPTEMBER 1943

During these early years of the war the senior Abwehr man in Italy was Colonel Otto Helfferich (see plate section), who lived with his wife at Via Archimede 128 in Rome. Helfferich had been a captain in World War I and had rejoined the army in September 1935. As a linguist (he had been born in Trieste in 1888, so spoke fluent Italian, besides English, French and Spanish) he was at once posted to AST Stuttgart. In January 1937 he took part in the Spanish Civil War as a liaison officer between the Abwehr and the Italian Expeditionary Force under Roatta; injured in a car accident, he returned to Germany at the end of the year. In March 1939 he was posted to AST Prague as head of Department III-F (i.e. security and counter-intelligence work against enemy espionage) but after only a month was pulled out and appointed Head (Leiter) of KO Italien. This appointment was something of a misnomer in terms of 'classic' KO work: his main job was to act as liaison officer between the Abwehr in Berlin and the Italian military intelligence organisation, the SID. He had an office of his own inside this latter establishment.

Described as 'a military man of the old type' (his photograph calls to mind that well-known pre-war Hollywood actor of German officer rôles, Konrad Veidt), he was a great admirer, and friend, of Admiral Canaris, and played a certain rôle in maintaining one of the latter's attempted links with the British Government. He had a great contempt for the Nazis, whom he loathed, and at the end of the war he made a formal request to the Allied authorities to be allowed, when released from POW camp, to live in Italy and not be obliged to return to Germany. His request was granted, and he died in Italy some years later.

As LO to the SID he concerned himself with the exchange of purely military information, most of it consisting of SID reports on French troop movements on the Riviera, French garrisons in N. Africa, British garrisons in Egypt and Order of Battle in the UK. He was also receiving, at the time of the North Africa campaign, shipping movement reports from Madrid and some operational intelligence transmitted direct from Tunisia. He had, however, no secret sources of his own and merely acted as a channel and filter for information. He also maintained his interest (it was, indeed, his only Abwehr expertise) in the III-F sector, being kept informed by SID/CS on intelligence about Allied agents in Italy.

Naval intelligence at this time (1940-41) was handled by visits to Italy by Fregatten-Kapitän Hermann Balzer from Abwehr I-M Berlin and did not involve Helfferich's office. Air intelligence too was initially run direct from Berlin, with visits 3-4 times a year by GAF majors Brede and Brasser to Italian Air Command. At the beginning of 1942, however, I-L Berlin sent Hauptmann Lewinsky to Rome as a permanent air representative, working under the direct orders of I-L but operating alongside the German Air Attaché in the Rome embassy.

With the arrival of larger numbers of German troops in Italy at the end of 1941, consequent upon the regular passage of troops and supplies to the Afrika Korps, it was found necessary to institute some form of security intelligence back-up, and KO Italy was set up in more formal shape. Its main tasks were the prevention of sabotage and espionage within the Wehrmacht in Italy, and the security of shipping between Italy and North Africa. Military history aficionados will recall that 1941-42 was a period when Axis shipping to North Africa was being increasingly destroyed by Allied submarines and aircraft, with the German High Command constantly attributing these losses to Italian 'treachery'. In fact it was the Wehrmacht's own security failings, i.e. the breaking of their Enigma codes by the British, which were largely to blame for these sinkings.

Since early in the war Abwehr I-H had in fact been operating in Italy (though not in respect of Italian matters). Sonderführer Rabe, using the cover name of Emilio Rossetti, had arrived at the German Consulate in Genoa in early 1940, his tasks being to administer agents coming from France, and to recruit new agents for use against France. For this he worked direct to Berlin, being placed under Helfferich only for administrative purposes. In June 1940 he took on as secretary a German girl, Elisabeth Tabbo-Petzel (see plate section), who had come to Italy from Bremen when aged 26 for reasons of health, and who before long had married an hotel proprietor in Alassio; she took on the job quite unaware of the work that Rabe was engaged in (in fact it was only two years later that she discovered that Rossetti was not his real name) but in due course was to become one of the most active Abwehr employees in Italy. Her aliases, 'Annabella' and 'Baroness von Hodenberg', were before long constantly cropping up in the interrogations of captured GIS agents.

It will be realised that while agents A and B were being despatched on missions, agents C and D would be under training and a search was having to be made for agents E and F – in other words, to maintain an effective and on-going organisation, a considerable 'back-up' of 'talent-spotters', trainers and administrators was essential. This was particularly so once Allied CI in Italy began achieving success in arresting large numbers of GIS agents, so that the attrition rate called for a constant supply of new bodies. Such persons usually held the honorary rank of Sonderführer. It was in such rôles that Elisabeth Tabbo figures so often, her fluent Italian, and ability to assess the Italian character, proving of great help to the Abwehr.

Over the next months she was busy vetting and administering Rabe's agents. Soon his tasks were switched from France (since the Germans had now a grip on the whole of the country) to the Middle East, and at Helfferich's suggestion he moved down to Naples as being a more profitable location from which to attack Turkey, Syria, Iraq, Palestine and Egypt. Elisabeth Tabbo went with him, and an Abwehr office was set up in Naples at Via Alessandro Manzoni 146, complete with W/T station. Rabe also installed his family in an apartment immediately above the office. Here 'Annabella' was busy as before, helping to manage the agents and also acting as a courier to Helfferich in Rome, collecting mail and secret funds, and carrying Abwehr mail for Berlin.

In September 1941 it was decided by I-H that Rabe would be more effective if he operated from AST Athens; but 'Annabella', who was by now highly estimated in Abwehr circles, was left in charge of such agents who were still in Italy, besides being encouraged to look out for new ones. She found however that Naples was a poor hunting-ground for Middle

East agents and decided to include Rome in her operational area. Here she got an introduction (using the phoney title of 'Baroness von Hodenberg') to Amanullah, the ex-King of Afghanistan, and members of his immediate family, where she became a frequent visitor; her aim was to get suggestions for any Middle-easterners who might be suitable for use as agents by the GIS. No names were forthcoming, but the ex-King's brother and his brother-in-law became interested in carrying out such missions themselves – indeed, even Amanullah himself considered doing so, with the proviso 'that he would have to travel incognito and the Germans would have to find a means to ensure his safe return'. In the end, these grandiose plans failed to get off the ground.

At the end of April 1942 she left Naples and set up permanently in Rome, occupying an apartment at 25 Via Archimede, only a few doors away from Helfferich, and continued to administer Rabe's agents and to cultivate Arab and Persian circles in the search for new recruits. Finally, at the end of January 1943, she was posted to Athens in order to help Rabe set up an I-H stay-behind network in Greece. The gentle reader may well surmise that Rabe was behind this posting, and that the relationship between the two of them was by now not entirely platonic.

We shall hear more of her later on (see p.95). Allied CI already had her in their sights, their card on her reading:

> TABBO alias PETZEL Elisabetta alias Annabella.
> Daughter of ENERT Ernesto and STUEBEL Gianna.
> Born Bremen 1898. Resides at Via Archimede 25, Rome.
> Recruiter for Abt. I agents.

With the departure of Rabe, Abteilung I of the Abwehr appointed in mid-1942 a number of independent officers to supplement the intelligence they were receiving from SIM. These officers reported direct to Berlin, so that Helfferich did not control their reports or even see them – a curious situation which might be taken to infer a certain lack of confidence in Helfferich's ability. The officers in question were:

For Abwehr I-M: Freg. Kaptn Baltzer (photo, see plate section), Korv. Kaptn Klaps, Lt. z. See Georg Sessler (photo, see plate section), Korv. Kaptn. von Wettstein

These officers were all located at La Spezia and later at Florence, with the exception of von Wettstein, who covered the Adriatic and worked from Bari and Brindisi. Their tasks were mainly Allied troop and shipping movements, especially in the Western Mediterranean; they were also charged with seeking intelligence on Allied intentions in respect of amphibious landings.

For Abwehr I-L: Leutnant (later Hauptmann) Hoermann, who was based at Kesselring's Air HQ at Frascati, south of Rome. This link increased in importance when, at the beginning of April 1943, Kesselring became the Supreme Commander of all German armed forces in the region (OBSW: Oberbefehlshaber Südwest). Hoermann was given his own W/T link, code-named TOGO. He himself was later replaced by Oberleutnant zur See Rhotert.

For Abwehr I-H: Leutnant Häusgen: based on Spezia, he had the special task of planting post-occupational agents in Sardinia and Corsica, since it was felt that the Allies would probably attempt to seize these at some point. He does not appear to have had a great deal of success in this.

THE SABOTAGE ORGANISATION IN ITALY

At the beginning of 1943 Abteilung II of the Abwehr set up a sabotage organisation in Italy. This was placed under the direct control of the Ic of OBSW, at that time Colonel Schwednitz, with Helfferich once again cut out of the chain of command. Initially it was commanded by Major Pachtl, who had previously been engaged in training sabotage agents for North Africa; he left, however, in September 1943 to take command of the Lehr Regiment Brandenburg, his place being taken by Major Graf Thun von Hohenstein.

The task of Abeteilung II was, as has been stated, sabotage and the organisation of minorities. There was not much scope for the latter function in Italy, and the sabotage at this stage was only of a preparatory nature, consisting of concealing quantities of explosives in waterproof containers for use later on by post-occupational agents. However, a start was made in the recruiting of suitable Italians for this latter rôle; they were trained either in Germany by the Lehr Regiment Brandenburg, or at the X Flotilla MAS sabotage school. An additional Abwehr II Trupp, under Oberleutnant Schmid-Burck, also made an appearance in Italy during the summer (about which little seems to be on record), and a company of the Brandenburg Regiment was sent to Corsica for coastal defence.

THE SICHERHEITSDIENST

So much for the Abwehr's groundwork before the onset of the Italian campaign. What of the Sicherheitsdienst?

There were already two names of significance in Rome by 1939. One of these was Standartenführer Eugen Dollmann, Himmler's personal representative with the Italian Government, whose rôle has already been described in Chapter VI. Dollmann settled into a house at Via San

Sebastianello 17 and provided directly to Himmler, through personal contacts at the highest level, high-grade political and personality information on the Italian scene. This was not, of course, 'secret intelligence' in the accepted Sicherheitsdienst sense of the subject, but rather the type of information normally picked up by a country's ambassador and reported back through Ministry of Foreign Affairs channels; but the latter, in Nazi Germany, had fallen low in esteem – and in any case Himmler hated von Ribbentrop, the German Foreign Minister, and would hardly wish to rely on him for 'inside information'. Dollmann plays therefore no significant part in the story of German espionage operations in Italy, emerging only, in the final days of the war, in the context of the covert surrender negotiations.

The second figure is one of greater significance – and notoriety – in the history of GIS operations in Italy. SS Obersturmbannführer Herbert Kappler was born in Stuggart in 1907 and studied electro-technics. In 1931 he joined the SA, passing on to the SS in 1932. In the following year (see plate section) he entered the Würtemberg police and in 1937, after doing well in police examinations, was admitted, as the first non-Prussian, to the SIPO Leaders' School in Berlin/Charlottenburg. He then became a Kriminalkommissar (Detective-Superintendent) and in 1939 was posted to the German Embassy in Rome as Police Attaché. He was also, in 1939, involved indirectly in two of the more sensational political incidents of the period: he was recalled to Berlin in November to assist in the interrogation of Georg Elser, who had placed the time-bomb which narrowly failed to kill Hitler in the Munich Bierkeller, and also, during the same visit, in the interrogation of Stevens and Best, the two British MI6 officers in Holland who had been lured to the Dutch frontier at Venlo and kidnapped by Schellenberg in person – the famous 'Venlo Incident'.

His duties involved liaison with the Italian police, the exchange of political police information and duty as political adviser to the German Embassy. Unofficially he was also required to send to Berlin regular reports on political tendencies and the general state of morale in Italy.

Until October 1943 Kappler himself carried out no direct Amt VI activities, with the exception of collecting a certain amount of information from the Vatican (one of his contacts there was a man called Kurtna, an ex Soviet agent who was studying to take holy orders). However, a number of Amt VI men were sent to Italy in 1942 and were loosely attached to Kappler's section, or worked outside the Embassy. One Amt VI man who arrived at this time was a Dr Groebl, whose task was to prepare a post-occupational network of agents in Italy. A more sinister Amt VI operation was heralded by the arrival in Rome of a book publisher named Bierback, who ran a number of agents who travelled by air to and from South

America. On one occasion Bierback left behind in his hotel a sealed box which had been too heavy to carry by plane; Kappler was asked to get the box back to Berlin because it was beginning to stink out the hotel room. Kappler investigated the matter and finally learned from Bierback that the box contained bacteria intended to be used on meat sent from South America to Britain, in order to render it unfit for consumption by the time it reached the UK.

In March 1943 Kappler received a direct order from Schellenberg, head of Amt VI, to prepare a stay-behind network for Sicily, leaving Groebl to be responsible for Southern Italy. He applied to Berlin for trained Italian-speaking W/T operators and W/T sets, but was told that neither were available.

OPERATION 'ACHSE' ('AXIS')

Immediately after the resignation of Mussolini and his arrest by the Badoglio government on 25 July 1943 (only a week after he had held a conference with Hitler in the Dolomites) Kappler and Dollmann were summoned urgently to Berlin for a meeting with General Student, commander of the German airborne forces; he told them that Hitler was determined to rescue Mussolini, and that they were to assist Otto Skorzeny and his men in the planning of this operation, which was given the code-name 'Achse'. Doll-mann and Kappler's role was to keep Skorzeny informed of Mussolini's whereabouts, so that the rescue could be carried out as soon as Hitler gave the green light. Interestingly, while in Berlin Kappler was called to a conference with Himmler to discuss the turn of events in Italy. He persuaded Himmler that it would be a fatal mistake to set Mussolini (when rescued) up again as head of an Italian government, and suggested the name of Tassinari, a moderate and ex-professor of Economics, as government leader. Tassinari was known to both Himmler and Dollmann, and Himmler agreed to put the idea to Hitler. Tassinari was later called to an interview with Hitler, but the idea seems to have got no further.

The first information on Mussolini's location came from a contact of Kappler's – two brothers who owned a spaghetti factory in Naples and also ran a small number of coastal trading boats: they reported that he had been taken to the Island of Ponza, off the Naples coast, and then to the Sardinian naval base of La Maddelena. Skorzeny planted a man in La Maddelena under cover of the MEK stationed there; but the man then reported that Mussolini had been taken away by seaplane for an unknown destination. For some 16 hours all trace was lost. Kappler, however, knew that a police officer called Gueli had been entrusted with the security of the various zones in which the ex-Duce was to be held, and found out at the Ministry of the Interior that Gueli had just sent in a report from the Gran Sasso area of the Abruzzi Mountains, east of Rome and two-thirds of the way across the peninsular. Kappler's staff were sent to reconnoitre the area and confirmed Mussolini's presence: the rescue operation was then launched successfully by Skorzeny. It was supposed to have been followed by the arrest of the Italian King and some 120 other Italians connected with the coup d'état which removed Mussolini, but this sequel to the operation was never carried out, for reasons which are now obscure.

Kappler's staff had by now expanded and included SS Captain Erich Priebke (see plate section), aged thirty, who had joined the GESTAPO in December 1936, having previously been in the hotel business – including working from February to November 1935 in the Savoy Hotel in London, and a spell in the Grand Hotel Europe in Rapallo.

Unlike the cultured and intellectual Dollmann, Kappler was a tough and ruthless man who embodied the worst German traditions of the militarist Prussian ethos, and who had made the most of the opportunities offered to him by the Nazi regime; his photograph (see plate section), showing the sabre-cut scar from student duelling days when this was the badge of the macho cult, is revealing. We shall hear more of the brutal side of his character later on.

9

Phase II: September 1943-May 1944

Most of the Abwehr who had managed to escape from Tunisia in May 1943 now found themselves in Naples and were attached to the Abwehr station there. The small out-station which had been set up in Sicily had to be evacuated when the Allies landed there on 10 July, and Dr Meyer took over as CO of the Naples Station, hitherto run by Hauptmann Heidschuch. The invasion of the Italian mainland and the Italian armistice in early September (events for which the Abwehr, unlike the SD, was unprepared) raised a host of urgent problems. A change-over from a static to a mobile system, which would work in close support of the armed forces now hurrying south to confront the Allied armies, had first to be effected; but not only did the Abwehr not have any well-established system of fixed stations on which to base such a re-organisation, but it was expected that Rome would have to be abandoned. Helfferich flew back to Berlin on 12 September for a meeting with Canaris; at the end of the month he flew back to Rome, having been appointed Liaison Officer with the newly reconstituted SID, and also CO of AST Italy, which had just been formed with its HQ at the Hotel Bernina in Merano – designed in fact as a reserve station for Rome in case the latter had to be evacuated. This dual role for Helfferich was absurd in operational terms, and no doubt arose from Canaris's support for his old friend; in fact what happened in real terms was that Helfferich remained in Rome and concentrated on his SID liaison, making only very rare visits to the North, while Major von Tarbuck became Deputy Head of AST Italy and Leiter III.

Hefferich's first task on his return to Rome was to get the incompetent Foschini removed as Head of SID and, after negotiations with Marshal Graziani, have him replaced by Lt-Col De Leo (a task which took him until January 1944). It was agreed with Graziani that the SID should limit its activities to safeguarding the security of the newly-reorganised Italian Republic forces, and should refrain from all offensive intelligence activities in the future.

The deep mistrust felt by the Germans for the Italians, which existed before the latter changed sides and was redoubled afterwards, the necessity of obtaining information about the sympathies of prominent Italian personalities and about the extent to which Italy would support the Allies, resulted in the northern Abwehr stations, which were hurriedly set up in Turin, Milan, Genoa, Spezia, Leghorn and Florence, being at first preoccupied with C/E tasks and provided perhaps another reason for the appointment of von Tarbuck, an experienced III-F officer.

Helfferich's responsibilities now involved liaison both with the forces of Kesselring in the south and with Rommel (later General Toussaint, who took over when Rommel moved to Normandy) in the north. In fact AST Italy, especially as it concerned Helfferich in the south, was something of a misnomer, since he only had direct responsibility for Abt III work, comprising the following main tasks

(i)   Safeguarding the security of all German armed forces in Italy
(ii)   Security of the Lines of Communication (transport, telephones etc)
(iii) The safeguarding of all Italian industrial establishments working for the German war industry.
(iv)   Prevention of sabotage and espionage in the rear areas under the command of the OBSW, with the exception of an area 30km deep along both east and west coasts of Italy.

Abt I work was largely directed by Abwehr I in Berlin, while Amt II work, as has been said earlier, was the responsibility of Ic at OBSW. Nevertheless AST Italy had some hand in the initial formation of the new units on the ground.

The main Abwehr I unit to be formed for the collection of tactical intelligence was FAK 150, with subordinate Trupps (FATs) under its command, designated FAT 150, 151, 152 and 153. The unit was commanded by Captain Berger (an I-H officer sent down from Berlin), with the Trupps commanded by Leutnants Hoehle, Mohr, Plaaten (see plate section) and Lossen (the later, a good-looking man, won the sobriquet 'Il Bello' from his female agents (see plate section). In the early weeks there was a lot of changing of locations until the military picture settled down and it became clear that the front line was going to hold firm on the Cassino front; by the beginning of 1944 the Kommando itself had its headquarters at the Pensione Flavia, Via Collina, Rome, (see plate section) with a training school for agents at Via XX Settembre. The Trupps were located as follows:

> Trupp 150 at Bussi (20 miles south of Chieti)
> Trupp 151 at Piombino (45 miles to the south of Leghorn)
> Trupp 152 at Arpino, just east of Frosinone.

Trupps 150 and 152 were thus close to the front line areas, well-placed to launch line-crossing operations. The whereabouts of Trupp 153 at this time is uncertain.

A new station was also set up in Trieste by Kdo 150 (Aussenstelle Trieste) code-named 'Erika' and commanded by Hauptmann Paimann, alias Pitter (subsequently replaced by Leutnant Buddenbrock, alias

Busoni). Initially its tasks were to set up a network of sub-units throughout Istria and to penetrate the partisan organisations which were active in the Trieste hinterland; but subsequently it was given a major role in the recruitment of post-occupational agents. In order to penetrate the Yugoslav partisans the station persuaded an Italian army intelligence officer to put at their disposal an agent network, known as 'Baldo', which he had already been running in the region prior to the Italian surrender; it was able to build up a good picture of the Communist partisan units. Each sub-centre was in radio contact with 'Baldo' HQ (in two offices at 10 Via S. Nicolo and 6 Via Cassa di Risparmio, Trieste) while the latter was in direct radio touch with FAK 150's W/T base station 'Lilli'. Intelligence collected by the 'Baldo' network was handed over to Paimann, who processed it and sent it back to 'Lilli' over his own radio station 'Orion'.

The liaison station which had been located at Frascati now moved to Morlupo, about thirty miles north of Rome, and the Naples and Sardinian stations were disbanded, although the latter enjoyed a brief existence at Monte Carlo before its dissolution. The small Bari station under von Wettstein joined Helfferich in Rome, while the I-M station under Korvetten-Kapitän Klaps at Spezia was given the special task of co-operating with the X Flotilla MAS, in conjunction with Kdo 212. A new station was also set up, FAK 190 (L), to assist Luftflotte II, to which it was attached; it was initially located at Malcesine, on Lake Garda, but later accompanied the Luftflotte when the latter moved to Padua, and set up its own HQ a few miles away at Abano. Originally its main function was to provide the German Air Force in Italy with intelligence coming from other Abwehr stations (not necessarily only those inside Italy), and it was not until later, when the energetic and resourceful Hoermann took charge, that it assumed its predominant role as the centre for all air intelligence on Italy, its agents concentrating also on air targets in AOT. Hoermann also retained control of his old station, now working on a restricted scale at Morlupo. Under his vigorous direction the Padua station embarked on an aggressive policy in the field of air intelligence (not, it must be said, that this was to be of much help to the Wehrmacht: all the air intelligence in the world can hardly affect the situation when, as would be the case before long, the Luftwaffe had been virtually swept from the skies of Italy (or removed in order to counter the Normandy landings) and Allied bombers roamed northern Italy at will, save for the unpleasantness of heavy flak defences). 'Luftkommando 190', as it became known, set up two subordinate Trupps, one at Padua and one, under Leutant Bucholtz, using the alias 'Dr Bauer' in his dealings with agents in Rome.

A further appointment of importance was that of Hauptmann Hofmaier to be 'Funkleiter Italien', i.e. in charge of all the radio training and communications of Abwehr agents operating behind the Allied lines.

Abwehrkommando 212, the sabotage unit, had moved its HQ to Florence in December, but before long had moved again to Rignano, 20 miles north of Rome, leaving Trupp 254 (Leutnant Hagleitner) in Florence and Trupp 253 (Leutnant Lorenz) in Perugia, although the latter had an Advanced HQ in Rome, in close liaison with Kesselring's forces. The whereabouts of Trupp 256 (Leutnant Grassel) and Trupp 257 (Leutnant Pfannenstiel) at this juncture is uncertain.

In addition to the various training schools run by the individual Kommandos, centralised training facilities for agents of both Abwehr I and II Kommandos were established in Florence in early 1944. One of these was run by our old friend 'Annabella', who had been called back from Greece at the end of 1943, along with Rabe: both of them joined Abwehr Kommando 150 and resumed their activities. The agent W/T training school there was run by Baron Schumann.

So much for the organisational arrangements. We can now turn to the Abwehr's actual intelligence-collecting operations over the end of 1943 and the early weeks of 1944. As a result of the Italian armistice there was considerable delay before Abwehr agents were actually despatched into AOT; gradually however the machinery began to function and agents, recruited and trained in the rear areas, began to come across the lines. One group was recruited by Kdo 150 in Genoa and, after training, despatched to the Ic post at Ovindoli for infiltrating through the front lines. The Kommando's training camp at Via XX Settembre, Rome, was preparing agents for both short and long-term missions, and these were in due course passed forward, either to Trupp 150 at Arpino, or to one of the Ic despatch points along the front line.

A few more valuable and highly trained agents were, however, being sent into Allied territory by sea, as a convenient way to avoid the perils of the battle zone and its tougher security controls. A party of three arrived in a boatload of refugees, which had set out from Gaeta, some 40 miles north-west of Naples, and beached at Mondragone, 17 miles further to the south (at a time when the front line lay halfway between these two points). The US 88 Division had just moved into the Monfalcone area; their Counter-Intelligence officer was Harry Rieback, a fine Chicago lawyer who quickly discovered, from a tip-off by two of the genuine refugees, that three of the group were suspect and had hidden something in the sand-dunes just after landing. A search revealed a buried radio transmitter, and the three men were arrested.

Two of the arrested agents agreed to work for the Allies; the third – an Italian Air Force lieutenant – refused. The operation was called Alpha/Primo; 'chicken feed', or deception material, was provided by 'A' Force and the play-back was so successful that after some time the GIS sent in a trusted messenger with a considerable sum of money, having received a signal from the team that they were short of cash. Instead of acknowledging receipt of this, and at the suggestion of the French Deuxième Bureau (who were also 'in on the act'), the SCI control sent a message complaining that nobody had arrived. This in turn caused the GIS to send in a second agent with money, who was also arrested.

The operation ran successfully until the end of the war, and one of the two agents remains in touch with his former British controller until the present day.

As an example of the way in which quick thinking and imagination could help sustain the credibility of a 'play-back' agent, the following incident is worth recording. It was extremely rare for a German reconnaissance aircraft to reach the port of Naples, so that when sirens and anti-aircraft fire indicated that one such had flown over, the Alpha/Primo control officer quickly encoded an intelligence report which, without mentioning the passage of the German aircraft, gave accurate details of the Allied shipping moored in the port at that time. In the normal course of events such intelligence would be kept from the Germans in every way possible: but since they were now about to obtain it from the air photographs taken by the intruding plane, it was available for use as confirmation of the 'play-backs' bona fides. The report reached Abwehr HQ well before the plane's photographs had been developed and delivered to the Luftwaffe's photo interpretation section, so that, when they finally did reach the Abwehr, they provided solid 'confirmation' that the agent's report could be trusted.

Two other agents who were sent across the Allied lines during February were instructed to make a 45-mile circuit and to report back five days later. Of two other 'line-crosser' agents ('Frontläufer', in the German term) one was given a mission of reconnaissance as far as Bari, the other the collection of information on troop movements, dumps etc in the Naples area. All these agents were provided, as was normal practice, with passwords to facilitate their return through the German lines, but on the whole as little consideration was shown for their security as had been displayed in their selection.

The chief Kommando 150 recruiters in Rome included two men of special interest to Allied counter-intelligence. One of the most active was Giovanni Zanetin, thought to be of Swiss origin and to have worked for Rabe for many years. The other was an Italian of evil reputation, Lieutenant-Colonel David (see plate section), who ran a recruiting organisation specifically for Trupp 152. Its official title was Gruppo Segreto Attentatori Fascisti Reppublicani, or Gruppo SA for short. It served mainly to provide, from among misguided and idealistic Fascist youths, short-range line-crossers for the Abwehr's forward posts. Previously Lt-Colonel David had been active in a similar organisation in North Italy, the Centuria Del Fascio Crociata (see p.77).

Kdo 212 sent a number of sabotage agents across the 8th Army lines, using a despatch point at Aielli, near the Adriatic coast, known as Dienststelle Kaiser: this was one of the aliases of the CO of Trupp 254, Oberleutnant Hagleitner. Some of the agents were local recruits from this area, but Abt II was also making efforts to recruit a better type of saboteur from among Italian shock troops, who were given instruction at a sabotage school. One of these, captured at this time, even tried to knife the troops who captured him. Missions were in some cases merely a 'dry run' to identify future worthwhile targets; but in other cases they had been equipped with incendiary devices and were given specific objectives, mostly in the Foggia area.

It is not without interest that even by September 1943 Allied Counter-Intelligence possessed details of a large number of Abwehr staff in Italy, even down to secretaries and drivers, with their locations and, in many cases, their background; details of 35 W/T operators were available who were believed to be in the Abwehr, plus information on around one hundred other agents, contacts, informants and employees in major towns of Italy, with their addresses, dates of birth and even, in many cases, the names of their parents.

A characteristic feature of the Abwehr effort, both in Kommando 150 and Kommando 212, was its lack of security. No attempt seems to have been made to segregate agents or to restrict their contacts to those Abwehr officials whom it was necessary for them to meet for training and operational reasons. Even short-range agents were often acquainted with the personnel and plans of more important missions, who were thus seriously compromised when captured. This failure to discriminate between small-time agents with only a slender chance of success, and those who might with luck produce worthwhile results, was seen by Allied security officers at the time as 'one of the most encouraging features' of Abwehr operational methods.

Meanwhile the Rome office of Kdo 190, under Oberleutnant Hans Buchholz (using the alias of 'Dr Bauer') had been actively preparing stay-behind networks of its own in the city, with the assistance of a sinister figure called Dr Kurt Martens, alias Werner, said to be a Frenchman who had formerly worked for the Abwehr in France.

Ic OPERATIONS

As a result of the Italian Armistice and the Allied invasion of Southern Italy the Abwehr's plans for the introduction of agents in that region were, as we have seen, seriously disrupted. The result was that fighting units were seriously deprived of tactical intelligence, being further handicapped by German inferiority in the air and the consequent difficulty of maintaining regular aerial reconnaissance. To try to improve this situation a special effort by General Staff Intelligence, Ic, was called for, and resulted in the expansion of an Ic station to co-ordinate these operations. This was given the name of Dienststele Schistler, derived from the name of its commanding officer, Oberleutnant Schistler. It was also known as 'Kommando Fritz', possibly as a security measure to avoid mention of Schistler's name when dealing with Italian agents.

It was first identified in early November 1943, when it was located in the Albergo d'Italia, Avezzano, at a major road-junction east of Rome and half-way across the peninsular. The principal task of the unit was to obtain military information of immediate tactical importance (Aufklärung), both from the reports of short-range informants and from the interrogation of prisoners of war.

A considerable number of agents were therefore sent across the lines through the winter of 1943-44. They were mostly of a low-grade type whose reports, even if their trip was successful, could only be of value in the absence of any other sources of information. Many of them were captured, and during March and April the flow appeared to cease altogether, though it later picked up again. The manner in which they were recruited

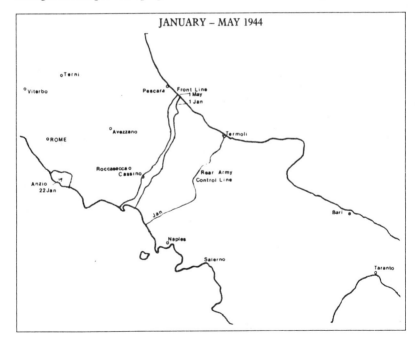

JANUARY – MAY 1944

bore all the hallmarks of hasty improvisation. All were Italians and all were very young, the majority being youths of 17 or 18; they were given little or no training and appeared to have been chosen with little regard for their suitability for the work. Indeed, apart from sometimes receiving a short course on the recognition of Allied equipment (guns, tanks etc.) and unit signs, little seems to have been done other than virtually press-gang them for the service and send them across the lines with a small sum of lire and a warning that, if they failed to return, their relatives in German hands would suffer. Their normal assignment was simply to wander about in the forward areas behind the Allied lines and bring back as much information about troop movements, unit locations and types of equipment as was possible in the limited time allotted to them, usually 5-6 days. In a few cases deeper penetration was attempted, with agents sent as far as Bari and Naples.

After a final briefing by an Ic officer they were taken by car to the front and guided through the mine-fields by a soldier from the unit manning that sector of the line, being given at the same time a password which they were to quote when stopped by German troops on their return. In sending over these youthful agents, ill-trained and ill-equipped, the object was presumably to achieve results by strength of numbers, in the hope that a proportion at least would return with some information of interest. These perilous trips must, however, have been most unpleasant for the participants, with the broken terrain, winter snows, the considerable risk of stepping on a mine or of being shot by one side or the other on the outward or return trips. There was, too, the even greater risk of being captured and executed as a spy – a risk, no doubt, which was not much stressed by their German recruiters in Ic. In a letter dated 22 February Major-General Strong, Head of Allied Intelligence in Italy, reported a summary of the above facts to the Director of Military Intelligence (DMI) in London and stated that six captured agents had so far been sentenced to death, two had been executed, one reprieved and given 20 years, while the other three were under appeal against the death sentence.

The Dienststelle Schistler appears also to have been used regularly by the Abwehr, and even the SD, for the launching of line-crossing agents of their own. By the early spring of 1944 it seemed that Dienststelle Schistler was confining itself to very short-range tasks in the Cassino region, leaving to the Abwehr the task of collecting military intelligence in the rear areas – intelligence of a type that would still be of value even if it was two or three weeks old.

The other side of the work of the Dienststelle is also worth noting en passant. In addition to his permanent staff Schistler appeared to maintain a floating population of half a dozen renegade Allied POWs to act as 'stool-pigeons' in prisoner of war 'cages', together with three or four Sicilians who were sometimes used as agents and sometimes on camp duties at the HQ. The following 'stool-pigeons' featured in Allied reports on the Dienststelle at the time:

(a) Sonderführer Anton Dobrot. Posed as a Canadian; known as 'Tobruk' to the German staff.
(b) Private Bill Pearson. Essex Regiment, captured before Naples.
(c) 'Bob the Regular': a Scotsman with the Military Medal.
(d) Jean Dumas: a French Arab, nicknamed 'Carole' by the Germans.

Both (b) and (c) appear to have been effective at the work, enjoying considerable popularity among the British POWs in the camps into which they were infiltrated.

The information came in this case from a Private Parest, of 1 Canadian Division, who in order to escape from German captivity had agreed to a suggestion that he collaborate as a stool-pigeon and was employed there from 3 March-5 April, before making his escape back to the Allied lines. Pearson's claims that he was a member of the Essex Regiment who had been captured near Naples seem however to have been false, since no battalion of this regiment was engaged in the Naples sector. Parest seems, in any event, to have effectively sabotaged Pearson's and 'Bob's' activities: shortly before escaping he told the Germans that they were providing false information, and they were alleged to have been sent to a Concentration Camp in Germany.

THE SICHERHEITSDIENST

The SD had meanwhile not been idle. As soon as the Italians changed sides the Germans rushed forces south to disarm their erstwhile Allies and occupy the country, treating it thereafter not very differently from the other countries of Europe which they had seized and plundered. An HSSuPF Obergruppenführer Karl Wolff (see plate section), moved at once to Fasano, on Lake Garda, to take charge of all security (as opposed to military) measures. Wolff, a cultured and intelligent man, who had earlier been Himmler's Chief of Staff, made great efforts after the war to prove that he had not himself been involved in any war crimes or artrocities; nevertheless in September 1964 he was convicted by a West German court for personally arranging delivery of 300,000 Jews to the gas chambers. Nor were his hands exactly clean in Italy, although his rôle in facilitating the negotations for the German surrender in Italy spoke in his favour. Three of his immediate subordinates – Harster, Kappler and Rauff – were convicted of war crimes after the war. His high-level rôle as security overlord plays only a minor part in the history of GIS activities in Italy: he acted as little more than a channel for the orders from Himmler and Kaltenbrunner in Berlin.

Shortly after Wolff's arrival SS Obergruppenführer Dr Wilhelm Harster arrived hot-foot from Holland to take up the post of BdS, immediately under Wolff. Born in Bavaria in 1904 (so 39 at this time) Harster had entered the SS in November 1933; by 1941 he was head of the Sicherheit-polizei and SD in Holland and thus responsible for the rounding up, and shipment to concentration camps, of Dutch Jews. He has been described, therefore, as the man who brought about the death of Ann Frank. On 18 September, a week after Mussolini had set up his new Fascist government at Salò, on Lake Garda, Harster was pulled out of his post in Holland and, after a briefing in Berlin which lasted three weeks, he left for Italy and set up his HQ in Verona. He became thereby the man with the most direct influence on the security and intelligence situation in EOT (if one excludes Wolff's higher and more remote sphere of responsibility). Harster was described as 'a typical policeman turned officer, who had risen more by perseverance than brilliance'; while showing contempt for the Italians and their intelligence work, he is said to have 'displayed a respect approaching worship' for General Wolff.

An outline of the organisation and personalities of Harster's empire will be left until a later chapter: for the moment, all eyes were on Kappler, who due to his drive and ruthlessness already enjoyed a status well above that of his rank. Rome became the centre of the SD's sabotage and intelligence operations for the next nine months. Kappler was relieved of his Police Liaison post at the Embassy and appointed head of a new Rome Einsatz-kommando, with a considerable increase in staff.

This included Obersturmführer Tunnat, together with an explosives expert named Negroni, who ran an explosives training school for Kappler at Viale Rossini 11. The total strength of the Aussenstelle was 12 officers, 60 NCOs and one private.

At the beginning of November Abteilung VI was given as its main task the building of a post-occupational network for Central and South Italy. Nevertheless, the directive coincided with orders from Himmler, declaring that the time had now come for large-scale sabotage operations, since the Allies were now fighting in occupied territory, 'a fact which should make conditions roughly equal for Germans and Allies alike' (the comment shows how little Himmler knew about actual conditions in AOT). Wolff nominated Kappler to be responsible for sabotage operations in addition to his other commitments. In fact, Kappler already had a sabotage organisation in being, which even before the Italian armistice had been recruiting agents from the Fascist Harbour Militia; three such agents were sent in

August 1943 to Berlin for training, returning to Italy in September. One of them was despatched soon afterwards across the lines via Dienststelle Schistler, but was captured and revealed to Allied CI this new aspect of SD operations.

A second group of 12 agents, mostly from Trieste and recruited by Commandante Caruso of Trieste Harbour Militia, left in mid-November for Berlin, whence a number of them were sent on for a month's course at Scheveningen, near The Hague, where the SD had an agent's sabotage school. At the end of the month Kappler himself went, with Hass, to Scheveningen to study the problems of sabotage work; when he returned to Rome he was ordered by the SD to take with him a Dutch girl, Helen ten Kate Brouwer – of whom more anon – for use as an agent.

In December another party of ten men, once again all members of the Harbour Militia but this time from Venice, plus fifteen men recruited in Rome, were likewise sent to Scheveningen, followed by a further party of twelve from Venice a little later on. Some of these agents were actually received inside the German Embassy by Kappler, as were several prospective recruits, before being passed on to Ovindoli for despatch on their missions. A group of three such agents who were captured in January 1944 had been given the combined mission of blowing up, with delayed actions bombs, a petrol dump in the 8th Army area, for which purpose they had been issued with two bombs each; securing information on AA sites, vehicle markings etc.; obtaining specimens of civilian ration cards and currency issued by the Allied authorities; and reporting on the behaviour of the Allied troops towards the civilian population. They had no sooner crossed the lines, however, than they ran into a British control-post and were arrested – a premature ending to their mission which may have been due to their failure to follow the route chosen for them by Dienststelle Schistler.

A surprising feature of this particular mission was that all the foregoing (except for its final failure) was known in considerable detail to a fourth agent, captured separately, who was not a saboteur and whose mission was of a relatively long-range variety. In the course of training for his own mission he had in fact been allowed contact with many other agents and SD staff, of whose identity it would have been more prudent to keep him in ignorance.

Kappler was also busy with other sinister schemes. One of these (perhaps sparked off by the recollection of the poisoned meat operation of Bierback?) was to despatch rats, infected with some pestilential disease, into the Anzio Bridgehead: the plan is said to have been vetoed by Kesselring himself – no doubt wisely, since the average rat is no respecter of front line boundaries.

One interesting SD operation during the period is, however, fully documented. On 8 February 1944 a note was sent to Schellenberg, head of Amt VI of the RSHA, by Kaltenbrunner, which ran as follows:

The Reichsführer SS[1], in his telephone call of 8th inst, showed himself to be very indignant (ungehalten) that no progress or results have been achieved in sabotage behind the enemy lines.

He was especially indignant about the use of candidates for execution ('Todeskandidaten' in quotes in the original) who could not be employed as saboteurs with any prospects of success: it would be better to have their sentences carried out.

The Reichsführer wishes Kappler to be encouraged ('zur Aktivität angelhalten') to get on with it.

On 26 February Schellenberg reported back to Kaltenbrunner as follows:

SS Obersturmbannführer Kappler reported on 22.2.44. that he had allocated tasks to some sabotage people and sent them off. At the present time there is however no communication with these people. He is therefore obliged to hold back his reports of the results until the line-crosser (Grenzgänger) sent off by him has returned. Due to especially heavy falls of snow on the central sector of the front, which is where crossings with material have to be made, passage through the lines at this time is much more difficult. This is also the reason why further missions have been delayed.

With Himmler breathing unpleasantly down his neck, Kappler was doubtless under some pressure to produce results. At some point during early February he had paid a visit to Field Marshal Kesselring's HQ and asked General Westphal, the Chief of Staff, and Colonel Zolling, the head of Ic, to suggest two or three worthwhile targets which, if they could be attacked, would give support to the German forces fighting in the Anzio sector.[2] Westphal and Zolling suggested two targets of importance, on the basis of intelligence reports available to them:

1. 'The HQ of the Commanders of the V and VIII Anglo-American armies – Clark and Alexander'
2. A tank repair workshop in Anzio town.

1. i.e. Himmler
2. Always referred to by the Germans as the 'Nettuno' bridgehead; the town of Nettuno lay immediately beside Anzio.

Zolling was instructed to prepare the necessary documentation (air photos, POW statements etc). On the basis of the intelligence available Kappler decided to attack both targets from the sea and ordered the following steps:

1. Procurement of a sea-worthy, light boat with as shallow a draught as possible, in order to cross the minefields
2. Preparation of 4 saboteurs, who must be explosives experts, good swimmers and rowers
3. Preparation of the necessary sabotage materials, in watertight packing
4. Procurement of four English uniforms, with all the appropriate bits of equipment
5. Final training of the men, especially in respect of the two buildings to be attacked, and their precise briefing on the basis of air photos and maps
6. Report when ready
7. Final planning and execution of the operation, up to the start time of the men, to be under SS Obersturmführer Tunnat

Curiously, there is no mention of any requirement that at least one of the saboteurs should speak some English, which would seem to be a fairly important requisite, given the possibility of their being challenged by sentries at some point.

That the SD, or indeed Zolling, had got the idea that there was a 'combined 5th and 8th Army HQ' actually inside the Anzio bridgehead, with the possibility of both Clark and Alexander being present, seems, in the light of reality, extraordinary. Commander of the bridgehead forces was General Truscott (replacing the discredited General Lucas) at VI Corps HQ in Anzio town, which is where Clark or Alexander would go on the occasion of their visits to the bridgehead, and where there was also V Army Advanced Command Post; to imagine that both the latter, with the Battle of Cassino raging, would be located in a remote building (as shown on German sketch) on the coast, within easy range of German artillery, in a precariously-held bridgehead, shows only too clearly the weakness of German intelligence assessments. Moreover, Alexander had never, in Italy, commanded 8th Army, as the Germans were stating; this had previously been Montgomery's command, and he had been succeeded, early in 1944, by Sir Oliver Leese. What is more, 8th Army held the eastern (Adriatic) side of the Allied front: the suggestion that their commander should be sitting in a villa on the west coast (and presumably commanding his troops from there) is laughable. It is surprising that Kappler was able to get away with such errors without being rapped by Berlin; it is surprising, also, that Kesselrings HQ seem to have originated this gaffe.

The situation is further confused. An article just after the war in a Czech paper, based on SD documents retrieved from the depths of an Austrian lake, describes the villa as being 'in the north of Anzio town, at a spot where the road connecting Anzio with the inland cuts a road running along the coast in a northwesterly direction'. If the target were indeed in Anzio town this would at least make the story a little more credible; but the sketch map, drawn by Kappler's office when submitting his report on the operation, clearly shows the target ('successfully attacked') as being half-way along the road between Anzio and the Moletta river – some 7-8 kilometres out of Anzio, and a similar distance from the German front line. Worse is to come, as we shall see.

In the RSHA the operation was given the title 'Sonderunternehmen Anzio' (Special Operation Anzio). Kappler, reporting subsequently, stated that he had had considerable difficulty in getting hold of the boat, the uniforms and men who were suitable in all respects. The final briefing and training was carried out by Negroni, an explosives expert who was already logged in the Allied CI card indices as running a sabotage school for Kappler at Viale Rossini 11, Rome. One of the saboteurs was described as being 'three times a European champion both of swimming and rowing'.

Tunnat, put in charge of the operation by Kappler, drove, together with Sturmbannführer Hass of Kappler's staff, to the HQ of the German 4 Parachute Division, which was holding the north edge of the Anzio Bridgehead. The Divisional Commander, Colonel Trettner, thought the plan looked feasible and appointed Hauptmann Kühne to accompany the two SS men on a reconnaissance of the locality. It was decided that the best place to launch the operation would be at the mouth of the River Incastro.

On 24 February Tunnat's little group, helped by a squad from the German division, launched their boat at 9pm and put out to sea. During the afternoon the surface had been calm, but in the evening it became rougher. It was known that the coast between the mouth of the River Incastro and the target building was mined, and they intended to use a narrow strip which, on the basis of an earlier reconnaissance, was believed to be safe. They could not, therefore (stated Kappler in his first report) risk being driven by the waves to a place where there was a risk of mines, and after an hour the boat was forced to return to base.

Two similar attempts, on 26 February and 3 March, likewise failed. On the latter occasion Tunnat himself went out with the boat to convince himself that the attempt would be impossible. Then he went back to Rome to consult Kappler. The latter suggested that they choose a different starting-point, further to the north. Under the guidance of Para Leutnant Lammer a fresh spot on the coast was selected, near to the village of La Fossa. On the evening of 8 March, when the weather forecast was good, a further launch was made. This time only three saboteurs were available: the fourth had meanwhile 'got lost somewhere'.

Kappler reported how Tunnat and Negroni gave a final briefing to the team, including a special password to use with the German sentries when they returned. At 8.30pm the boat set forth in a flat calm sea. After reaching a point some 500-600 metres from the shore it was seen to turn south and disappear into the darkness. Tunnat and Negroni betook themselves to the HQ of the Paras near La Fossa. Had they but known it, they were only a mile or two away from the SOE out-post at Torre San Lorenzo, where Malcolm Munthe, (son of the author Axel Munthe) of No 1 Special Force, was waiting to infiltrate an agent through the German lines.

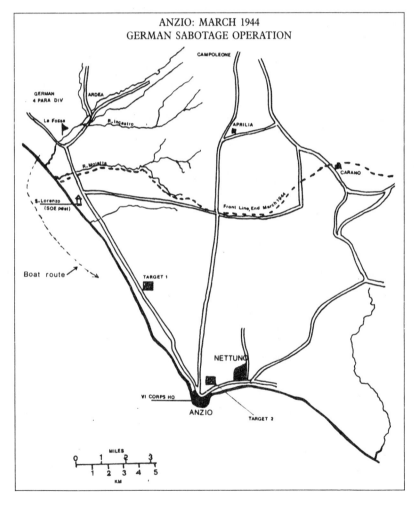

ANZIO: MARCH 1944
GERMAN SABOTAGE OPERATION

At 1.40 the next morning the German watchers observed a 'sharp, yellow-white flame, as high as a house' ('haushohe gelbweisse Stichflamme') precisely in the direction of the target. Because of the darkness, it was difficult to judge the distance, but it was estimated to be at a distance of some 5 km from the German observation point on the German front line (no mention, in Kappler's reports back to Berlin, of the incompatability between this figure and the carefully scaled sketch map, which showed the target to be at least 10 km from the observation pont: nor of the ludicrous inference that Alexander and Clark would have set up an HQ only 3-4 kms from the German forward patrols).

The names of the several Fallschirmjäger NCOs who had also seen the explosion were carefully noted in order to confirm the incident. Various of them claimed, independently of each other, 'two detonations, which sounded virtually as one'. Further confirmation was sought, and obtained, from sentries on the extreme right wing of the German lines.

In addition to these explosions two long bursts of Allied machine-gun fire were heard, with the tracer bullets directed out to sea. Kappler's men decided this was probably directed at the sabotage team as they escaped in their boat, and explained why they never got back to base.

On leaving the area Negroni was wounded by Allied shell-fire and his vehicle was destroyed. Tunnat however returned to Kappler and reported the sequence of events; on 16 March Kappler sent off two signals to the RSHA, summarising these facts and adding: 'Conclusions: the attack as such can be seen as having been successful'. There is no indication of why he waited a week before despatching these signals.

Back in Berlin, however, they do not seem to have been entirely convinced. While Schellenberg, Head of Amt VI, quickly prepared a report for Himmler (omitting, however, the final sentence claiming success) it was decided to hold up this report until a more detailed account had been received from Kappler, who was given until 1pm the next day to submit this. On 30 March Kaltenbrunner's office completed the text of their own write-up, based on Kappler's information, and submitted it to Himmler, with a copy to Hitler's adjutant Fegelein. On the same date Kappler sent back a full written account by courier. It contained a full section headed 'Conclusions', which, over his personal signature ran:

On the basis of available reports and reconnaissance (espionage) results (air reconnaissance has not to date been possible) it can be presumed that the three saboteurs were able to reach Target No 1 (HQ of Generals Clark and Alexander) without being seen, and there, as instructed, to place two explosive charges, linked to each other by a fuse, with a thirty-minute delay timer, on either side of the building and to get back to their boat. Orders had been given not to attack the second target (tank repair workshop in Anzio) on this particular night, since due to the considerable distance both missions could not be carried out on a single night. The way things went, it can be taken that the three men succeeded in getting away from the shore by boat, but that they were then spotted by the enemy and shot up. This is how, on the basis of the observations made – explosion in the direction of the target, time of the explosion and time of the burst of enemy firing aimed at a target out to sea – the operation presumably took place. Whether the explosion which was quite definitely observed, really was the blowing up of Target No 1 cannot as yet be confirmed as certain. All the signs point to this however. Final confirmation may perhaps shortly be possible on the basis of air photos and statements by prisoners of war.

KAPPLER'S SIGNAL TO THE RSHA ANNOUNCING THE 'SUCCESS' OF HIS SABOTAGE TEAM'S ATTACK ON THE ALLEGED 'HQ OF THE 5TH AND 8TH ANGLO-AMERICAN ARMIES' INSIDE THE ANZIO BRIDGEHEAD. 'IDA NEUN' WAS THE CODE FOR SD HQ IN ROME; GAETANO WAS THE CODE FOR AMT VI OF THE RSHA IN BERLIN.

Reichssicherheitshauptamt 23

Fernschreibstelle

Aufgenommen			Raum für Beschränkung		Bestätigt		
Zeit	Tag	Monat	Jahr				Zeit	Tag	Monat	Jahr
16 März 1944				ƒUЧК				

FS.-Nr. 7118

Telegramm — Funspruch — Fernschreiben Fernspruch

+ IDA NEUN /33 EINFACH 16.3.44 2200 – HAH –
AUFGEN: 16.3.44 1910 –
     AN G A E T A N O BETR: SONDERUNTERNEHMEN A N Z I O –
START DER DREI SABO-MAENNER NACH VIERMALIGEN VERGEBL.
VERSUCH GEGEN OBJEKT EINS (STABSQUARTIER DER FUENFTEN UND
ACHTEN ANGLOAMERIK. ARMEEN) AM 8.3. – 20.30 UHR GELUNGEN.
1.40 UHR WURDE SEHR HEFTIGE DETONATION UND HAUSHOHE
GELBWEISE STICHFLAMME EINWANDFREI BEOBACHTET. ENTFERNUNG
VON MEINEM STANDORT EIGENE HKL BIS ZUM DETONATIONSPUNKT
LIESS SICH IN DER NACHT NICHT AUSMACHEN, GESCHAETZT WURDE
ETWA FUENF KM. GEGEN 1.20 UHR WURDE MG FEUER DES GEGNERS,
FEUERUEBERFALL AUS ZWEI MG'S MIT L-SPURMUNITION ETWA 300
SCHUSS AUF ZIEL IM MEER UNWEIT KUESTE BEOBACHTET. MAENNER
SIND BIS HEUTE NICHT ZURUECKGEKEHRT. ......
  FOF. FO. +++
  + 9/33/16.3.44 2200 AMT VI / OH+

108

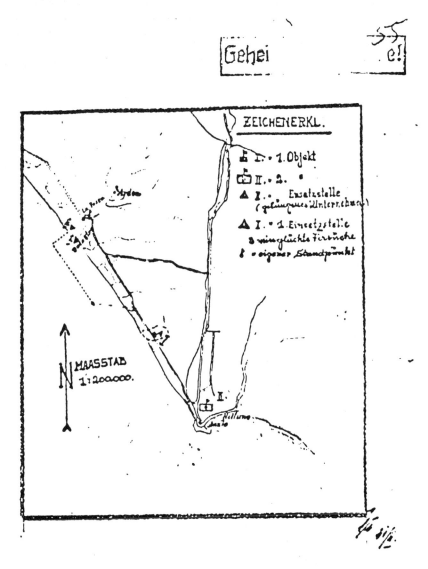

Alas for Kappler, the reality was very different. In a message timed at
8.16am on 9 March the Advanced Command Post of 5th Army in the
Anzio Bridgehead sent a message back to main HQ 5th Army worded as
follows:

Recon Unit of 1st US Armored Division apprehended during the night a dinghy with three Italians at (map reference) 799255 carried demolitions. Now being questioned.

There is some reason to believe that one of the original team of four saboteurs (the fourth man who had 'got lost somewhere' would appear to be a likely candidate) was in touch with the Italian Resistance and had reported the intended operation, news of which reached Peter Tomkins in Rome and was passed on to AAI by radio. This no doubt would have resulted in increased vigilance along the Anzio coastline, although, given the several postponements forced upon the attackers, the precise date of the operation could not have been predicted with any certainty. As for the 'explosions' observed: German shells – some of them from long-range guns – were arriving in the bridgehead day and night for weeks on end – might not one of them have scored a lucky hit on, for example, an ammunition limber or a dump of shells?*

Although nothing to do with Kappler, mention should be made at this point of a major attack on the shipping at Anzio on the night of 22 January, where X Flotilla MAS and the German KdK (Small Battle Units) made a combined assault with frogmen, 2-man torpedoes and assault motorboats. Only a limited success was achieved. Other attacks followed in February and April (see chapter 6 for details).

The SD's main activities concentrated less on current operations, however, than on planning 'stay-behind' networks against the day when the Allies would occupy Rome. Kappler's plans envisaged a vast espionage network, divided into several groups, each with its own W/T operator. These groups were to collect not only political and military intelligence for transmission to Germany, but also information to be passed on to groups for saboteurs. The latter had their own dumps of explosives established throughout Rome, one of the largest being in the gardens of the German Embassy, which was to be left, on the arrival of the Allies, under the protection of the Swiss. Additional groups of saboteurs were to move into South Italy, while a further team was to be dropped by parachute into Sicily.

Kappler had great problems in getting hold of the essential W/T sets for his planned P/O agents. Berlin calmly said that they were unable to provide any – hardly a very efficient back-up to their demand that these networks be established. The resourceful Kappler, however, was able to locate an Italian radio engineer, Lucci, who could build W/T sets; these proved very successful and Kappler even sent a model to Berlin, where it was received with much enthusiasm – so much so that the RSHA placed an order for 500 of them. Lack of time and materials, however, prevented

---

*Not for nothing was the Torre San Lorenzo area dubbed 'Stonk Corner' – a stonk being an artillery term for a heavy concentration of shells on a pinpoint target.

Lucci from fulfilling the order. Training of W/T agents was carried out at the Aussenstelle radio station in the grounds of the embassy, with the senior W/T operator of the unit, Rottenführer Boehm, in charge of the training.

In addition to Italian agents, Kappler also attempted to use any Germans whom he and Berlin could find, who spoke fluent Italian. Hauptscharführer Otto Lechner, who had been in Rome since 1940 and who had been sent in July 1943 to Amt VI in Berlin by Looss for training, returned to Rome in readiness for an espionage mission. He was installed in a monastery near Cassino, pretending to be an Austria émigré, and was to allow himself to be overrun there; he was then to make his way to Naples. Unfortunately for Amt VI the monastery was evacuated, so that Lechner could not stay on without arousing suspicion; he returned to Rome for a fresh plan. It was then decided to put him into a troupe of actors, but this proved unfeasible and he went back to Berlin. In November he was back again; this time the plan was to set him up as a bee-keeper on a farm just outside Rome. There was difficulty in finding a suitable spot and Lechner then developed back trouble, so that in February 1944 he went back once again to Berlin. He re-appears some time later as a W/T instructor with the BdS headquarters at Verona, a rather safer occupation.

One of the early plans of the Aussenstelle involved the setting up and staffing of a monastery in Rome which was to serve as a centre for post-occupational activities. In August 1943 the SD began negotiations, through a Georgian nationalist leader in Berlin, Michael Kedia, with a certain Father Michael Tarchnisvili, who was prepared to set up a Georgian monastery in Rome, for which he had apparently obtained, through misrepresentation, the Pope's blessing. The SD undertook to purchase the necessary property for him, while Father Michael was to furnish facilities and cover for one of their agents – initially in the shape of a private room reserved for a stay-behind W/T operator. A house was bought, and 'monks', presumably of Georgian origin, were being recruited by Amt VI in Berlin; the hope was that the Vatican could be persuaded to grant the monastery extra-territorial rights, i.e. to turn it virtually into a diplomatic premises. The strain of all this covert planning proved, however, too much for Father Michael, who disappeared. There seems to be no record of the final outcome of the scheme: probably it folded, like so many of the other over-ambitious projects.

Another plan involved leaving Obersturmführer Ellig, an Amt VI officer, inside the Vatican in order to direct espionage operations from inside this diplomatic sanctuary; the indications are that diplomatic pressure from the Allies brought about his departure in due course.

Hass, assisted by Dr Meyer and Schubernig, was very active in recruiting and training Italian agents – Scaccia, the brothers Flandro, Stroppa, Cipolla, Baron Evola, Fontani, Grossi, Antonucci, Della Rovere, Aschieri, Rizzi – the list rolls on and on.

Agents in training were usually paid 300 lire per month, and many of them had direct dealings with Kappler and the leading members of his staff. Some of them, while awaiting despatch on missions, also acted as recruiters for the Aussenstelle. Kappler even suggested to Meyer that one of his several Italian mistresses should be taken for a stay-behind rôle, but she refused to accept an espionage task.

Agents from this group, later captured by the Allies, reported under interrogation that they had been told that they would be controlled by a mysterious German, 'Colonel Falco', who was said to speak all Italian dialects perfectly and would make himself known to them when the time came. Allied CI staffs speculated that this might be Elling, or on the other hand might be merely a 'bogey-man' invented to make the impressionable Italian agents think that they would be under some form of supervision in their S/B roles, in order to make them toe the line. In fact, later interrogation of Kappler shows that 'Falco' was none other than Cipolla senior, whose son was one of the 'stay-behind' agents; Meyer had conceived the idea of leaving a sort of 'inspector' to keep an eye on the groups and to verify statements they might be reporting back. 'Falco' was present in the SD waiting room in May 1944 when Meyer was carrying out his final agent briefings, so that he could at least get to know the various agents by sight, without them being aware who he was.

Mention was made earlier of a Dutch girl, Helen ten Kate Brouwer, whom Kappler had brought back to Rome with him after a visit to a sabotage training school in Holland: doubtless it was her knowledge of Italian which had suggested her for an agent rôle in Italy. She was trained in W/T and installed by Kappler in a Rome apartment in order to act as a stay-behind agent once the Allies had occupied Rome: her SD code-name was 'Hoffman'. Her brief was to supply military intelligence – although Kappler was never entirely convinced that her allegiance to the Nazi cause could be relied on.

Allied CI was soon on to her once Rome had fallen, and she agreed to change sides and work for the Allies as a 'double agent' – although like the SD, the SCI officers handling the operation were equally unsure where her real allegiance lay and whether she could be trusted. She rejoiced in the SCI nickname of 'Ten Gun Kate'.

Kappler's instructions to her were that she should make her way back through the lines by 25 August. On SCI instructions she established W/T contact with the SD in the North, and was used regularly for passing deception material: but she became increasingly reluctant to do so. At one point it became important to deceive the Germans about certain movements of Allied divisions: but 'Ten Gun Kate' refused to transmit. The SCI officer in contact with her was a tall Scot, somewhat addicted to the bottle but with what has been described as a fatal fascination for women, although he was not a man to exploit this. It was known in the unit that Kate had quite a soft spot for him, and it was enjoined on him that his patriotic duty lay in winning her round by amorous means.

A colleague who shared his Rome apartment recalls him leaving the premises that morning with a heavy sigh and the muttered protest: 'The things I do for England . . .'

Apart from 'Ten Gun Kate', none of the other SD agents in Rome ever made W/T contact with their control stations in Northern Italy once Rome had been occupied by the Allies – a depressing outcome, from the SD's standpoint, of the considerable efforts put into this task by Kappler and his minions.

Before leaving the SD side of GIS work in Rome, the uglier aspects of Kappler's responsibilities must be put on record – i.e. those pertaining to his GESTAPO work. These, constitutionally speaking, involved the maintenance of law and order, and security in the rear areas – 'protecting the backs of the German troops at the front', as he was later to describe it. One might comment at this point that it is hard to assess where exactly the dividing line runs between the work of Abt IV, Abwehrkommando 309 and Helfferich's Abt III in this overall field of activities, nor to establish to what extent there was any effective liaison between them on the ground.

Kappler found that the main Italian gaol in Rome, 'Regina Coeli', was useless as a security gaol for the Germans, because messages could be passed in and out with the greatest ease; he therefore took over the former buildings of the German Culture Institute at 155 Via Tasso as a prison for GESTAPO use. This was to acquire a sinister reputation as a torture centre – a reputation that, there can be no doubt, it fully deserved. Under interrogation at the end of hostilities, Kappler claimed that the 'terror' of Via Tasso was exaggerated by the Italians, and that no torture was carried out *with his knowledge*. He only, he said, allowed one form of 'physical persuasion' (sic), namely blows on the bare soles of the victim's feet; he justified this treatment by claiming that (a) all Italians were liars, (b) all Italians were afraid of physical punishment and were willing to talk to avoid it, and (c) in order to save the lives of thousands of German troops at the front 'almost anything' was justified. He claimed that it was only many months after the withdrawal from Rome that he had learned that Hauptsturmführer Schuetz (in charge of Abt IV activities, i.e. the GESTAPO side of the SD's work) had, in his words, 'exaggerated' physical persuasion against his orders.

113

According to Kappler, General Wolff, the HSSuPF, once expressed concern, while on a visit to Rome, at the stories circulating about Via Tasso, mentioning a rumour he had heard that a prisoner had had his teeth pulled out to make him talk. Kappler had been able (he claimed) to prove that this story was unfounded, but gave Wolff his views on 'physical persuasion'. Wolff had agreed that it was a matter of necessity, and had suggested that a soundproof room should be built in the prison so that screams should not be heard by the inmates or by people outside. General Harster, the BdS, had also visited the Via Tasso and had been present at the beginning of an interrogation in which the prisoner was thought to be lying. It was decided that a little 'persuasion' should be used. Harster had continued on his tour of inspection, but had expressed a desire to return to the interrogation room to see if satisfactory results had been obtained; he had appeared quite satisfied and had expressed no disapproval of the methods used. For these 'and other reasons' Kappler had concluded that his superiors, who were all informed, had agreed with his own views on 'physical persuasion'.

Kappler's attempts to show that his actions in this field were not unreasonable carry little weight against the mountain of direct evidence from Italian victims who survived, showing a constant pattern of extreme and bloody torture. Given that his SD office was in another wing of the same building, any claim that he was unaware of what went on is unconvincing. Even in the restricted sphere of beatings on the soles of the feet, there is direct evidence of a 64-year old solicitor being given 100 such lashes to make him talk.

Leading members of the Resistance suffered far worse. General Simoni, captured on 22 January and aged 64, was tortured all night, whipped and beaten with spiked mallets and had the soles of his feet burned with gas jets. The fiancé of the Duchess of Cesaro's daughter had his nails ripped out, while another victim had 14 teeth torn out by Schuetz and his assistants. The building is kept today as a museum of the Resistance, with much bloody evidence still visible on its walls. Combatting the resistance movement was, as we have said, the chief preoccupation of Abteilung IV under Schuetz (as well as the penetration of Allied espionage and sabotage organisations, and the rounding up of the many Allied escaped prisoners who were being hidden by Italian families and in the Vatican), working largely through informers. Among those penetrated and destroyed was the Montezemolo group and its successor, the organisation under Bencivegna (through an agent named Perelli, later left in Rome as a P/O agent) and the discovery of a large arms and explosives dump in the Via Giulia area.

On 24 March – a month after the abortive SD sabotage raid against the Anzio Bridgehead – an event occurred which was to result in Kappler being imprisoned for life as a War Criminal after the end of hostilities. An Italian resistance group in Rome exploded a bomb (concealed in a dust-cart) in the Via Rassella as a company of SS police marched by. Of the 156 SS men 33 were killed outright or died of wounds shortly afterwards. Hitler, informed immediately, demanded a reprisal 'that would make the world tremble', and called for it to be carried out within twenty-four hours of the attack. General Mackensen, GOC 14th Army, laid down that ten Italians should be executed for every German killed. Kappler, asked for his views on how the victims were to be selected, suggest that they should use a basis which he had previously discussed in theory with Harster, namely that they should execute people who had already been sentenced to death or to life imprisonment, as well as those who had not yet been tried but who were expected to receive the death penalty when they were. Mackensen approved this basis for action, adding that if there were not enough prisoners in these categories it would be all right simply to shoot as many as there were, and later to publicise falsely that the full number had been executed.

Kappler, as security chief for Rome, was given the task of drawing up lists of names of the chosen victims. Not only that: when Major Dobbrick, commander of the SS police regiment involved in the Via Rassella attack, refused (under various excuses) to provide the firing squads for the execu-tion, and 14th Army also refused to get involved (arguing that it was purely an SS matter), Kappler was told that he himself would have to carry out the reprisal, using his own men.

For the next 24 hours Kappler hardly slept, but worked frantically on his lists of names, in order to be in time to meet the deadline laid down. He had in fact only three prisoners who had been sentenced to death as parti-sans, plus 16 who had been tried and given prison sentences (even though these were not the life sentences suggested in the original proposal). He added, with Harster's authority, 65 Jews who were awaiting deportation to Auschwitz, and a further ten people who had been dragged from their homes in the Via Rassella, although totally innocent of any involvement in the attack. Koch was able to contribute a few victims, including Peter Tompkin's W/T organiser, who had been captured and severely tortured. Kappler added whatever other names he could scrape up, both from prisoners held at Via Tasso (none of whom had been brought to trial, let alone convicted) and from people held in the German wing of the Regina Coeli goal. By 3am he had managed to assemble a total of 270 names, and was still 60 short. The only possible source for the balance would be from Italians held by the local police. Caruso, the Chief of Police for Rome, was told early next morning to prepare urgently a list of suitable names; by 4.30 in the afternoon, when the deadline arrived, he had still not completed it.

Ostuf Tunnat (the officer who had led the Anzio raid) lost patience and began taking prisoners from Regina Coeli at random; among them were ten men who had been arrested some time previously on non-political charges, which had been dismissed: they were just collecting their belongings prior to leaving the gaol.

The actual executions were carried out by the light of torches, under horrific circumstances, in an underground tunnel network in a hillside south of Rome, the so-called Ardeatine Caves, which forty years earlier had been used to mine a sandy volcanic dust employed in the making of concrete. Kappler's men had to be fortified with cognac as the mound of bodies, shot in the back of the head, grew to a great pyramid. Schuetz was in charge of the killings, SS Captain Erich Priebke with checking off the names of the victims, who, hands tied behind their backs, were dragged inside in groups of five, one German executioner to each victim. Kappler and four of his officers, to set an example to their men, each killed a victim personally; Schuetz warned the rest of the NCOs that if anyone refused to fire, he would be executed alongside the Italians. Only one, Sonderführer Amon, could not go through with it: he fainted, and one of his comrades took his place.

In the chaos and urgency of getting together the lists of names and assembling victims, 335 men were found to have been executed instead of the 330 authorised. These extra five were to be Kappler's undoing at his future trial: for the 330 he could plead he was only obeying orders, but for the extra five he had no defence.

General Eugen Dollmann, Himmler's representative in Rome, when the subject was raised during his interrogation at the end of the war, put the blame for this massacre squarely on Mackensen, although in his view 'Kappler could have refused to carry out the order, or could have done it differently'. But he described the method used as 'dreadful, humanly and morally absolutely frightful'.

Fifty years later Priebke was arrested in Argentina, as reported in the *Herald Tribune* on 11 May 1994:

ROME (Reuters) – Argentina police have arrested a former German Nazi SS captain, Erich Priebke, who is wanted in connection with the worst war crime committed in Italy, the Italian Interior Ministry said Tuesday.

A ministry official said the arrest took place in the southern Andean resort of San Carlos de Bariloche, where Mr. Priebke, 81, had lived peacefully for 46 years until he was traced to the town by the U.S. television network ABC.

His arrest followed the issuance on Monday of a warrant by an Italian military prosecutor who wants to try him in connection with the reprisal killings in March 1944 of 335 Italians at the Ardeatine Caves near Rome. Italy said it had begun formal extradition proceedings.

On 1 March Himmler, with Hitler's agreement, ordered the RSHA to take over control of the Abwehr – something which Himmler, at loggerheads with Admiral Canaris, had been striving to achieve for a considerable time. This final step was helped along by an incident just before the Anzio landings, when on 21 January Canaris had been paying a visit to Kesselring's HQ.

Allied deception channels, using a cypher which it was known the Germans could read, and well aware that the invasion fleet might easily be sighted while on its way, were busy persuading the Germans that the landing was going to be at Civitavecchia, on the coast north-west of Rome. Canaris was pressed for any intelligence he might have about Allied intentions in respect of a landing, especially about the positions of aircraft carriers, battleships and landing craft. Canaris was unable to produce any such intelligence, but expressed the view that there was no need to fear any new landing in the immediate future. A few hours afer his departure for Berlin, the Anzio landings began.

The text of a German report from OBSW dated 3 February (see Appendix 'A') shows that no usable Abwehr link in S. Italy was working by January 1944, and that two agents with a W/T set, sent to Naples, had been unable to provide any information about the landings. This, coupled with a total lack of air reconnaissance of Naples, the main Allied port of entry, for the previous six weeks, indicates all too clearly the failings of the GIS apparatus at this juncture.

In any event, AST Italy was formally dissolved on 1 March. Helfferich retained his appointment as Liaison Officer to SID; he was placed under the German Army Commander for disciplinary purposes only, but like all other Abwehr officers was immediately seconded to the RSHA, which established what was in effect a new Abwehr department, the Militärisches Amt. This had the following effects on the units previously under Helfferich's immediate command:

(i) Abteilungs III-F, III-W, III-C and III-N were placed under the command of BdS Italian in Verona (Sturmbannführer Kranebitter: see plate section). The departments were taken over complete with personnel, all members of the Wehrmacht being seconded to the SS and offered one SS rank senior to the army rank they had held hitherto (a subtle form of bribery to lessen internal Abwehr opposition).

(ii) Abteilungs III-H, M and L (i.e. the three sections concerned with the Armed Forces) were placed under command of the Wehrmacht commander in Italy, General Toussaint.

(iii) Abteilung I-G was placed under command of the senior Air Force commander in Italy, General Pohl.

The RSHA laid down that work must proceed without interruption on the same lines as before, until such time as new policies had been worked out for intelligence and security operations. But in fact the RSHA seems never to have issued any new directive on the policy to be followed in Italy, and with the removal of Colonel Hansen, Director of Abwehr III (later executed as a supporter of Canaris), Helfferich found that the situation became very confused and nobody in Italy was sure who his counterpart in Berlin actually was.

Shortly after the absorption of the Abwehr into the SD, the latter began to prepare for the total elimination of the Italian SID. The RSHA was apparently opposed to the existence of the SID because it was the only military security organisation in Italy which had powers to arrest independent of the Germans: according to Helfferich they also resented the fact that he, an Army man, was able to exclude all influence of the SD within the SID. In June/July 1944 a plan called Operation 'Gardasee' was to have been carried out without the knowledge of Helfferich: it involved the arrest and internment of all Carabinieri functioning in North Italy, whether working for SID or not. Helfferich got to hear of the plan from a German Town Commander in N. Italy a few hours before it was due to be launched; he drove at once to Fasano, where Wolff had his Forward HQ, and after negotiations with Wolff's Chief of Staff, Standartenführer Wieht, Wolff agreed that the plan should be shelved. The order countermanding the operation did not in fact reach all areas in time, but virtually all the arrested Carabinieri were soon released.

Helfferich did however get permission to retain control over one particular agent with whom he had had direct contact from early on: this was a Colonel Aletti and his wife. Aletti, who had been a commercial pilot in the USA before the war, had joined the Italian Air Force and was eventually posted as SIM representative in Turkey, working in the Italian Embassy there. After the Italian Armistice he returned to Rome and offered his services to Helfferich (with whom he had of course direct contact in the SIM offices) as a stay-behind agent in Rome, if and when the city was evacuated by the Germans. Berlin approved the operation, and the couple were given the cover name of 'Antonia'; they were both trained by Herz in W/T and codes and installed in an apartment. Their mission was to report troop movements and unit identities, working to 'Jakob', the Abwehr I base station in the Alps. Helfferich considered 'Antonia' to be a very good agent, and the radio link remained operational until the end of hostilities, sending back military information.

Unfortunately for Helfferich and the Abwehr, Aletti was working all the time for the Allies; he had been recruited by British Intelligence in Turkey at the time of the Armistice and had agreed to undertake this penetration mission.

The case of Emilio Cappellaro (cover name 'Mozart') was similar; he was a night-club singer and an agent of Rabe since June 1942 – working purely from a desire for adventure and not for any pro-German or financial reasons. He carried out a mission for Rabe in Athens, and was then sent to Istanbul, where his sister was married to a Turk: his mission there was to spy on Anglo-American activities in Turkey. He established good contacts in these circles, and Elisabeth Tabbo considered him to be one of the most intelligent agents with whom she was in contact, and Rabe too had a high opinion of his work. In November 1943 Cappellaro went back to Italy and worked for Kdo 150 in Rome, acting as despatcher for a number of their agents across the lines; finally he was installed in Rome with a W/T set to act as a P/O agent, working in harness with another agent named Renato Aliquo. It was yet another case of a 'double agent' operation: he too had been recruited by the British in Istanbul, and given a password and a rendez-vous by which to contact them in Rome.

While the monthly Counter-Intelligence Surveys of the early months of the Italian campaign were less informative than those later on, they do provide a number of statistics to fill out the picture of GIS agent-running operations and CI successes. Details (which up until March 1944 cover incidents in the 5th and 8th Army sectors only) are as follows:

1-15 December, 1943: Three Ic agents, aged 17-18, were captured. All were Fascist supporters, who had left Bari on the arrival of the Allies, hoping to join Graziani's Fascist army further north; they were however picked up by the GIS and sent together on three short-range missions, which they carried out successfully. They were then despatched on a longer mission to Naples, where they were to report on shipping. They aroused the suspicions of a Field Security NCO en route, and were arrested.

16-31 December: Records not available.

January 1944: 18 agents captured, three of them saboteurs. 8th Army alone captured eight in the first two weeks of the month. Of nine captured earlier, four were tried and given death sentences.

February 1944: Nine agents captured; details were not given.

March 1944: There were 24 arrests in the first 20 days of the month; these were mainly line crossers, but two separate parties arrived by boat. They were described as mainly young and inexperienced, but included a few higher-quality individuals, ten of the total were caught on the 8th Army sector, 11 by 5th Army (including two at Anzio) and two by 5 Corps. Polish troops in the 8th Army were praised for being commendably 'spy conscious'.

Fifteen of the agents had been sent by the Abwehr, two by the SD and five were on short-range missions for Ic.

The above figures were given in a 15th Army Group survey; at the same time an 8th Army summary gives a figure (for their sector alone) of 27 agents arrested during the whole of the month, 13 of whom were stay-behind agents. Two of them were saboteurs, named Bruno Brigido and Giovanni Soro, who had crossed the lines together on 5 February. Both were former Italian commandos, aged 31 and 28; Brigido appears to have been a talented character, speaking English, French, Arabic and Spanish besides his native Italian. Soro's identity card was, however, enough to raise a modicum of suspicion on the part of his CI interrogators: it had been issued at a village called Celano. A glance at the map showed this to be in the immediate vicinity of Ovindoli, where the Dienststelle Schistler was located. This fact in itself of course proved nothing; but it singled them out from the run of ordinary refugee line-crossers as worthy of a fuller interro-gation, and few line-crossing agents – at least at this stage of the campaign – had been sufficiently well briefed with a cover story which would stand up under rigorous questioning, especially when there were two men together whose stories, if genuine, would need to confirm each other in great detail.

April 1944: Ten agents captured, all of them working for the Abwehr. Four of them had W/T sets – one destined for Foggia (where there were several large Allied airfields), one for Naples and two for Sicily.

During the month 12 agents were sent to trial; nine were convicted and six executed.

No CI Summary was issued in May 1944, due no doubt to the disorgani-sation inevitable on the capture of Rome and the move northwards of 15th Army Group headquarters.

In reviewing GIS operations up to this time, it can be said that the tacti-cal, and indeed strategic, intelligence contributions coming in to the German commanders in Italy from agent-running missions – both from Ic, Abwehr and (in so far as it was passed to them) Sicherheitsdienst were relatively slight and certainly not cost-effective. The cynical use of untrained young local lads, who were liable to be shot if captured, does not reflect particularly well on Ic, although it might be expected from the SD.

10

The GIS in Italy: Phase III: June 1944-October 1944

So far we have mainly looked at the GIS effort as it was seen from the German side of the lines; the Allies over this period had acquired a fairly detailed picture of the GIS effort as far as it concerned attempts to gather current military intelligence, but were of course still largely in the dark in respect of GIS plans for stay-behind networks, while nevertheless in possession of a considerable number of names of Italians believed to have been preparing for this rôle. Once the Gustav Line was breached early in May it was clear that Rome would fall to the Allies in the very near future, and preparations were made by Allied CI units to exploit the openings which this would offer, both by arresting enemy P/O agents and by seizing and searching the large number of premises occupied by the Abwehr and SD units.

No I ICU ('S' Force) had assembled as early as 20 January in the Naples area, expecting to be operating well before now (the tough German resistance at Cassino having delayed the projected Allied time-table); but the additional time enabled very detailed target lists to be drawn up, based on the interrogation of captured agents, and on intelligence from Allied agents working in conjunction with the Italian resistance inside Rome. Arrest lists of German agents were prepared and passed to SIM/CS, who were to carry out the actual arrests. The team, which consisted by now of 204 officers and 1085 Other Ranks/Enlisted Men, with 268 vehicles, had moved up into the Anzio Bridgehead and was standing by in readiness. By 0015 hours on 5 June they had moved to the outskirts of Rome, and by 0320 had established their Command Post on Monte Pincio, close to the Piazza del Popolo in the centre of the city. Their report at that time states coolly: 'Sub-Task Force C was forced to fight for its Command Post, in that it arrived there four hours before the infantry, but established itself without loss after disabling and capturing a Mark VI (Tiger) tank with carbines and hand grenades'.

It must have been an exciting and exhilarating night for those concerned.

In the days immediately following, 249 arrests were made by 'S' Force; 336 buildings were seized and searched. One useful capture was that of a German 'Enigma' cipher machine.

Overall figures for agents rounded up in Rome, from all branches of enemy intelligence, showed the following by early July (figures differ slightly in different records, depending on the 'cut-off' date for sending in the statistics):

> 75 enemy agents arrested, of whom:
> 28 were SD agents with espionage missions
> 14 were SD agents with sabotage missions
> 23 were Abwehr agents
> 10 were listed as 'miscellaneous'

Of the above persons arrested, 13 were in possession of W/T sets.

THE ABWEHR NETWORKS

Of the 23 arrested, one group had already started operating when caught, another gave himself up at once, complete with his Abwehr training notes. From initial interrogations it became clear that the plan was for some 8 separate groups to operate, each with its own W/T operator and in some cases with secret ink communications. The majority had already been rounded up by early July. The primary mission of these agents was military intelligence, although one or two had been instructed to report on political and economic conditions. Nearly all of them had received some instruction on aircraft recognition, but their main task was to send back information on the movements and identities of army units, their weapons and equipments, and the location of headquarter buildings. In general, however, their assignments were vague and non-specific.

The W/T operators had all been trained in a relatively simple 'transposition code', which did not prove too much of a problem for Allied code-breakers, and in the one or two cases where Abwehr agents managed to survive for a few weeks without being caught, their messages were being read; the intelligence they were sending back proved to be so minimal and inaccurate that CI staffs were hardly worried by their own failure to locate them (except in so far as it impugned their professional competence).

There were clear indications that the Abwehr had departed from Rome in some haste and disorder, in spite of their awareness for some time past that an evacuation would soon be necessary. Thus at their agent training school in Via Severio Mercandante valuable documents were found by 'S' Force, while the HQ of FAK 150 (its code name was 'Kommando Lilli' and its unit sign, a wide open Eye, was painted on the front door) left its name board behind and the names of all its officers and NCOs posted on the doors of their respective offices. So much for security in the Abwehr.

The occupation of Rome was also particularly fruitful for the light which it threw on the SD, which up till then had been something of an uncertain quantity. During the first week of the Allied occupation more than half the members of the SD's stay-behind network were in custody, and further arrests continued as the days went by. More than a dozen members of their sabotage group were under arrest: one of these was to have been the leader of a squad to be dropped by parachute onto the Plain of Catania in Sicily. One agent, who was to have operated outside Rome, was so overcome by panic on reading Allied leaflets (which had been dropped by air over the city) announcing the execution of German spies caught earlier that year that he smashed his W/T set and abandoned his mission.

One of the SD teams, consisting of three men, was found on arrest to be in possession of five phials and two boxes of potassium cyanide – the first instance known in the Italian campaign of saboteurs being equipped with poison. One allegation at the time was that this was to be used in an operation to poison the King of Italy and the Crown Prince: records do not, unfortunately, reveal whether or not this was in fact a specific mission of this team, but with memories of the poisoned meat and the bubonic rats one can only say that Kappler might well have had some such operation in mind.

SCI EXPLOITATION

A start was made by the SCI units, whose role was to utilise arrested (or surrendered) agents by 'playing them back', wherever judged worthwhile and feasible, to their German 'control' in North Italy. Such operations had three major objectives:

(i)   to pass strategic or tactical deception material to the Germans. Scope for this became increasingly limited as the front line moved northwards, but one of the continued aims was to make the German High Command believe that further landings from the sea could take place (in the style of Anzio), with Genoa a likely location, in order to oblige OBSW to hold German (and to some extent Fascist Italian) forces available to counter any such move. Deception as to the sector of forthcoming major attacks along the front, and movements of divisions connected with these, was also carried out, and the Allied landings in the South of France also provided scope for such work; Abwehr networks were preferred for this type of deception, since they provided a more direct 'feed-in' to OBSW, who was the more important target for the deception.

The officers responsible for overall deception planning in Italy were Col Noel Wilde and Col Dudley Clark, representing 'A' Force – the Mediterranean offshoot of the 'London Controlling Section' (LCS) which carried out the much more vital Normandy deception plans. Apart from false intelligence supplied over 'turned' agent W/T channels, other operations involved dummy signals traffic to create non-existent formations, false divisional and corps shoulder-flashes and road signs.

(ii)   to induce the GIS to send over more agents, money and (where applicable) sabotage supplies to reinforce an existing network under Allied control. The arrest of the new arrivals would enable Allied CI to broaden its knowledge of GIS operations, personnel and methods, and not infrequently to learn in advance of the identities of further agents who were currently under training or awaiting a mission in the near future.

(iii)   to reduce the apparent need for the GIS to send in additional agents in independent operations (about which we might be in ignorance), by persuading them that their existing networks were functioning sufficiently well to reduce the need for major new intelligence operations.

To run such deception agents was time-consuming (since their messages had to be a mixture of truth and falsehood) and needed great care; for this reason there was a limit to the number which could be handled securely and effectively. Though much of the material concerning these deception agents is still classified, it is believed that between eight and ten were operated for extended periods.

There was a satisfying conclusion to this work for the Counter-Intelligence staffs involved. After the German surrender in May 1945 Lieut-Colonel W.D. Gibson, who commanded the Allied CI effort at HQ Allied Armies in Italy (General Alexander's HQ) went up to Bolzano for an informal meeting with General Wolff, the HSSuPF, overlord of the GIS operations in Italy. Wolff boasted to him: 'Your security was bad, Colonel: I had seven agent teams in the South, sending me intelligence messages by radio!'

Lieut-Colonel Gibson was able to riposte, no doubt with some satisfaction: 'I'm sorry, General: each and every one of them was in fact working for *us* . . .'

OPERATIONS OUTSIDE ROME

The rapid advance of the Allied armies no doubt necessitated a hasty revision of the Abwehr's plans for the penetration of Southern Italy, but it offered certain compensating advantages, in that it created a state of fluidity and temporary confusion favourable to espionage operations. During the month of June Kdo 190 in particular attempted to exploit the situation, and prior to the May offensive it had been clear that this Kommando alone was preparing to send some 15-20 agents into the South, some of whom were thought to be still in Rome when the city fell, awaiting an opportunity to make their way southwards.

Kdo 150 had also left a number of W/T parties south of Rome to be overrun by the Allied advance; they were instructed to make their way to various widely-scattered points in S Italy and Sicily, including the naval port of Taranto. Two of these agents were already in Allied hands by early June; one was arrested in the 8th Army area, the other gave himself up in Naples. Both were equipped with W/T sets. Three other stay-behind agents surrendered to the Polish Corps in the first half of June; they were not themselves equipped with W/T sets, but had been instructed to contact, through intermediaries, a W/T operator already established in the area, and to pass the intelligence they collected to him for encoding and transmission to N Italy.

Parachute operations were a feature of the period: approximately a dozen agents were dropped over the three months April-June. Several of these were despatched from Jugoslavia by AST Belgrade, flying in across the Adriatic. Most of them had W/T sets with them. The majority gave themselves up without attempting to carry out their missions. One Kdo 190 parachutist, dropped in the Salerno area, had instructions to make his way north, gathering information as he went; among other tasks he was to look out for any indications of preparations by the Allies for an amphibious landing further up the coast. Agents were also parachuted into Sardinia, apparently a joint operation by the Abwehr and the Fascist Republican authorities.

Conditions were less favourable for short-range agents, partly because the Forward HQs of both the Abwehr and Ic had had to move back in a hurry, and also because it would have been very difficult for agents to return across the lines, in view of the speed with which these had receded and the impossibility of giving such agents any advice on where they should best try to cross the lines on the return journey. Nevertheless a few agents on this type of mission were arrested; two of them had been recruited by Kdo 150 in Rome.

As in Rome, Allied CI was quick to seek out other places where it was known that the GIS had located their forward units. In general, these yielded little of value; an exception was at Arpino, near Frosinone, where an excellent piece of investigation by 412 Field Security Section gave a complete picture of the functioning of Abwehrtrupp 152 (one of Kdo 150's subordinate Trupps). Known in Arpino as 'Dienstelle Hans', its CO was

Oberleutnant von Weiss; his recruiting organisation in Rome was run by the notorious Italian, Colonel David, its cover title being 'Gruppo Segreto Attentatori Fascisti Italiani'. Colonel David had placed several groups at the disposal of the Abwehr and his organisation served in general to provide, from among misguided Fascist youths, short-range line-crossers for the Abwehr's forward units. Two of his agents were brought to trial at this time and convicted.

Abwehr II, as represented by Kdo 212, seems conspicuously to have failed to carry out its sabotage programme for this period. Five members of X Flotilla MAS, operating on behalf of Kdo 212, were caught on the Polish sector; their task was to wait for the arrival of the Allied troops and then to select suitable vehicle targets for sabotage – a singularly poor choice of target in cost-effective terms, when a Bailey bridge, a fuel dump or an airfield could have caused some disruption to the Allied forces, whereas the loss of a couple of vehicles was neither here nor there.

A further two saboteurs had been installed at Pontecorvo, just west of Cassino, but were soon in Allied hands; their instructions were to await the arrival of Allied troops and then to sabotage 'any suitable targets'. None of all these seems to have intended to carry out their missions; it seems to have been a frequent practice for saboteurs to dispose of their explosives and return to EOT with an entirely fictitious account of their exploits, which the Germans would have little ability to verify.

On the other hand, Allied CI organisations were aware that a number of German dumps of explosives had been left hidden, both in territory already overrun, and in that about to be occupied, so that it was expected that further sabotage attacks would be launched before long, utilising these materials. Dumps in Rome had even included a large number of altitude-triggered bombs for the sabotage of aircraft – a highly sophisticated form of attack.

All told, by mid-June, there were 25 arrests, excluding the Rome agents held; 14 of these were Abwehr with espionage missions, nine with sabotage missions. Six of the total had W/T sets with them. As was to be expected, the majority (15) were 'stay-behinds'; five were line-crossers, and an equal number had parachuted in.

One final statistic: since the beginning of December 1943 the number of enemy agents who had fallen into Allied hands was by now approximately 200. Of these, 40 had been brought to trial, 35 of whom had been found guilty and 16 had been executed.

THE SICHERHEITSDIENST ORGANISATION IN N ITALY

Before moving on to the actual operations over the next two months, it is time to establish the details of the SD's organisation and network in North

Italy. The overall command, as has been indicated, was with the HSSuPF, General Wolff, whose HQ was set up at Fasano, on the west side of Lake Garda and not far from Mussolini's government location at Salò. With him were some ten senior staff officers. Under him came the BdS, Gruppen-führer Dr Harster, with his headquarters in Verona and a considerable organisation under his direct control.

His immediate staff consisted of 35 officers, about 40 Warrant-officers and 20 NCOs – although at the time of the final surrender in May 1945 the total staff figures provided by Harster listed 110 Germans, 80 local employees and 50 Italian guards, giving an overall figure of 240.

Abteilung IV (Gestapo) was headed by Stubaf Dr Kranebitter (see plate section), with Oberstuf Schwinghammer as his deputy; under them came Oberstuf Anders (running the V-Männer, or informants), Oberstuf Walch, in charge of interrogations, and Oberstuf Didinger (Partisans). Rittmeister Lang, absorbed from Abwehr III f, was also employed on interrogations at the interrogation centre at 2 Via dei Mille, Verona. It was Didinger who had the responsibility of organising the anti-partisan drives ('razzias' in Italian, a word which embodied a high element of terror at that moment in history) in co-operation with the GNR and the UPI of Verona. Such drives became an increasing preoccupation of the German and Fascist security forces in the North, and absorbed a major proportion of their effort; they also resulted in many of the nastier atrocity incidents which figure in subsequent histories of the period.

The head of Abt VI (Foreign Intelligence) was Stubaf Huegel, with Hauptstuf Schoenpflug as his deputy. The head of Personnel was Stubaf Wiehan (see plate section). The BdS also had its own W/T transmitting station, in the charge of Ustuf Moeller.

Other dependencies were the former Abwehr station at Borghetto, where Major Dirlam (ex-Abwehr III-N) was employed on technical intelligence and control of the telegraph and radio service, and Major Heymann (ex-Abwehr III-H), collecting intelligence on Italian political and military personalities. From November 1944 onwards the HQ also ran a small anti-Partisan training school, about 100 strong, at Padua, under the command of Major Carita.

Harster himself also had various links to other security authorities:

Colonel Helfferich	:	Liaison with SID
Hauptstuf Goebl	:	Liaison with the German Embassy
Hauptstuf Koehler	:	Liaison with X Flotilla MAS
Oberstubaf Kappler	:	Liaison with the Italian police

In addition, there were direct links with Lt-Colonel Schwednitz, the Ic of Army Group Southwest, and with Lt-Colonel Walz, of the GFP.

After his powerful position in Rome one might have expected Kappler to have become Head of Abt VI at the BdS, but this was not to be; he was relegated to the job of Liaison Officer to the Republican Fascist Chief of Police, setting up his Dienststelle at the Villa Titynino at Maderno, close to Salò. His duties consisted creating in effect an efficient Italian Security Police system, so that his direct connection with intelligence operations appears to have thereby come to an end. His total command now consisted of two sergeants and a secretary.

From the Allied CI point of view the most important adjucts of the Bds HQ were:

(a) an agent-training school at Parma, called 'Einheit IDA', which was run by Kappler's previous deputy in Rome, Stubaf Hass, together with Oberstuf Schubernig (an Austrian who had joined the SS as early as 1932). This was treated in fact as an Aussenkommando, with six officers and 25 NCOs, a total strength of 70.

(b) a training school for agents at 2 Via Pasubio, Verona, run by Ustuf Dr Herbert Meyer (ex-Rome) with Ustuf Lechner as W/T instructor.

(c) an Abt VI S (sabotage) school at Villa Grazzani, Campalto (near Verona), and later moved to Chiusa.

The last named school was headed by one of the more notorious SD figures, Dr Otto Begus (alias Ragen, Wills, Gerbel, Beck, Benck, Bertolli, Beng, Goeblers, Major Bock and Major Fellner . . .; see plate section). Begus, who was at first believed by Allied CI to be the head of Amt VI in Italy, had had a chequered and wide-ranging career. Born in 1899, he was a native of Posen (present-day Poznan) who while in the army in World War I had been bayonetted in action on the Italian front. Possibly for this reason he was violently anti-Italian, although he spoke the language well. Having studied law after the war, he ended up as an Austrian police official from 1928.

In September 1933, when serving as a police chief in the Schmeltz district of Vienna, he was arrested on charges of engaging in illegal Nazi activities. Given six months gaol, he escaped to Germany. In mid-1934 Austrian Nazis in Munich (where Begus was working as a private detective) asked him to return to Austria to direct Nazi underground work. He did so, but was eventually re-arrested for this work and for alleged complicity in the murder of Austrian Chancellor Dollfuss. He was held for six months, but once again managed to escape and flee to Germany.

In Berlin, through an Austrian Nazi holding an important position with Berlin Police HQ, he was able to get a job with the police as an adviser on political affairs for Austria and Italy. Part of his work consisted in obtaining information on the Italian-Abyssinian crisis, then approaching a climax, and when shortly afterwards the Abyssinian Government officially requested police personnel in order to train and organise an Abyssinian police force, Begus accepted one of these positions and served as a 'European Captain' in the 'King's Army' on the Northern front, and for a time was personnel bodyguard to Haile Selassie.

He returned to Berlin in July 1936 and was appointed Commissioner in the Criminal Police in Frankfurt, and then in July 1938 in Salzburg. In November 1939, drafted into the German army, he was assigned to the Geheime Feldpolizei (GFP) as a captain. In May 1940 he was in action with the GFP in Rotterdam, Amsterdam, Dunkirk and Paris, and was eventually in charge of the security of XVIII Army Corps in the Bordeaux area until January 1941.

After three months with the GFP in Rumania and Bulgaria he travelled with a panzer division through Yugoslavia for the invasion of Greece, finishing up in charge of a GFP unit in Athens. A turning point in his career came in February 1943, when he was posted across to the RSHA Amt VI F (agent operations); he spent two months being briefed in Berlin on the organising of sabotage and espionage networks in Greece, and then went to Athens to carry out this work. In June 1944 he was recalled to Berlin and directed by Skorzeny to take command of Operation 'Zypresse' (Cypress) in Verona, i.e. the training and infiltration of saboteurs through the Allied lines (it is not clear why this should have been designated as a new and special operation, given that the SD in Italy had been carrying out this type of work for months past; we only have Begus's word for it, and possibly he was only trying to boost his own importance). It is not perhaps without relevance that a later CIC report describes him as 'Heavy smoker, drinker, double-crosser, gambler of sources'. (This latter phrase doubtless means that he committed his agents recklessly, without paying sufficient attention to the risks they would be running.)

SUBORDINATE UNITS

Under the BdS came the various Einsatzkommandos of the main towns and cities of North Italy plus a separate group based at Bolzano, concentrating on anti-partisan work.

Special mention must now be made of another sinister SD figure in the War Crimes catalogue: SS Standartenführer Walter Rauff (see plate section), who was based in Milan as area head of 'Gruppe Oberitalien West' (Upper Italy West) i.e. Piedmont, Lombardy and Liguria. Rauff, born in 1906, was a cultivated and intelligent polyglot, who had been an officer in the German Navy in 1924, but (like his subsequent boss Heydrich) was dismissed in 1937 for immorality. He joined the SD in the following year, and is said to have owed his rise in the SD to his being one of the few men who were aware of the Jewish ancestry of Heydrich. He served in the SD headquarters in September 1939, and achieved subsequent notoriety for being credited with the invention of the 'mobile gas chamber' for killing Jews when serving in Poland in 1941. In 1942 he commanded the SD in Tunis at the time of the Allied invasion of French North Africa, and at the end of 1943 was posted to Milan, where his office was established on the first floor of the Hotel Regina.

In Italy Rauff, a fierce anti-Semite without scruples or pity, left a lurid record behind him. His deputy, Theo Saevecke, organised on Rauff's orders a series of massacres of Jews, and Rauff became known as 'the Butcher of Meina' (where 17 Jews were massacred). His biggest coup was the capture of Ferruccio Parri, head of the Italian Resistance Movement, in January 1944; he then followed this up by capturing resistance men Edgardo Sogno and his companions when, dressed in German uniforms, they burst into the Hotel Regina and tried to free Parri. According to a modern press report, the pretty French waitress who served him meals was in fact an agent of the French Deuxième Bureau.

After the war Rauff managed to escape from Allied POW camp and made his way to Chile, where in spite of exposure and attempts to extradite him to face War Crimes charges he died of natural causes in 1984, at the age of 78.

EINHEIT IDA

To return to Einheit IDA, which (like the SD school at Verona) was providing training both for current agents and for post-occupational networks. After the fall of Rome Stubaf Hass had lost the confidence of the SD in Berlin because of the failure of his S/B organisation there. Harster was visited in Verona by Stubaf Reinhardt Wolff, of Referat VI b(i) Berlin (no relation to the HSSuPF), who told Harster that they were greatly displeased with the results of the P/O in AOT and that he, Wolff, had been instructed by Amt VI to study the matter on the ground. Harster put a car and petrol at his disposal, and at the end of October Wolff (who had no doubt been enjoying his three-month holiday in the sun, on a nicely unsupervised mission) reported that he was confident that Hass had been let down and possibly 'sold' by an Allied penetration agent (it is not clear quite what he meant by this expression, in practical terms). Wolff also told Harster that he would arrange to introduce agents into AOT through the islands off the Dalmation coast, as 'he did not think Hass could produce anything profitable himself'. Wolff returned again early in November 1944 and visited Milan and North-East Italy, but Harster never heard any more details of such plans as Wolff may have had.

Rauff, sinistro inventore degli «autogas»

Il colonnello si distinse anche in Italia per la sua ferocia: ordinò le stragi di ebrei sul Lago Maggiore nel settembre del 1943

SANTIAGO — È morto ieri a Santiago, stroncato da un infarto, il criminale nazista Walter Rauff. Ultimamente la sua estradizione era stata sollecitata dai governi di Israele, Francia e Germania Federale. L'ex colonnello delle SS risiedeva da 26 anni in Cile.

Figlio di un ufficiale di cavalleria caduto durante la Grande Guerra e nato nel 1906 a Kothen, presso Dessau (Germania), Hermann Julius Walter Rauff, il «carnefice di Meina» e l'SS che inventò le camere a gas mobili per lo sterminio degli ebrei, era uno dei Fuhrer-SS che dal momento del crollo del Terzo Reich era riuscito a farla franca: invano Simon Wiesenthal gli aveva dato la caccia per oltre quarant'anni cercando di ottenere l'estradizione dal Cile dove si era rifugiato.

La sua è stata la carriera di uno di quei «gangsters» intellettuali che, al pari di Wisliceny, braccio destro di Eichmann, erano ricercatissimi nelle sfere medio-alte del Terzo Reich. Poliglotta, colto e intelligente, uscito nel 1924 con pieni voti, dalla «Bismarckschule» di Magdeburgo e divenuto ufficiale della Marina Militare (finché, nel 1937, non ne era stato cacciato per immoralità), Rauff fu uno dei pochissimi uomini delle SS a conoscenza dell'ascendenza ebraica di Heydrich e tanto bastava per farne o un prigioniero o un condannato a morte. Ma ebbe fortuna.

L'Italia conobbe Rauff nella seconda metà del settembre 1943. Richiamato dall'urgenza da una missione in Turchia, il colonnello venne inviato a Roma agli ordini del generale SS Wolff il quale gli affidò l'incarico di responsabile della polizia di sicurezza (SD) per la Lombardia, il Piemonte e la Liguria. Rauff chiamò attorno a sé tre sinistri figuri, tutti assassini di professione: il capitano Schmidt, che inviò a Torino, il capitano Engel, al quale assegnò il comando di Genova, e il capitano Saevecke, che nominò proprio sostituto a Milano: fu Theo Saevecke che, su disposizioni di Rauff, organizzò e coordinò le stragi degli ebrei di Meina (17 vittime), di Baveno (14), di Stresa (4) e di Arona (4), avvenute sulle sponde del Lago Maggiore fra il 15 e il 30 settembre 1943.

Feroce antisemita, poliziotto senza scrupoli e senza pietà (fu suo comando di Milano, l'hotel «Regina», vide la tortura di centinaia di patrioti), Rauff riuscì a mettere a segno il più grosso colpo della propria carriera quando, all'inizio del gennaio 1945, identificò in un italiano arrestato, che si qualificava per «professor Pasolini», il capo della Resistenza, Ferruccio Parri. Tuttavia Rauff ebbe l'abilità di non mettersi mai in mostra e non gli fu difficile fuggire dall'Italia. Al New York Times narrò di essere stato «aiutato da un prete cattolico a raggiungere Roma, dove rimasi nascosto per un anno e mezzo in conventi del Vaticano» riuscendo inoltre a impiegarsi, come insegnante di francese e di matematica, nell'orfanotrofio romano «Villa Pia».

Da quel momento solo un uomo gli diede ancora la caccia: Wiesenthal. Il governo italiano, che pure avrebbe potuto cercare di stabilire quali e quante fossero le responsabilità di Rauff nel Lago Maggiore, lo fece interrogare una sola volta, nel 1953, da un funzionario della nostra ambasciata di Quito, in Ecuador (tuttavia per una questione diversa: una giornale di estrema destra aveva vergognosamente calunniato Parri scrivendo che aveva ottenuto la libertà da Rauff, tradendo i propri compagni, ma l'ex colonnello SS smentì seccamente i fascisti nostrani).

Con paziente tenacia, Wiesenthal risalì tutta la carriera di Rauff e individuò in lui l'uomo che, in Polonia, fra il 1941 e il 1942, aveva inventato i sinistri «gasauto», grandi autobotti che — con la croce rossa dipinta ai lati, sul letto e nella parte posteriore — nelle quali venivano fatti entrare dagli 80 ai 100 ebrei per volta. Chiusi gli sportelli a tenuta stagna ed avviato il motore, i gas di scarico erano comvogliati attraverso due grossi tubi nell'interno del veicolo e nel giro di mezz'ora l'ossido di carbonio uccideva tutte le vittime.

Il tribunale di Hannover, nell'ottobre 1963, processò dodici ex aiutanti del «gasauto» e uno di questi, Friedrich Pradel, ex maggiore della polizia di sicurezza, dichiarò: «Non sapevo a che cosa servivano quei camion, io ricevevo semplicemente ordini dal mio diretto superiore, il colonnello Rauff». I giudici tedeschi chiesero l'estradizione di Rauff accusandolo dell'eccidio dei 97 mila ebrei di Chelmno e di Kulmhof) ma il Cile, nel dicembre 1962, la negò. Un secondo tentativo, compiuto personalmente da Wiesenthal quando in Cile andò al potere Allende, non ebbe miglior risultato: nel settembre 1972 il presidente sudamericano scrisse a Wiesenthal una lettera in cui, dopo aver condannato i crimini nazisti, affermò che gli era vietato dalla legge esercitare funzioni giudiziarie o avviare cause penali. Andò al potere Pinochet e da allora Rauff si stabilì a Santiago senza più nascondersi, con la moglie e i due figli, ottenne a Punta Arenas l'amministrazione di una società di pesca oceanica e diventò intoccabile come se non avesse mai compiuto alcun delitto.

Giuseppe Mayda

131

Hass continued on in a small way with IDA, sending line-crossers on short-range missions, the longest of which reached Rome. By means of small successes he won back some support from Berlin, which agreed to supply him with W/T sets. These sets arrived in February 1945 (we are getting ahead of the general story here, but include these details at this point in the interests of unity) but it was found impossible to establish contact with the Control Station at Bamberg from Verona,, so that the sets were never in fact distributed, either to IDA or to the school at Verona.

Before we move on finally to the run of actual operations, there is one final by-product to be recorded. In April/May 1944 the Second-in-Command of the 'Baldo' network in Trieste was called to FAK 150's head-quarters in Florence and told that 'Baldo' must now create a pool of agents to be used for stay-behind missions. The individual agent was given a cover name, usually formed on the basis of the initial letters of his real names; pay rates depended on his social status or army rank, the maximum being 12,000 lire a month. Training in identification of Allied uniforms, badges of rank etc, with particular stress on shoulder flashes and divisional signs, was given from books provided by FAK 150. W/T training was also given, the aim being to link each agent with the FAK 150 base station 'Jakob'. By September agents had been installed in a number of towns, not only in Istria and Northern Slovenia, but also further afield: In Ancona (Miceli, alias 'Ireneo'), Venice ('Italico'), Treviso (Furlani, alias 'Ignazio') and Ravenna (Mangia, alias 'Marte').

OPERATIONS JUNE-JULY 1944

The front line moved swiftly northwards once Rome had fallen; the 150 miles between Rome and Florence were covered in exactly two months as the Germans carried out a fighting retreat towards their main final bastion, the so-called 'Gothic Line' (see map p.134). Work on this had been going on for months, under the energetic direction of Field-Marshal Kesselring, and it was to bring the Allied armies up to a fairly abrupt halt, based as it was along the main backbone of the Appenines, with harsh rocky moun-tains rising to as much as 7,000 feet, and before long to be aided by the bitter winter snows. In the final months of the summer, however, GIS agent activity continued unabated. In July, 14 agents on espionage missions in Rome itself were unmasked, together with five saboteurs – most of the latter being SD agents. Excluding Rome, 12 were arrested on espionage missions, one on a sabotage mission. Of the overall total of 32, 16 of them were stay-behinds (four of them with W/T sets), 11 were line-crossers and five were parachuted in. Two Abwehr W/T stay-behind agents, who signed themselves in their messages as 'Riga' and 'Heini', who subsequently

132

turned out to be South Tyrolese serving in the German Army, were still operating and had so far eluded RDF operations to locate them: the only consolation for Allied CI was that their codes had been broken and it was clear that the intelligence they were sending back was of minimal value to the enemy. They were finally tracked down some time later, tried and executed.

GIS MOVEMENTS

In consequence of the Allied advance there was perforce a general falling back of GIS headquarters towards the Po Valley. A short intermediate stage involved the use of Florence, and here both training schools and unit offices had been set up in the Spring of 1944, before finally being obliged to evacuate by the end of July. The final move back to the Po Valley saw them ending up as follows:

> FAK 150 at Verona, with two Trupps at Padua, two at Milan
> FAK 212 at Verona, its Trupps at Verona, Padua and Milan
> FAK 190 at Padua
> FAK 309 at Verona

Allied Intelligence staffs were in no doubt by this time that the Abwehr had been discredited to a considerable degree, and it was clear that the comparative independence that it had hitherto enjoyed in Italy was being drastically curtailed. In comparison the Sicherheitsdienst, although its post-occupational plans for Rome had met with virtual disaster, seems to have suffered a less serious blow to its prestige which, unlike the Abwehr's, did not depend exclusively – or even mainly – on espionage and sabotage. Moreover, the fortunes of the SD were so closely linked with those of the Nazi Party that the latter were forced by pressure of events to assume ever greater control, both within Germany and without, so that the SD found itself taking on ever-expanding responsibilities.

OPERATIONS AUGUST 1944

During the month 52 enemy agents fell into Allied hands; some 20 of these were in Florence, 24 in Rome and the remainder being captured in widely-separated parts of Italy, Sardinia and Sicily. Fifteen of the total were SD agents, 21 were Abwehr and the balance were grouped under the 'miscellaneous' heading. Ten of those arrested were on sabotage missions. Five had arrived by parachute, 11 had crossed the lines and the remainder were stay-behinds. Curiously, all of the SD agents were in the latter category and all had been installed either in Rome or in Florence. Equally curiously,

133

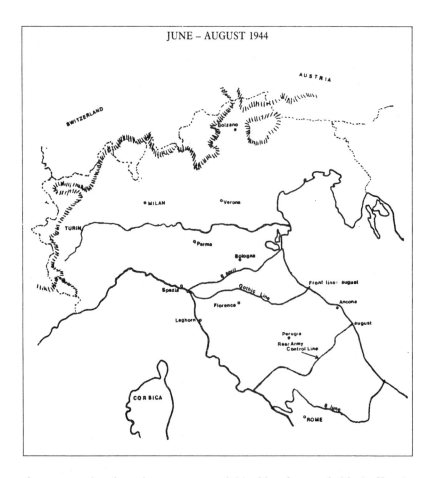

there seemed to have been no appreciable Abwehr stay-behind effort in
Florence – a city which had been their main HQ and training centre for
nearly six months, besides being an important conjuction of road communications through which the bulk of Allied military traffic for the 5th
Army could be expected to pass; they had had, therefore, ample time to set
up stay-behind networks at this strategic location. Only a small number of
those arrested had W/T sets, but this may in part be explained by the fact
that a number of them belonged to groups whose W/T operators had
already been arrested. Their espionage missions were, as usual, concerned
for the most part with the gathering of long or short-term military information, although in Rome a small proportion of the agents captured, all of
them SD, had been instructed to collect political information. There was a
conspicuous absence of Ic activity, limited to one or two agents. In general,
their briefing had been vague and casual, except in the case of one agent,

134

who was sent a long distance for the sole purpose of ascertaining whether or not a particular airfield was being used by the Allies – a brief which could have been more accurately answered by a single aircraft sortie, pointing up the now complete failure of the Luftwaffe in this theatre.

The Italian partisans, who had already proved their worth in Rome and elsewhere, were especially useful in Florence, where they were instrumental in the capture of several important GIS agents. It was found that the Partito d'Azione group in the city had organised a very efficient counter-intelligence service of their own, with further contacts in other towns of N Italy. A Security Summary issued at the time concluded: 'It appears likely that we shall in future receive some really valuable and well-organised assistance from this quarter, and it is proposed to take full advantage of this co-operation, which is readily forthcoming'.

One agent, who was dropped by parachute in Apulia (the 'heel' of Italy) – an area much favoured by the GIS for this type of delivery – had first been taken by air from Bergamo to Belgrade, then to Tirana (Albania) before finally crossing to Southern Italy. However, although the aircraft kept low over the Adriatic, at a height of some 600 feet, it was picked up by radar and attacked three times on the way by Allied night-fighters, apparently without being damaged. It can hardly have been an encouraging beginning for the agent concerned.

One group of three agents was briefed to obtain jobs in Allied military HQs, both as cover and, presumably, in the hope of gaining access thereby to useful intelligence. One agent was found to have been working in an Allied Forces Club in Rome. Another suggestion made by the GIS, to an agent who had had some journalistic experience, was that he should launch a Review in English and Italian – work which would bring him into contact with useful sources of information and gain him an entrée into Allied headquarters. A second agent was to have been used as a translator on the staff of the review.

While a few of the agents arrested were of higher grade and of a more determined calibre, the rest were described as 'poor stuff'. One point of interest was an Abwehr agent who said that his despatching organisation was anxious to collect Mediterranean shipping information for the Japanese.

SABOTAGE OPERATIONS

It became clear, as successive sabotage agents were arrested, that the members of X Flotilla MAS who had been left in post-occupational rôles to carry out missions had received but scanty instruction in the use of the sabotage devices issued to them. Others who had been through a sabotage school in Belgrade, although more thoroughly trained in such matters as tactics, explosives, arms, ju-jitsu and self-defence, driving and W/T operating, had not in the first place been selected with any degree of discrimination and in many cases showed considerable distaste or lack of enthusiasm for their missions. A highly successful penetration of this Belgrade SD sabotage group was made by four young members of the Partito d'Azione, which itself carried out the arrest of several members of the group and handed them over to the Allied authorities. The missions which had been allocated to the sabotage agents were vague and general.

GIS CHANGES

August also saw the arrival in Italy of Colonel Hans Engelmann (see plate section), sent up by the Militärisches Amt in Berlin with the object of uniting all Abteilung I departments in Italy under one command, called 'Führungsstelle Italien', in order to give the SD a closer control of what the Abwehr Kommandos were doing. Engelmann, who used the aliases 'Enzian' and 'Angelo', seems to have found it difficult to achieve this, particularly in the case of FAK 150; however, the Führungsstelle was finally operational in Feb/March 1945, after which intelligence collected by Abt I agencies was passed through Engelmann (located at Merano) via the W/T station 'Jakob' to Berlin.

OPERATIONS – SEPTEMBER 1944

During this four-week period over thirty enemy agents were caught. Around half of them had crossed the lines on foot, three were dropped by parachute (two in Sardinia, one in South Italy) and the remaining 12 were stay-behind agents. There was an increased emphasis on the use of W/T, with eight of the 30 captured being equipped with radio sets. The short-range Abwehr and Ic agents were, as usual, all instructed to recross the lines after a few days spent in the Allied forward areas.

There were indications that the SD appeared to be assuming greater responsibility for military sabotage, but in the main it seemed that the Abwehr was being allowed to continue its operations much according to the old pattern, although an analysis of past failures should have convinced an objective critic that many of their operations would stand little chance of success. Many of them, too, illustrated an apparent lack of any direct relationship with the military situation, with some missions, both sabotage and intelligence, appearing rather pointless.

The front line did not advance to any great extent during the month; in consequence the GIS had little opportunity for planting agents with stay-behind missions, and concentrated on the despatch of line-crossers with short-term sorties. It was plain that agents of this type were more likely to satisfy the immediate needs of the German Army for tactical intelligence than were agents equipped with W/T sets and sent into AOT by parachute or small boat, although it was in fact in respect of the Allied rear areas that the higher German formations, lacking any air coverage, were most lacking in knowledge. In spite of the not inconsiderable numbers of line-crossers who were falling into Allied hands, the GIS continued to employ them with what was accepted as a moderate measure of success, although the information they were able to bring back was very limited. One courageous German agent arrested during the month was a girl called Costa: she was only seventeen years old, but proved to be one of the toughest nuts to crack when under interrogation: it was five days before she could be persuaded to talk (it should be added that the type of 'physical persuasion' favoured by Kappler was not used on the Allied side). She had been arrested when on her way back to EOT from her third mission: she had earlier been awarded the Iron Cross, and had been received and congratulated by Mussolini.

Those arrested during the month numbered 23, 14 of them being Abwehr agents, six from the SD: the remaining three were Ic. Nine of this total were stay-behinds, and only two had sabotage missions. A survey of the agents captured that month showed that almost all of them had been trained prior to June, suggesting that the GIS had a reserve pool of agents which it was using up, even though their training was not specifically adapted to the current military situation. One factor which stood out in the overall picture of GIS operations during the month was the enterprise shown by the Abwehr I-M (Marine), and the higher quality of the agents used by this section. As evidence of this was the uncovering in Rome of a complete W/T reporting group, the detection of which was due more to the loss of its leader's nerve than to any lack of preparation by I-M. Again, there was the case of two agents who had been despatched to obtain information on shipping and troop movements in the port of Ancona. The operation was, unusually, a joint enterprise by Abwehr I-M and FAK 150, and was noteworthy in that one of the two agents was of a particularly high standard, having previously been in Italian Naval Intelligence as well as Vice-Consul in Switzerland. But the weakness in the operation lay in the other member of the pair, a woman, who denounced her partner in a fit of jealousy over the fickleness of his attentions . . .

Another agent was sent to Leghorn, to report on shipping in that port; two were instructed to obtain information of a political and economic nature in Rome and Florence, while two others had a somewhat vague mission to 'organise rebel bands and sabotage groups' in Southern Italy. These latter four were said to be the only SD agents captured during the month.*

The above pair's sortie to raise rebellion was tartly described by the CI Branch as 'somewhat impetuous'; needless to say, it did not get off the ground.

The remaining agents, with the exception of one who was to note the numbers of aircraft on airfields in Central Italy, were to collect information of a purely military nature, mostly concerned with unit identifications. Four agents were equipped with W/T sets; all the others had been told to come back through the front line.

SEABORNE OPERATIONS

While some attempt had been made back in January 1944 to attack shipping at the Anzio Bridgehead by underwater swimmers (one of whom was only 17 years old) there was no further discernible seaborne sabotage raid until October, when an abortive sea attack was made on the port of Ancona, involving the use of midget submarines and frogman-saboteurs. While this was a strictly naval operation, in that it was carried out by members of the Marine-Einsatzkommandos, the latter units were closely associated with Abteilung II of the Abwehr and largely derived their intelligence from Abwehr I-M.

This attack was followed up – possibly quite independently – by another attack, almost certainly seaborne, on the night of 13/14 October near Rimini. In the early morning the driver of an army Tank Troop Workshop was inspecting his truck when he discovered that an explosive charge, with time detonating device attached had been placed on the front axle during the night. A search among other vehicles revealed a second set of explosive on another truck ten yards away. The plastic explosive was thought to be British in origin, with the detonators and time delays of German or Italian manufacture.

The workshops were sited very close to the sea, and tracks ran from each of the two vehicles to the water's edge. A few feet inshore six German

---

* There is a clash of statistics here between the figures issued by HQ Allied Armies in Italy (AAI) in their monthly 'Notes on Counter-Intelligence', and those published by 15th Army Group in their monthly 'Security Summary' covering the front line areas. The latter's figures claim six SD arrests. Since neither publication specified the precise dates covered, but only 'monthly' figures, there is probably some discordance in the time-span parameters.

anti-vehicle mines (Teller mines) were found, and a service haversack containing fuses, detonators and primers; the mines must have been fitted with some form of time delay, because they exploded shortly after their discovery, without doing any damage. There were further indications that a heavy object (doubtless a rubber boat) had been dragged up onto the beach nearby. It was thought that possibly the arrival of a tank transporter in the vehicle park in the early hours of that morning may have scared the attacking group into beating a retreat seawards before they had completed their mission. The enemy unit involved was not identified.

Yet another sabotage attempt took place on the night of 18/19 October, on the same lines as that at Rimini a few days earlier: this was against the vehicles of a searchlight battery at Viserbella, 6km to the north of Rimini. At 6.30am on the 19th two 3kg explosive charges were found to have been attached roughly to the front axle of each of two vehicles parked on the beach; each charge was fitted with an acetone delay-action igniter and a detonator which had in fact exploded, but had only broken the charge instead of setting it off. Three 'S' mines ('jumping' mines, a particularly lethal German army anti-personnel mine) and three Teller mines were also discovered in plain view at various places in the unit area. Between 6.30 and 7.30am three explosions took place on the beach, having apparently been caused by further mines of some description buried in the sand. No damage was done and no casualties were caused.

Two more charges were then found attached to the tracks of an old abandoned Italian Army SP gun, which was lying nearby. These were left where they were, in order to avoid any risk to personnel; eventually the detonators exploded but, once again, the main charge was not set off.

It was evident that the attack was the result of yet another 'hit-and-run' seaborne sortie; nevertheless the failure of any of the essential bombs to go off seemed to indicate a lack of skilled operators, or a failure to give sufficient training.

11

GIS Operations – Phase IV

The month of November produced a virtual flooding of the front-line areas by line-crossers; no fewer than 55 were arrested in the forward zones. Forty of these were espionage agents, while eleven were on sabotage missions.

In spite of this 'mass production', however, there were indications that the enemy intelligence effort was undergoing a transition from a state of merely coping with the current situation in a somewhat extempore fashion, towards a more determined aggressive policy, which the now comparatively stable battle front made more feasible. An interesting feature of the recent policy was that it included 'deep-roving' line-crossers, sorties from which they were expected nevertheless to return through the lines, having presumably memorised all the information they had collected. Formerly, such longer-range agents had tended to be equipped with W/T sets and to be fed in well behind the lines by parachute or small boat. Such operations had been few and far between in the preceding months; the absence of parachutists may of course have been due to a shortage of suitable aircraft, and the absence of sea landings in rear areas due to a combination of past failures and increased Allied vigilance (a special coast-watching service of SIM/CS had been set up by Allied CI in May 1944). It may on the other hand be that the Abwehr had come to the conclusion that their W/T missions were not paying a dividend and this new modus operandi might produce better results. Be that as it may, the only W/T agent known to have been despatched during the month had been parachuted into Sardinia, 'an area beyond the scope of mortal line-crossers', as a contemporary report put it. The report went on: 'In this connection, it may be noted that the enemy has only once insulted us by despatching an agent across the lines on foot with a W/T set'.

Most of this line-crossing activity (48 agents) took place in the US Fifth Army area (see map on p.142) due no doubt to the fact that the western sector, in particular that area lying between Pistoia and the coast, was thinly held and mountainous; what became known as 'the Abetone Pass route' was the favourite entry point for feeding agents into Allied territory. Even some agents who had been given missions in the Eighth Army and Adriatic coastal areas were despatched via the Abetone Pass, with instructions to move across thereafter to their destinations over on the eastern side of the peninsular. Moreover, they were also told to return by the same route.

In the main, the line-crossing agents had been despatched by Trupps 150 and 152 of FAK 150; their missions were to Florence, Arezzo, Pisa, Leghorn and Rimini, and to other smaller towns in the forward areas, their instructions being to locate and observe concentrations of troops, gun positions, HQs, vehicle and uniform insignia, types of tanks, fuel and ammunition dumps etc, and to report on airfields across the whole peninsula. One agent had a specific mission to reconnoitre the location of civilian Control Points in the forward areas, so that these could be avoided by future line-crossers.

Abwehrkommando 190 (I-L) used the despatching facilities of the FAK 150 Trupps. Its agents were still primarily briefed for air intelligence, although they were expected to collect military (and, where appropriate, naval) information while en route to and from their primary air targets. Three FAK 190 agents were despatched during this month to visit the ports of Rimini and Ancona and the airfields at Iesi and Falconara: at these latter they were to find out the identity of the air force units stationed at the field, the type of aircraft and the insignia painted on them. Another FAK 190 agent was to travel to Naples and Salerno, observe shipping activity and to attempt to locate a specific Allied Airborne unit.* Another was to go to Leghorn to observe shipping and any air installations which might be seen en route, while two more were to travel to Rome on long-term missions.

The majority of FAK 190 agents were found to have been equipped with a handkerchief carrying secret ink writing in the form of a Laissez-Passer, which identified the bearer and made it easier for him to move in the German-occupied part of Italy. Needless to say, it also made it easier for Allied interrogators to 'break down' any suspected agent; once a test had revealed the invisible ink message, the agent had little option but to confess. As a result, such agents naturally did their best to get rid of such evidence surreptitiously when they were arrested, so that security forces had to be alert to such ruses. A Security Circular of the period posed an acid but rhetorical question as a 'tailpiece': 'In which Carabiniere station was the lavatory found to be bunged up by secret ink handkerchiefs disposed of hastily by *three* different agents after their arrest?'

---

* It is interesting to note in this context that Field-Marshall Kesselring, in his Memoirs written after the war, expresses astonishment that the Allies 'did not use this powerful weapon available to them'. However, an Ic assessment made at the time stated firmly: 'An airborne operation in conjunction with the ground offensive is considered unlikely, owing to small numbers of airborne troops available (at most, one Airborne Division)'.

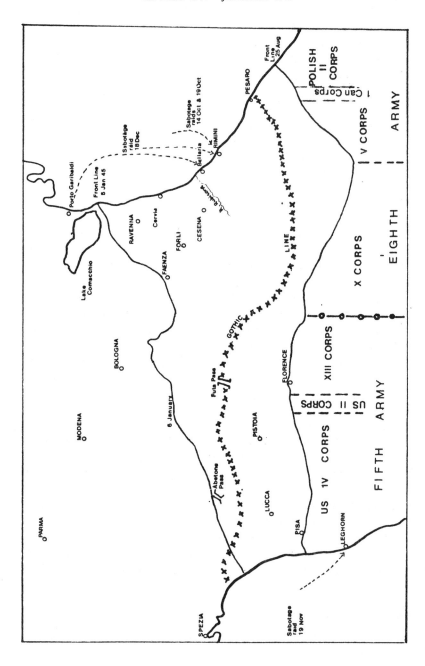

The Abwehr Marine Kommando (I-M) did not appear to have been very active during the month, although no doubt it had a hand in the briefing of FAK 190 agents for the naval parts of their missions. However, one stay-behind agent of this Kommando was arrested during the period: he had been installed with a W/T set in Leghorn and had been transmitting his observations for some time before he was unmasked.

An unusual operation was mounted by one unit, believed to be Abwehr, involving two Poles who had been recruited in Poland and sent down to Italy expressly for the purpose. They were to cross the lines into the sector held by the Polish Corps and attempt to join these forces; after a period of two months or so they were to desert back to the Germans, taking with them information about the Polish forces – troop strengths, morale, relations with the other Allies etc. Both were arrested and confessed. Their operation had not been made any easier by the fact that neither of them could speak any Italian.

At some point Lieutenant Pfannenstiehl, already known to Allied CI as OC of a forward HQ for FAK 212, appears to have decided to do a little espionage on his own; he disguised himself in the tattered clothes of an Italian shepherd and, driving a herd of some twenty sheep, moved across into the Allied forward areas and back again – an exploit for which he allegedly was awarded the Knight's Cross by the Führer. The source of this anecdote was an ordinary German soldier, taken prisoner, whose CO was friendly with Pfannenstiehl.

This was not FAK 212's only activity during the month. Ten of its agents, all of them on sabotage missions in the forward areas, were arrested; they had been despatched in pairs, with instructions to sabotage vehicles, dumps, bridges, railway rolling stock and equipment in the Lucca-Pistoia area. Sabotage material for their use had been previously hidden by the Kommando before withdrawal from the sector; each dump, when uncovered by Allied investigators, was found to consist of a small metal box containing explosives and fuses. The boxes in each of three different sites were identical in content. They also contained a list of contents and an identifying number, which the agent was to report when he returned to EOT on completion of his mission – thus providing his controlling officer with confirmation that he had at least got that far in carrying out his orders.

The Sicherheitsdienst meanwhile showed some recrudescence of interest in straight military intelligence. One agent was instructed to attempt to penetrate the British Intelligence Service, having first surrendered. He admitted immediately that he had been recruited by the GIS and had come on an espionage mission. The information which he gave about the SD unit which had despatched him was sufficiently accurate to make it credible, for the GIS had clearly made allowance for a fair measure of

Allied knowledge about their organisation. It was, however, only a 'cover story', and one in which the agent had been carefully coached; later he admitted that his real mission had been to get himself recruited by the British Intelligence Service, with the aim of being sent back to EOT as an Allied agent, when he could pass on to the GIS such information as he had been able to pick up about their activities.

Three other SD agents were despatched through the lines with the help of a forward Abwehr Trupp; under interrogation they admitted that they were to travel to Naples on a 30-day mission, and once there, were to spread anti-Allied propaganda. They were also to look for incidents indicating bad relations between Allied troops and Italians, and for any problems in Allied administration. They were also to determine the extent, and needs, of any existing or potential Fascist group. After a month one of the party was to return to EOT across the lines, and report any progress made.

There was one major sabotage operation launched during the period – an attack by X Flotilla MAS against Leghorn (Livorno) harbour. At 1am on 19 November a Royal Navy rating, one of three 'mine-watchers' stationed in a small lighthouse on the end of the northern breakwater of the port, walked along the mole and threw into the water an anti-frogman explosive charge – as was part of his routine duties. As he did so he noticed a dark shape alongside the mole and heard a slight cough. He returned to his post, alerted his mates and the party of three advanced on this figure, one firing a shot as they did so. Three men emerged from the water and surrendered. They were wearing green felt skull-caps of the Balaclava Helmet type, with dark camouflage netting attached, and their faces were blackened. When they were later examined to better advantage their clothing was found to consist of dark blue overalls, over which was fitted underwater breathing apparatus, rubber skin-suits set in rubber shoes with large flippers attached, and next to the skin thick woollen under-garments. In addition, each carried a money-belt containing nearly 50,000 lire in newly printed and consecutively numbered Banca d'Italia notes, a knife, wrist-watch and two metal clamps hanging from a weighted belt. The leader of the party had the badges of rank of an Italian Sottotenente on his overalls, and all wore a service identity disc around the neck. When the question arose of treating them, not as members of the armed forces but as saboteurs out of uniform, it was to this disc, rather than to their badges of rank, that they referred in order to establish their military status.

Immediately after their capture they were segregated, searched and questioned individually. It was found that they had entered the water some three hours earlier from an X MAS Flotilla craft which had brought them from their starting point at Castagno up the coast to a point two or three kilometres northwest of the entrance to Leghorn harbour. The Naval authorities took immediate steps to alert the port, and the illumination was increased, the dropping of charges intensified and keel searches of all ships in the vicinity were carried out, while a PT Boat put to sea in the hope of making contact with the parent craft of the limpeteers. As the events of the night were more fully revealed by subsequent interrogation of the captives, however, it became clear that no damage would have resulted from the attack, which was barely under way when its would-be authors surrendered. But they were evidently in earnest, for each had swum with two bilge-keel bombs of a new type on his belt, and had assisted with the towing of a large rubber sack containing four sets of civilian clothing and various personal effects for use on shore, including false identity cards, three Beretta pistols and a quantity of concentrated food. The swim had proved more exhausting than they had anticipated, as their leader explained, for the unexpected brightness of the port lighting prevented a closer approach by their boat. They were also unprepared for the frequency and strength of the anti-limpeteer charges used in the harbour, and in general their briefing had been inadequate for the task before them. The three were therefore in rather poor shape as they rested at the mole (one was suffering from convulsions resulting from a torn suit) and when the sentry opened fire they promptly abandoned both their equipment and their mission.

The limpeteers, Sottotenente Malacarne, Sotto Capo Bertoncin and Marinaio Sorgetti, all of X Flotilla MAS, had first been brought together in the Valdagno office of Lieutenant Wolk, CO of the GAMMA group, early in November. Previously they had undergone extensive swimming training, two of them on the island of San Giorgio, near Venice, the third at Valdagno. For the planning of their attack there had been available a set of air photos taken over Leghorn about 20 October, and this appears to have been the most concrete piece of operational intelligence on which their mission had been based. The aim had been to put the party into the water fairly close to the harbour mole and for them to swim towards it in order to deposit the rubber sack in hiding there; they were then to re-enter the water on the other side of the mole and to swim about three-quarters of a mile to attack the ships in the stern-to holding berth at the Curvilinea mole, each tackling one ship with his two bombs; they would then return to the cache of equipment and head across the harbour, swimming with the sack into the waters of the Pisa Canal until they reached a pine wood about two miles up the canal. Here they were to change into civilian clothes, hide their equipment in some convenient place and await events. The fourth set of civilian clothing which was found to be in their sack was intended to be used by another GAMMA man named Pavone, who had trained with them; Pavone was to further the operation by swimming into Leghorn a few days later, dragging with him ten large sacks, each weighing some 40 kilos, containing spares in the shape of bilge-keel bombs, clamps, floats, respirators, a spare suit and rubber solution (presumably for punctures), sulpha drugs, first aid kit and several bottles of cognac. One of the earlier arrivals was to contrive to be on the breakwater, flashing a light to guide Pavone in, help him store the sacks around the harbour (in wrecks or under the water) until they were needed, and then lead him to the rendez-vous in the pine wood.

Thus while Malacarne and his men were undergoing a six-day interrogation, Pavone was waiting at La Spezia for his follow-up mission. The weather remained unfavourable, and it was decided to postpone the attempt until the December moonless period. Pavone spent the interval in a journey to Milan and Genoa, where he contracted VD, and in getting his gear in order at Castagna. By the evening of 10 December he was ready to start off, declining the substitute whom Wolk had provided in view of his medical condition. Wolk had informed Pavone that the Malacarne trio had successfully established themselves* and had cached their equipment among the burned-out oil tanks in the port. Engine trouble postponed departure until 11 December, when at about 9.30pm Pavone was put into the water a mile off Leghorn, together with his ten sacks and some sulpha tablets (presumably for his illness). Once more (hardly surprisingly, in view of the size of his load) the necessary effort proved greater than had been expected, and it was a very exhausted swimmer who got ashore nine hours later, close to the derelict Marzocco oil tanks at the north end of the main harbour. Naturally, no Malacarne was there to receive him, and he abandoned the sacks on the beach together with his flippers and breathing apparatus, donning over his blue overalls a light brown waterproof which he had been carrying separately. It is not clear whether he was setting off to find his associates or whether, as he claimed later, he was beginning a long trek to Taranto, his former home, when at 8.30am he was arrested by a US Military Guard on the west bank of the Pisa canal: the sentry had noticed the tell-tale rubber shoes with large eyelets, joined to the rubber trousers. Malacarne's party was forthwith reunited under Allied auspices.

From their various interrogations valuable information was obtained about other possible operations of a similar nature at Leghorn, for which appropriate reception measures were then taken. Fresh light was thrown on the training methods and technical developments in limpeteer warfare

---

* One can only presume that the original trio had had a W/T set with them, with which to report progress, and that this was now being used by Allied CI in order to 'collect in' the final swimmer. There was no mention of this, however, in the account given at the time in an Allied CI bulletin.

as conceived by Wolk, and on the relations between his German and Italian trainees. It appeared that the Italians had been starved of essential equipment since their stores at La Spezia were destroyed, and consequently they had had to beg, borrow and steal from the Germans the explosives, oxygen, rubber suits etc without which a limpeteer remains grounded. Wolk had even had to buy petrol on the Black Market in order to keep his trucks on the road.

A CI account of this incident drew attention to the following aspects worth special mention:

> Firstly, the sentries' prompt segregation of their prisoners, which made it impossible for the latter to arrange a concerted cover story; then the production during their interrogation of several homely details on life in the X Flotilla MAS culled from Security files, which gave the impression that the interrogator 'knew it all anyway'; thirdly, the alertness of the US guard who captured Sottotenente Pavone after being told to watch out for individuals wearing limpeteer footwear. It was clear from the confessions of Malacarne and later of Pavone that far too little accurate information had been available on the sea and security defences of Leghorn when the operation was launched.

These arrests, with the attackers classified as military Prisoners of War, were not included in the statistics of agent arrests during the month. It is instructive to compare this correct handling, under the Geneva Convention, with a not dissimilar Allied operation in March 1944 in the same region, when two US officers and eleven Enlisted Men were landed near La Spezia in order to attack the railway. They were arrested by Fascist troops and Korvetten-Kapitän Klaps, of Abwehr I-M, was ordered to carry out their interrogation; this was conducted by Leutnant z. See Sessler.

General Toussaint, GOC of the German 14th Army, then ordered that the Allied party should be executed as saboteurs; Klaps however protested that they had been captured in uniform and should be regarded as POWs. Klaps sent a copy of his protest direct to Berlin by W/T; the execution was, however, carried out on Toussaint's orders.

It is sometimes suggested that atrocities of this type were only perpetrated by the SS, and that the Wehrmacht stuck strictly to the rules of the Geneva Convention, in which officers and men were well schooled. It seems clear that, where their careers were at risk, not all senior officers of the Wehrmacht were prepared to stand up and be counted.

Several GIS moves took place during the month. The SD's Abteilungen I and II had already moved from Verona to Colle Isarco, up in the mountains, as they had a large female staff and Harster wanted them removed from the air raid dangers of Verona; in November the Control Station for

147

the SD's W/T communications also moved there, under command of Ustuf Moeller. A small W/T link was set up between Colle Isarco and the remaining HQ at Verona. On the Abwehr side, FAK 190 opened an agent training school at Bassano del Grappa, north-east Vicenza.

The previous period had been a busy one for Allied Counter-Intelligence staffs; the succeeding month was to be no less so. There were 56 arrests,* of which 40 agents were captured in the forward battle zones (i.e. excluding those arrested in Rome and other parts of Italy). The fact that more than 90 agents had been captured in the operational zone over the two months must have caused the GIS considerable concern, and a more frequent use of parachutist agents was observable.

Moreover (and no doubt the influence of the RSHA was having its effect by now) it was noticeable that the GIS were starting to train and employ agents of better quality than before. The majority appeared more determined to carry out their missions, and this applied to line-crossers as well as to longer-term W/T agents and parachutists. At preliminary interrogations, for example, immediate confessions were now being more rarely obtained; 'cover stories' were almost always produced – a fact which in itself implied more serious intentions. Voluntary surrenders had become rare, and several of those arrested had shown considerable pertinacity in seeking to perform their allotted tasks.

All those line-crossers arrested had, once again, tried to pass (or had succeeded in passing) across the lines on the Fifth Army front. It was evident that the GIS were concentrating on this area, rather than over the Eighth Army side, although some stay-behind agents, some of whom had W/T sets, were uncovered in the latter area during the period, having been 'planted' in Adriatic towns by FAK 150 many weeks previously. Some fifteen FAK 150 line-crosser agents were arrested during the month, mostly on short-range missions, although two of them were to penetrate as far as Terni, some 150 miles away, for the purpose of locating a specific Allied formation.

Five agents of FAK 190 (I-L) were arrested – a considerable reduction compared with previous months, possibly as a result of the falure of so many of its agents during November. One of these agents was parachuted into the Perugia area and was arrested as he made his way back towards EOT; he was in fact on his second mission of this type, having already carried out a succesful one some time earlier. One of the other agents had been instructed to go to Rimini and Ancona on a 15-day mission to look for signs of any amphibious operations being prepared by the Allies.

*Eight of these were women agents.

One case of particular interest and importance was the arrest in Rome in mid-December of two stay-behind agents mentioned in Chapter IX. They were Austrians, and actually members of the Wehrmacht, who had already been installed in Rome by the Abwehr since February 1944, in order to be well 'bedded-down' before the city was captured by the Allies. They had worked as a team, equipped with W/T, and had transmitted a considerable number of messages between June and December. By early December they had almost been pinpointed by the Allied RDF organisation, which had narrowed down its search to a specific residential block in Rome, when their arrest was precipitated by the arrival of a courier from EOT with fresh funds, which they had requested in one of their messages. Since the Allies had been reading and decoding their signals, a 'reception party' was arranged for the courier, who was dropped in by parachute and was carrying details of how he was to make contact with the pair. The investigators were thus led straight to their goal.

Seven Abwehr II saboteurs, despatched by Trupps of FAK 212, were also arrested during the period; five of them had crossed the lines on foot, but two had arrived by parachute – a new departure in the sabotage field. The line-crossers were to work from previously laid-down dumps and carry out attacks on various targets in the forward areas; the parachutists were to move to the Cassino area, where they were to use explosives from another hidden dump to sabotage a petrol pipeline used by the Allies.

Some ten SD agents were apprehended during the month. One of them had remained as a stay-behind in the forward zone and, once over-run by the Allied troops, had proceeded south to Rome, Naples, Salerno and Sicily, where he had remained for several weeks: then he made his way north, and was unlucky to be arrested just as he was about to cross the front line into EOT. Another was parachuted in the Caserta area and made his way north to Florence, where he surrendered. The balance of SD agents all crossed the lines and were to go to Florence, Rome and Siena, mainly to collect economic and political intelligence. One of the spies destined for Florence was also, however, to find out what types of document were necessary to allow civilians to circulate (even at this late stage the GIS still seems to have been struggling with this relatively simple question) and to reconnoitre a suitable place in the mountains where explosives might be dropped in by parachute, presumably to supply existing or future groups.

Two agents among those despatched by the SD were of particular interest. One was an agent who had already completed two political espionage missions before being arrested at the start of his third. The other was a priest named Biondi, who was ostensibly carrying letters to the Vatican and funds to his religious order in Rome. Having persuaded his interrogators that this was his only reason for travelling, he was sent under escort to his order in Rome, where his letters were examined and arrangements made to prevent him from leaving Rome until N. Italy had been liberated. Biondi did not, however, remain long in Rome, and made off to Siena, where he was re-arrested. In the meantime his erstwhile companion, who had been captured in the company of another agent who had quickly confessed, made certain statements throwing suspicion on the priest, and under re-interrogation Biondi admitted that, while his main purpose in travelling had been as he had claimed, he had also, in return for the travel arrangements made by the SD, agreed to give them, on his return to EOT, information on the extent and development of Communism in AOT.

Intensive interrogation was then begun, with the result that he was found to be engaged in fact on a full-blown SD political espionage mission, his controller being none other than the redoubtable Dr Begus. He was to obtain the answers to a long political questionnaire which would provide the SD with material for their main propaganda campaign of splitting the Allies (i.e. Russia from Great Britain and the USA – a theme being much discussed in leading Nazi and Fascist circles at that time, as being the only way in which total defeat might be averted), and to exploit discontent in Allied-occupied Italy. He was also told to try to obtain from the Pope himself the latter's reactions to a certain aspect of the international situation. There was some suggestion at the time that Biondi might have been carrying a peace proposal from Himmler to the Vatican: Begus himself, interrogated after the war, claimed that Biondi had merely been briefed to 'sound out Vatican sentiments concerning a peace treaty' – a requirement hardly convincing in its vagueness.

As related in Chapter X, two sea-borne sabotage raids had been made in October in the Rimini area, directed against army vehicles. A third and fourth such missions were now launched by the GIS, with two groups of X Flotilla MAS personnel being despatched by sea on the nights 18/19 and 19/20 December against targets in the Eighth Army zone. Both parties were brought by motorboat from Porto Garibaldi, just north of Lake Comacchio, completing the last kilometre of the journey in rubber dinghies.

The first party of eight men, divided into two groups of four under command of 2/Lieut Kummer, had as their specific target a bridge carrying the main coastal road from Rimini to Ravenna, where it crossed the River Rubicone (of classical fame, as the scene of Julius Caesar's decisive step). Faulty navigation took the party too far to the south and the original target had to be abandoned. Instead, it was decided to lay charges in some RAF vehicles belonging to 244 Wing RAF – a Spitbomber unit engaged in close support bombing for the 8th Army along the Forli-Bologna road, whose landing-ground was an ad hoc airstrip along the sandhills just inland from the beach at Bellaria.

This task was successfully completed and four trucks were blown up; a signal line serving the airfield was cut at the same time. Both squads immediately re-embarked in their rubber dinghies, but after searching fruitlessly for the motorboat they finally returned to land, with the intention of escaping on foot back through the lines. They were not, however, successful; one group was captured three days later at Cesenatico, a few miles further up the coast, and the other on 26 December at Santerno, close to the front line.

The second party, five in number under 2/Lieutenant Zanelli, landed near Viserba, just north of Rimini, with the task of sabotaging any transport and armoured vehicles parked in the area. This party decided to abandon its mission even before it set foot on shore; they dumped their explosives in the sea, made a landing and set off on foot for EOT. Three were arrested in Ravenna on Christmas Day, having been brought in for questioning by the Partisans. The remaining two are thought to have managed to get back through the lines.

Both parties were dressed in Italian Republican uniforms and were treated as military POWs; it was believed that their operations had been controlled by Trupp 257 of FAK 212, located not far away at Padua.

One humorous and encouraging incident rounded off the end of 1944. By now, all fifteen student trainees who had attended an Abwehr sabotage course held near Como in October had been arrested, in twos and threes over a period of several weeks. To celebrate the capture of the fifteenth and last, a 'school photo' was taken of them all together in the yard of Florence goal. It was tempting to have this dropped over German lines in a message container, addressed to the Commandant of the school: but in the end it was felt more advantageous to leave him in ignorance of their fate . . .

12

GIS Operational Methods

Before describing the operations which took place in the final months before the German surrender in Italy, i.e. the period from January to May 1945, this may be a convenient point at which to study in more detail the operational methods used by the GIS in recruiting, training and despatching their agents to AOT. The first of these covers the various aspects of this latter subject: these can be summed up as stay-behind agents, line-crossing, air-drops and sea landings.

As far as 'stay-behinds' were concerned, the basic requirement was to provide the agent with some form of accommodation, money and, if possible, some form of cover employment. The latter was not absolutely essential, since unemployment in Southern Italy (as indeed in the North) was wide-spread, especially among refugees, and many lived from hand to mouth by black marketing and other fringe occupations. The agent also needed either to have a W/T set himself, or to be linked up with a radio-operator agent, so that the intelligence he was able to collect could be sent back to his control without delay (tactical intelligence quickly lost its value as it got overtaken by events). In the case of stay-behind sabotage agents, there was less urgency and a radio link was not in the short term essential, but might become so in the course of time, when the agent ran out of sabotage materials and/or funds.

One agent, who had been on a GIS training course for 'stay-behinds', described the following system favoured by the Abwehr in order to provide effective 'cover' for their agents:

A month or so before the Allied occupation of a city looked likely, several shops or business establishments would be selected by the GIS for their suitability as points of contact and centres for the collection of intelligence. In each case the shop owner received, through normal municipal channels, an order to evacuate his premises. The prospective stay-behind agent then approached him and offered to buy the shop, lock, stock and barrel. This was carried out in a proper legal fashion and the GIS then set up the store with all the merchandise necessary, provided a starting capital of between 800,000 and a million lire, and installed the agent (and if necessary his family as well) in adequate living accommodation. In some cases, rather than leave a large sum of money in the hands of the agent, with the risk of arousing suspicion, an equivalent quantity of gold and jewellery was supplied, which could be sold off later bit by bit. Wherever possible agents were installed in towns where they had lived in the past and could claim to be local residents.

Another agent, a medical student in the sixth year of his studies, had his knowledge turned to good account in the cover arrangements made for him. He was to set himself up as a doctor, and act as a collecting point for information gathered by other agents. After the arrival of the Allies GIS agents, who would be unknown to him, were to call on him 'professionally', saying that they had been sent by a certain Doctor X. When asked the nature of their complaint they would name a disease which would act as a code or password and which would vary according to the day of the month. Thus on 12 August agent-patients would be suffering from gastric ulcers, while on Christmas day they might be suffering from jaundice. The idea was certainly a good one, since nobody would normally suspect the many and varied callers who ring a doctor's doorbell.

PARACHUTISTS

Agent-dropping in Italy was carried out exclusively through 'Dienststelle Carmen', located at Bergamo. This was a part of the Luftwaffe unit KG 200, a special formation formed early in 1944, initially as a stand-by special transport unit at the disposal of the German intelligence services, but which rapidly expanded its rôle to include the operational testing of new weapons such as stand-off glide bombs, air-launched torpedoes and 'piggy-back' aircraft. Its main activities remained, however, the dropping (and sometimes the picking-up) of agents behind the enemy lines. The various sections were given girls' names as cover titles (Carmen, Olga, Tosca, Clara etc).

Detachment Carmen, which operated in Italy, had offices at Via Milazzo 11, Bergamo, and was in the charge of a Luftwaffe officer, Oberleutnant Kaiser, assisted by Leutnant Klinger. The main airfield used was at Bergamo/Seriate, but in March 1945 a new field was established at Ponte San Pietro, 4 km west of Bergamo. The original strength of the detachment was 9-10 Junkers 188s, but two were shot down on operations. Only two of the unit strength are believed to have been used for agent-dropping in Italy, the remainder being diverted to long-range reconnaissance, secret landings in North Africa etc.*

---

* In his book 'KG 200', P.W. Stahl, OC of Detachment Olga, states that it was planned that Dienststelle Carmen would be withdrawn from Italy in November 1944 and its duties be taken over by 'Olga', based in Germany. It is not clear if this did in fact occur; in any event, the Bergamo base seems to have remained open, at least as a staging or pick-up point.

Apart from the dropping of individual agents by parachute (for which no prior training seems to have been given), KG 200 also at times used parachute containers, slung under the aircraft and designed to hold three men. The advantages of this method were three: it lessened the danger of injuries during drops at night into an unkown area, the party (and their equipment) were not scattered widely on arrival, and it disposed of any need for any training beforehand. On the other hand, it was almost impossible to dispose of the container, which remained as visible evidence that agents had arrived. It must also have imposed a considerable nervous strain on the agents so carried.

The official German title of the container was the PAG (Personen-Abwurf-Gerät, or Personnel Dropping Equipment). It consisted of a double-walled plywood container, 1 metre in diameter and 4 metres long; it was designed to hold three or four persons lengthwise, slung in hammocks of strong webbing. In the upper part of the PAG were three parachutes packed inside a streamlined aluminium cover, which on release from the aircraft's bomb racks was pulled off by a strong ripcord and allowed the parachutes to deploy. In the lower part of the container was a compartment carrying the group's equipment (W/T set, explosives or whatever) while the bottom tip was covered by a semi-spherical aluminium cap filled with foam rubber, to minimise the landing impact (see Diagram A).

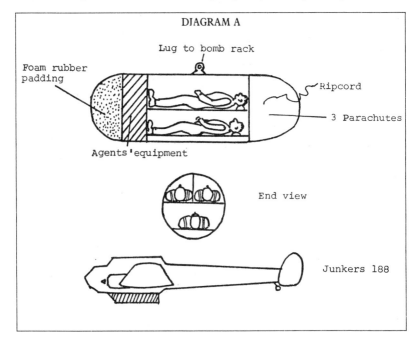

DIAGRAM A

154

Boat used by SD saboteurs of 'Sonderunternehmen Anzio'
COURTESY OF RALEIGH TREVELYAN

The saboteurs being taken away. It is clear from this photo that they were caught the moment they came ashore. PHOTOGRAPH COURTESY OF PETER TOMPKINS

Two of the saboteurs, Ernesto Catani and Mario Trifio, at the time of their capture.
PHOTOGRAPH COURTESY OF PETER TOMPKINS

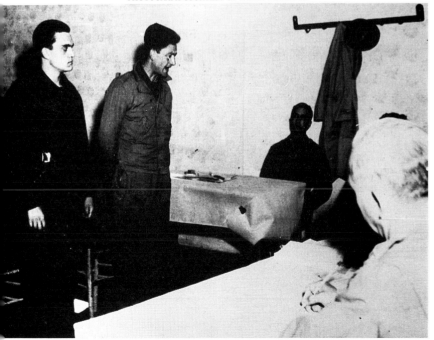

Catanio and Trifio at their court-martial. Arrested in British uniforms,
they had little chance of escaping the death penalty
PHOTOGRAPH COURTESY OF PETER TOMPKINS

The Sicherheitsdienst building at 155 Via Tasso, Rome. The lower row of open windows are those of the SD offices; the bricked-in windows above are those of the cells where prisoners were held. PHOTOGRAPH COURTESY OF PETER TOMPKINS

Inside the Via Tasso premises, showing the wooden doors to the prison cells.
PHOTOGRAPH COURTESY OF PETER TOMPKINS

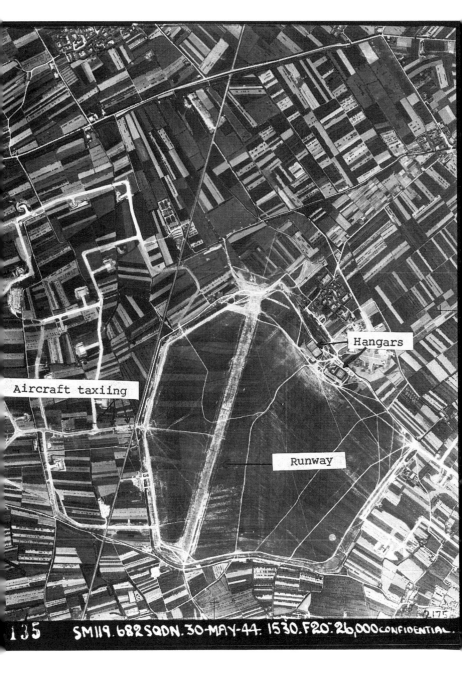

Aircraft taxiing

Hangars

Runway

135 SM119.682 SQDN. 30-MAY-44. 1530. F20". 26,000 CONFIDENTIAL.

Bergamo Airfield: 30 May 1944. Photo by 682 Squadron
(Photo-Reconnaissance Spitfires) from 26,000 feet
COURTESY OF KEELE UNIVERSITY

Photo-reconnaissance Spitfire flying over Mount Belvedere, south of Bologna.
It shows clearly the type of winter terrain over which line-crossers would
have to find their way in winter 1944.

*Standartenführer Eugen Dollmann: Himmler's personal representative with the
Italian Government. Photo taken at the time of the surrender negotiations
in April/May 1945.* COURTESY OF THE IMPERIAL WAR MUSEUM

Pensione Flavia (as it is today):
Rome headquarters of FAK 150

Another somewhat similar type of container was referred to by agents captured in Italy, although they had never actually seen it. It was described as a rectangular plywood box 2.2 metres by 2.5 metres by 1.4 metres, suspended by parachutes at each corner. While quite possible, there seems to be no proof that such containers actually existed, although they might have been made as a local 'lash-up' in Bergamo if the PAG was in short supply (see Diagram B).

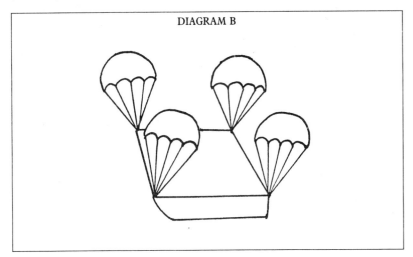

DIAGRAM B

LINE-CROSSING

Generally speaking, few GIS agents seem to have been warned of road blocks, travel regulations and security checks, although some were told that, when first entering AOT, they should avoid main arteries, stay away from all towns and move on country by-roads; once well behind the front line areas, however, they would be able to travel freely. During the winter months some were told to move along river beds, as snow made cross-country travel almost impossible and left main roads as the only other alternative. Little consideration seems to have been given to the question of the means by which they should travel once they were inside Allied-held territory. In a few cases agents were warned that hotel registers were subject to control checks.

Every GIS agent was given false identity papers. Either at the time of his recruitment, or shortly before despatch, he was instructed to obtain passport photos of himself and was later issued with an Italian identity card which bore this photo; if his home town was in EOT the GIS usually tried to give him a card issued by the civilian authorities of that town or of a nearby one, since under interrogation he would be expected to be familiar with his place of residence. If the agent was originally from a town in AOT, this condition was normally overridden – possibly because of the time and trouble necessary to forge AOT identity cards which would be good enough to pass expert scrutiny.

One delightful piece of forgery by the GIS came in the shape of a 'pass', carried by an SD agent. It was in the form of a card, printed at the top in bold capitals: 'Allied Military Government, Caserta Headquarters' ('Caserta' had been entered in manuscript over 'Eboli', which had been crossed out). The pass bore the official AMG stamp and was signed 'Major R.L. Lallar'. The following was then written in English: '. . . has been questioned by CIC and AMG. They can see no reason why he cannot be OK. He comes from Sicily and is trying to find his father in Rome. From a Security Angle.'

That the originator of this document did not feel too sure of his ground can be deduced from the fact that the agent was briefed to do his best to obtain a specimen of an authentic AMG pass while he was in AOT.

Over the months the GIS had clearly become aware of the suspicion that rested on 'refugees' who were carrying large sums of money on them. Various methods of concealing money were taught at one time or another, including the carrying of valuable postage stamps inside the back of a watch, but these were evidently judged insufficient. A system was then introduced whereby agents were paid only working expenses when despatched, the going rate being 3000 or 4000 lire every ten days. This practice had the additional advantage of encouraging the agent to return across the lines to claim the tempting lump sum which he would have earned. The GIS do not seem to have adopted the relatively secure system of putting down hidden caches of money before a withdrawal (as they regularly did with sabotage materials), of which agents could be given details before departure. This would have allowed them to cross the lines without arousing suspicion by the sums they were carrying. Such caches could also have been used as 'banks' in case, for example, a stay-behind network had run out of money: they could have been sent instructions by radio on how to locate these reserve funds. Possibly GIS pay officers were unwilling to fork out the large amounts necessary without some assurance as to precisely who would be getting the money, and for what.

Normally, agents expecting a return across the lines would be given either a password or a means of identifying their role. Several were given handkerchiefs imprinted with invisible ink; the agent was instructed that on returning through the German lines he should get himself taken to the nearest officer and have the handkerchief ironed with a hot iron or heated in front of a fire. The secret writing would then appear and would allow the agent to be taken back to his starting base a quickly as possible. A word of warning was added that if the handkerchief got wet, the writing would be eliminated for good. One agent captured during October 1944 clearly took the latter instruction to heart, as he effectively removed the incriminating evidence by continually mopping his brow with the handkerchief during interrogation. Some women agents carried as a means of identification a small piece of cloth about three inches by one inch, which had identifying particulars written on it and which was sewn into the hem of the women's panties.

In the latter context one must add that, apart from the actual physical difficulties of crossing the lines over rough country, especially in winter, female agents faced the additional hazards from the attentions of the sex-starved front-line soldiery. At least one reported under subsequent interrogation that she had found herself having to spend the night with a section sergeant in his pup tent. Since many of these girls were amateur prostitutes, it may be that no great protest was raised when such a situation developed.

Alive to the dangers of Allied searches, one group of agents in the early Spring of 1945 was advised to carry nothing in their pockets except one handkerchief and a pair of gloves – a circumstance which would, in fact, at once have aroused suspicion among Allied security personnel, since most people, if left to themselves, invariably carry a number of odds and ends of personal property in their pockets, especially if shifting their location from one part of the country to another.

A GIS document captured in September 1944 (although it carried an instruction that it was to be destroyed immediately after reading) was in the form of a warning to a forward German unit of the anticipated return of six agents across the lines in that sector. The documents listed the agents' cover names together with their pass-words or identification numbers. These took the form, in every case, of the word GHERO followed by a number. This word 'Ghero' had in fact been cropping up in agent interrogation reports for some months previously, although its significance had at first been obscure. The readers of the captured document were gratified to find that the possessor of every Ghero number listed was already safely under arrest, so that the front line units, and the GIS, would await their return in vain.

The methods by which agents were instructed to obtain information varied considerably. One was told to contact maids in hotels and officers' messes, and prostitutes who were associating with Allied officers; another was to treat Allied soliders to meals and drinks, and to buy them small presents. If opportunity presented itself, employment in any Allied unit was to be accepted. One woman agent was encouragingly informed that it was easy to gossip with soldiers and 'sleep' her way round her given target area. While it was true that relatively few of the female agents captured by the Allies met the classic requirements of the glamorous female spies of literature, it is clear that Allied soldiers could often be susceptible to feminine wiles. Although it was forbidden for Army vehicles to give lifts to civilians, one female agent who was captured in August 1944 in Bari had had no difficulties in this respect; during the course of extended travels in AOT she had journeyed as far south as Taranto, thumbing her way in a wide variety of military and civilian vehicles, ranging from armoured cars and DUKWs to little Fiat 'Topolinos'. She had then charmed her way through several interrogations and was on the point of climbing into an Italian army truck to make her way back to EOT with a wealth of information when she was arrested.

One problem with which a 'travelling' agent would inevitably be faced was that of having to remember the information he had collected without carrying obviously incriminating notes in his pocket. One agent had a kind of 'Pelmanism' system suggested to him during his training course, which worked as follows:

At the beginning of his mission he was to buy some small article in a shop and obtain a bill for it: on the bill he was then to add other bogus purchases, the quantities of which would indicate numbers of troops, tanks, guns etc. seen in the course of his mission. The agent in question stated that one of the 'school' examples given him was '100 tooth brushes' to represent 100 aeroplanes. As the security report acidly commented, 'one could hardly hope to find in a suspect's pockets anything more calculated to stimulate suspicion than a bill for 100 toothbrushes'.

SEA LANDINGS

This was not a method very much used by the GIS, except in the early days (Autumn 1943) of the Italian campaign, and again in March 1945, when there was a sudden surge of 15 agents in three separate parties. The usual technique was to land the agents by inflatable rubber boats, launched from motorboats standing off the coast, although in at least two cases agents were infiltrated into parties of genuine refugees making their way south.

An exception to the above statement is of course the sea landings carried out X Flotilla MAS saboteurs; such were not, however, agent infiltrations but 'in and out' operational sorties, except in one or two cases when agents were landed under cover of the attack.

RECRUITING METHODS

Mention has already been made en passant of various GIS methods of recruiting agents for their service. A number of these agents were culled from Fascist organisations, such as that of Colonel David, from the X

Flotilla MAS, the Blackshirt Brigades and so on. Many others were however induced to accept recruitment for less political or patriotic motives. Some of the main reasons may be listed as:

(a) to escape from being press-ganged for factory work in Germany
(b) to avoid being called up into the Italian Army
(c) to alleviate straitened financial circumstances, or to escape some marital or sentimental imbroglio
(d) as a means of getting back to homes, or girl friends, in AOT.

Many of the later agents were of low intellectual standards, and were waiters, prostitutes and suchlike, often picked up more or less at random by recruiters hanging around the local bars on the lookout for anyone who might fit the required bill. Another factor which undoubtedly played some part in encouraging volunteers was the attraction, for the Italian character in general, of having what would appear to be a starring role. Italians can be shown to make excellent racing drivers, fighter pilots, frogmen and so on, roles where the individual is not lost in the mass but has the chance to cut a 'bella figura' (and arouse the interest of the opposite sex as a fringe benefit). Recruiters often played on this aspect, while at the same time avoiding mention of the risk of being shot as a spy if they were captured. Even at payment rates of around £2000 per agent, it was still cheaper to sacrifice four agents in the hope that the fifth would succeed, than to lose a £20,000 reconnaissance aircraft and trained pilot over the dangerous skies of AOT. Moreover, life in North Italy was becoming increasingly difficult, with tight rationing, Allied bombing, German razzias and a general running-down of utilities and facilities: an apparent chance to break out of a humdrum, boring and often tawdry and hungry existence had a considerable appeal for many young people (most agents were aged between 18-30).

Two examples will serve merely to illustrate the wide variety of ways by which recruits might arrive in the GIS ranks. A certain Lancelotti had been making a fairly profitable living by Black Market activities. He met a pretty woman, struck up a rapid and intimate acquaintance with her, and in one of his less discreet moments betrayed to her the source of his money. Next day he was arrested by the local police. At the police station the woman's husband appeared, but instead of getting angry with the seducer, he offered him service in the GIS as an alternative to trial and imprisonment. Lancelotti, finding himself cornered, accepted the offer. He was later to regret the decision; early in 1945 be was tried for espionage in AOT and sentenced to death.

Another case was that of a girl who was working as an assistant in an antiques shop in N. Italy. The aging proprietor had contrived (so she believed) for her to knock over and smash a Chinese vase, which he claimed was of great value. Since she was too poor to pay for the damage, he insisted that she give up her lodgings and move in to share his bed, at the same time using the money, which she had previously paid out in rent, to repay him, in instalments, for the broken vase. Quickly fed up with this enforced prostitution, she readily agreed to work for the GIS as a way of escape.

It can be imagined that, apart from those who were working for political or patriotic motives, few of the GIS agents were of a type to provide faithful service. Certainly by the early spring of 1945 the Abwehr were in some despair at the small number of their line-crosser agents who made it back across the lines, particularly since they were in no position to know whether this was because they had been arrested, or had simply defected from their missions. One of the FAK 150 Trupps* was reduced to using schemes of high melodrama to try to prevent such defections. The newly-recruited agent would be blindfolded, told that he was being taken to meet 'The Chief' and driven round town for an hour (to give the impression of a long journey elsewhere). He was then led into a room and his blindfold removed. He found himself in a high room, draped with crimson curtains from floor to ceiling; facing him was a long table, covered with a crimson cloth, on which rested a skull, a Bible and two burning candles. Behind, seated in a heavy and imposing chair, was a masked man, who called on him to take a solemn oath on the Bible that he would return in two weeks, on completion of his mission. Thereafter he was again blindfolded and driven back to his starting-point.

When, over the weeks, this technique, too, failed to produce the necessary results, the melodrama was increased; the same initial rigmarole was gone through, but the agent was given an injection of water and was told: 'This is a deadly poison: if you are not back here in fourteen days for the antidote, you will drop dead'. The record does not, alas, show whether this method was any more effective; one takes leave to doubt it.

The end of the agents' training course was followed in many cases by a final 'end of term' alcoholic party, where in at least one case, when the celebrations were far advanced, the more attractive female agents were called upon to strip and take a 'Bath of Purity' to cleanse them symbolically for their mission. The sequel can safely be left to the imagination. Small wonder that by the time the course members were split up to leave on their missions, most of them knew not only each other's names, but a great deal about their backgrounds also; sometimes they had on them, when arrested, photographs of all their fellow-students on the course – a bonus for Allied Counter-Intelligence staff which made their task that much easier.

Under all these circumstances, Allied Counter-Intelligence was not

* Probably FAT 150, but memory fails.

160

always faced with a very difficult task in rounding up line-crossing agents; indeed, at one point the suspicion was voiced that surely these could only be 'cannon-fodder', sent deliberately to flood the security defences while higher-grade agents were somehow, somewhere, being brought into action. This does not, however, seem to have been the case.

In the later stages, when the RSHA began to exercise more professional control of such matters, the Germans became aware of the poor security reigning on such courses and began to issue false identities only after students had finished their training course and had been separated from their fellow-trainees.

INTERROGATION OF AGENTS: THE GIVE-AWAY INDICATORS

At its best, interrogation is an art, not a science: it involves psychological skills which cannot be taught, only acquired. In its simplest form it involves catching the prisoner out in a lie, and discovering precisely why he is lying. At Appendix E is a 15th Army Group guidance paper on the interrogation of suspects, which sets out to provide a framework for the successful identification of enemy agents. Paragraph 4 of the paper underlines one critical sector which led to the unmasking of many such persons: 'It is only the enemy agent who needs to lie about the manner in which he reached the front lines. It is only the enemy agent who is usually brought to the Front in a German vehicle or under German escort, and it is, therefore, only the enemy agent who must manufacture a cover story for this part of his narrative.'

As an example, if two line-crossers arrived together in AOT (very often the Abwehr would send a pair of agents over together, to give each other support during the tricky line-crossing period) they might claim that they had passed the previous night, before crossing the lines, in a certain house (whereas they had in fact spent it at a GIS despatch point or with a German front-line unit). The officer in charge of the RIP (Refugee Interrogation Point, one of a number spread along the Front, not far behind the fighting troops) would interview each of them separately and ask each to describe the room in which they had slept – a double bed? Two single beds? Carpet on the floor? Electric light, oil light or candles? The GIS did not, until very late in the campaign, take much trouble over such detailed cover stories, and when the two accounts varied, it did not take much pressure to obtain an admission from one or other of them that the story was false.

More than this, however, it was bits of actual equipment which could give them away, and the circulation to RIPs, FSS and CIC of details of what each individual (identified) agent had been carrying provided a highly effective 'pointer' to likely candidates among a crowd of genuine refugees. Mention has already been made of the GIS instruction that agents should only carry one handkerchief and a pair of gloves in their pockets – an indicator which it was easy to recognise.

In December 1944 15th Army Group circulated photographs of several typical items of clothing which were being issued to agents by the GIS before they left on their missions. Several agents, questioned in this context, reported that the clothing appeared to have been made in Germany and there were a number of differences between German and Italian styles of clothing. A German jacket was usually of the 3-button style, while the Italian model was generally 2-button and had longer lapels. German jackets had two upper outside pockets, whereas Italian jackets had only one, over the left breast. German trousers designed to be worn with braces (US: suspenders) were provided with six small strips of cloth, 4 in front and 2 behind, onto which the buttons were sewn, whereas Italian trousers had the buttons sewn directly onto the inside of the waistband. German trousers had two back pockets, Italian trousers only one, on the right. And so on.

It was noted that some GIS saboteurs had been issued with a large, handsome jack-knife made by J.A. Schmidt & Sons, Solingen. This had a single stainless-steel blade about 4 inches long, closing into a dark brown wooden handle. If such a knife was found on any subsequent suspect it could be taken as a fairly likely indicator of his subversive status.

Each of the same group of saboteurs had also been issued with twenty small paper envelopes, each containing 20 tablets of saccharine and bearing on the outside, printed in blue, details of the contents in English, French, Russian and German. This was in no sense an emergency ration, but was to be used to trade with civilians for food or lodging. Italian torches of the small 'dynamo' type were by early 1945 being issued as standard equipment to agents, as were leather briefcases (of German pattern!) for the carrying of documents and belongings. Another warning circulated to forward CI posts in December 1944 concerned a particular type of Italian-made brown boot which was being issued to agents of Abwehrtrupp 150 as they passed through the forward despatching point at Quaccio, near Ferrara, to equip them for the rough terrain they would have to cross; a sketch of the distinctive boot was sent round to the CI agencies concerned.

Frequently agents, issued with false identity cards, found themselves unable to recite the details which these carried – a lapse in which the psychological strain of arrest and interrogation doubtless played a major role. In the final months of the war the GIS was, however, paying greater attention to this aspect: some GIS training schools were now sending their students on a trip to the town to be shown on their forged identity cards, so that they could familiarise themselves with the location of their pretended home address, and with the names of other people living there. One agent was even given 1000 lire with which to buy himself an item of clothing bearing a label from a shop in the town in question.

A good example of the type of combination of small suspicions, leading to eventual arrest, was in the case of two agents who first aroused interest because they denied all knowledge of both German and Allied troop locations seen during a journey through the forward areas. Their identity cards were unusually clean, they had no luggage and they were clean-shaven in spite of what they claimed had been a three-day journey. Several times they slipped into German when trying to speak English, and were smoking Italian cigarettes which they even offered to British soldiers to try to disarm suspicion (something which no genuine refugee would ever do). All these facts taken together, left no doubt as to the nature of their trip.

Another small point which was regarded with suspicion by interrogators was the possession, when in AOT and especially if the person arrested was on his way to EOT, of quantities of newspapers and pamphlets; a number of agents had been briefed by the GIS to bring such items back with them, and at least one agent was arrested in possession of a considerable quantity of these, mainly consisting of left-wing publications.

COVER STORIES

The prevalent use by GIS agents of a rather standardised form of cover story gave further scope for 'breaking down' the agent and obtaining a confession. Such stories were often to the effect that the individual had been taken by the Germans for forced labour (the TODT construction organisation was frequently mentioned in this context) and that he had escaped – either to avoid deportation to Germany, or in order to join his family in AOT. It required, however, great care on the part of the agent to prevent inconsistencies coming to the notice of an alert interrogator or interviewer. The following are three examples of failures which led to the arrest of the person concerned:

> In November 1944 a man was apprehended by IV Corps CIC as he was making his way south. He told a fairly plausible story. He was, however, placed under immediate arrest by the alert CIC because of the following observations:
>
> His identity card was dated 8 April 1944. When the passport photo on it was removed it was found to have 31 October stamped on the reverse side.
>
> All the entries on the identity card appeared to have been made with the same pen and ink.

The identity card showed no signs of 'wear and tear', although it purported to be seven months old.

He was carrying a full packet of Italian cigarettes, which he said he had bought in Parma 15 days previously. They showed no signs of having been carried around for all that length of time, which was doubly suspicious because cigarettes were in extremely short supply at that time.

He was also in possession of a considerable amount of money.

No single one of these points would have been damning in itself, and a reasonable explanation could have been produced for each of them; all together, however, they provided ground for considerable suspicion. In fact, when he was confronted with the discrepancy between the date of issue in his identity card and the date on the back of the photograph, the agent confessed. His arrest was thus directly due to sloppy work by the GIS.

In another case an enemy agent was 'broken down' at an RIP in a somewhat similar manner. He stated that he had been taken prisoner by the Germans in September 1944 and had remained a prisoner for two months, when he had escaped and made his way across the lines. He mentioned the point at which he had crossed, and the last town in EOT in which he had stayed before making the crossing. The fact that several GIS agents caught earlier had followed precisely the same route already aroused a certain suspicion, which was strengthened when it was learned that he had previously been a student pilot-officer at Tradate Air Force base – a source of more than one earlier agent. Examination of the money found on him produced a 1000-lire note, of which the number was in the same series as a note found on another agent captured earlier in the month. Challenged with these facts, the suspect confessed.

Early in September 1944 an alert FSS NCO was responsible for capturing a German line-crossing agent in the forward area. He had been present when a civilian line-crosser was being interrogated by a GSI(a) officer (for straightforward military information, as opposed to counter-intelligence, which was the responsibility of GSI(b)). The man had volunteered certain military information abut the German forces which he had observed en route.

When the GSI(a) interrogator asked him about the calibre of a gun he had described, he replied that he did not know much about artillery, because he had served in the Italian navy, not the army.

When his interrogation for operational intelligence was over, the FSS NCO took over, in order to give him a CI interrogation. He noted the following inconsistencies:

(a) The man stated that he had served at Stalingrad – unusual for a sailor!
(b) He had on him an identity card issued in Italy in 18 December 1943,

whereas he had previously claimed that he had been in Germany in December 1943.

(c) The same card was clean and new, in spite of the fact that it was supposed to have been in use for nine months.

When these facts were pointed out to him, he broke down and confessed that he had been despatched on a short-range military espionage mission. He had attempted to establish cover for himself by offering certain limited tactical information, in the hope of being able thereby to win the confidence of the Allied authorities.

A more unorthodox technique for an agent to be brought to confess occurred as a result of the following incident. A pilot from one of the RAF photo-reconnaissance squadrons, who had been making a visit to GSI(a) 15th Army Group in Florence, in order to discuss what military targets the commanders might wish to have photographed, then called in to GSI(b), asking if there was anything for him to do, as he was rather short of jobs and didn't like sitting around doing nothing. The GSI(b) officers, more with a view to making him feel wanted than in the hope of any great contribution to CI work, suggested that he might like to take some low-level oblique shots of an Abwehr agent training school near Modena. Two days later the pilot returned, looking a little crestfallen because he didn't think his photographs were good enough. In fact, he produced an enormous enlargement of the school, with men running about in the garden and looking out of the windows at the sudden passage of his Spitfire over the rooftops.

GSI(b) already knew the identities of most of the agents who were training at this school at the time, so copies of the photo were sent out to RIPs and front-line security units. Some time later, one of the suspect agents was identified in a party of genuine refugees. Under interrogation he flatly denied ever having been at the GIS training school. The interrogator produced the air photo and challenged him saying: 'It's no good you denying it, we have this photo of you leaning out of that window there . . .'

13

GIS Operations: January-May 1945

The first month of the New Year was an eventful one for the CI field. A total of 58 enemy agents were captured. Nearly one third of these had arrived by parachute, of which 18 came in on the full moon period at the end of December/beginning of January. Of the remainder, one third were line-crossers and the rest 'stay-behinds' who had eluded arrest hitherto. Out of the total arrests, eight were once again women, and there were indications that a number more women were in training for use in the near future. Seven of the agents captured had been given W/T sets, confirming an earlier report that the GIS now intended to send in teams of three agents at a time, one of whom would be a radio operator and the other two responsible for the collection of information. The majority were, however, to make their way back across the lines with their reports.

Thirteen of the agents captured had been given sabotage missions. Two of them, working for the Abwehr, were aimed once again at the petrol pipeline near Cassino, while another pair, also Abwehr, who were members of the MGIR (a Young Fascist organisation) were to make contact with members of the movement in Florence and Siena, and to sabotage such military targets as opportunity offered. Virtually no damage attributable to saboteurs was reported in AOT during the month.

The tendency to increased persistence and boldness, noted already in the previous month, was maintained. Of the 58 agents arrested only four surrendered voluntarily; the remainder required searching out and, in some cases, careful enquiries and diligent interrogation before the real purpose of their presence in AOT was revealed. Until the later months of 1944 the normal conception of counter-espionage, as something usually involving long and elaborate investigation, had not generally applied in the Italian campaign (although there were a few exceptions). A large number of agents had surrendered, while in other cases the mere confrontation with a CI representative had in itself been almost enough to induce a rapid confession. The new hardening in the type of agent encountered had, however, come at a moment when counter-measures had had time to develop, so that although the task had become more difficult, the means with which to execute the task were now capable of meeting the challenge.

As can be seen, the number infiltrated by parachute was unusually high, bearing out an earlier theory that the GIS would probably be forced to adopt this method as a means of avoiding the ground controls in the forward areas. Although, of the 18 parachutists, only fourteen were captured (a fifteenth had in fact been dropped in August and had only now been arrested) interrogation revealed that there were four more somewhere on the loose. Of the 18, 13 had been sent in by FAK 212, two by the SD, while three were operating for KdM Munich, the Abwehr station in the homeland with constitutional responsibilities for Italy.

Arrangements for signalling the presence of intruding enemy aircraft over AOT were still imperfect, but it was found difficult to improve matters in respect of the detection of low-flying aircraft by radar and the impossibility of any extensive observer network operating by night.

The proportion of agents who arrived undetected is hard to estimate. Only three of those now captured had already been on earlier successful missions, but even allowing for treble this figure of enemy successes during the month, it was considered likely at the time that some 80% of agents despatched had been captured.

The line-crosser missions concentrated, as usual, on short-term tactical intelligence on the forward areas, with the major interest concentrating on the 2 Corps and 13 Corps sectors north of Florence where, as Kesselring's memoirs make clear, the Monte Belvedere position (see plate section) was seen as the most critical point on the whole front. It was clear to commanders on both sides that once a break-through was made here into the Po Valley, the German defence line would not be able to hold and would be forced to retreat at least to the north bank of the Po. Other agent missions were however aimed at Rome and as far south as Sicily, and there was renewed interest in the acquisition of Allied and South Italian identity documents and passes. One agent was even instructed that he was to obtain a copy of 'the secret Allied CI List of Suspected Agents' – a mission which smacks more of a spy novel by E. Phillips Oppenheim or Len Deighton than anything attainable in real life.

To give an indication of the scale of activity of the various GIS and Fascist Italian intelligence agencies, the following is a breakdown of the number of agents which each had launched during the month:

FAK 150:	14
FAK 190:	4
FAK 212:	11
SD:	13
MGIR:	2
Fascist Republicans:	1
Ic (76 Corps):	1
Fascist Group, Rome:	3
Not positively identified:	4

As indicated above, only four of the 53 agents surrendered voluntarily during the month; of the remainder, 17 were arrested as a result of routine checking at RIPs annd other controls, 21 were identified on the basis of information received from other arrested agents, while six were captured as a result of enquiries arising out of information circulated in the Monthly CI Bulletins.

The main targets given to FAK 212 saboteurs during the period were petrol pipelines and Army supply dumps.*

Four agents who were parachuted in near Ancona had been instructed to organise guerrilla bands in the Eighth Army area and to select a suitable dropping zone for further relays of parachuted agents who would augment such bands. The movement was to be based on San Marino, the GIS doubtless believing that, as a nominally independent Republic, San Marino would be less subjected to Allied security controls.

One female agent, who was arrested in Florence, had been equipped with a W/T set, which she had been trained to operate; she had already succeeded in obtaining a job with an Allied unit.

A small commando raid by MEK 71 took place on the night of 9/10 January at Porto San Giorgio, 30 miles south of Ancona. The railway bridge there was demolished, but the line was in fact relatively little used, so that no great problem was caused to Allied supply lines. The attackers were able to get safely back to base without loss.

GIS LOCATIONS

This may be an opportune moment to put on record the new Abwehr locations in N Italy, forced on them by the gradual edging northwards of the front line. FAK 150, which had its HQ in Verona until the end of 1944, moved up to Rovereto, near the north end of Lake Garda and received the title of Leitkommando (Control Commando), still under command of Major Berger. This title was given, according to Helfferich, in order to strengthen the hand of the IBSW against attempts by the SD in Berlin to gain control of the organisation through Engelmann. Of the FAK 150 Trupps, FAT 150 was in Verona, with a training school in Padua; FATs 151 and 152 were in Milan, 153 in Padua. FAT 151 also had a training school

---

* Although it was recognised that these surface pipelines could not be effectively guarded, damage to any section of the pipe would not have had serious consequences. Much more vital were the pumping stations, but these were few enough to allow for reasonable security measures to protect them. None of them was ever attacked.

in Alassio, under Leutnant Hoehle (alias Bergmann) for the training of line-crossers to be sent in to southern France, as well as for the training of P/O agents.

FAK 190, under Buchholz (alias Dr Bauer) was in Milan; in January its training school moved from Milan to near Bolzano, while a second school was opened at Bassano del Grappa, north-east of Vicenza.

INTERVENTION BY THE BDS

General Harster was by now not at all happy with the results achieved by Einheit IDA. The intelligence provided by the unit was published in report form – one for each agent. After the eighth or ninth report issued in January, Harster realised that the information, from whichever sector of the front it came, was in effect always the same: i.e. civilian controls, morale, prices, political situation, prostitution, relationship between troops and civilians etc, of very little use in prosecuting the war effort. He therefore called together all his sections for a conference in Verona, where he instructed them that they must be more active in looking around to find more suitable agents to send across to AOT. As he realised that internal jealousies were preventing one section from releasing personnel for use by another section, he arranged for two of his officers, Turowski and Heugel (Abt III and VI), to tour the various SD stations in Italy in a search for suitable agent material. What was needed, in his view, were agents from a variety of professions and industries, so as to enlarge the scope of the intelligence coverage. However, Turowski was transferred elsewhere, Huegel fell ill, and the plan never came to fruition.

COLONEL HELFFERICH

Helfferich, too, had his problems in January, although these were of a rather different kind. He had greatly resented the gradual ascendancy of the SD and the final decline of his own service; being a military man, he had begun to feel he was persona non grata in Berlin. He was not mistaken: on 9 January he received a radio message through Harster, summoning him to Berlin for an interview at the RSHA headquarters, and intimating that his further presence in Italy would not be required.

He arrived in Berlin two days later, for his first ever visit to the RSHA. He was closely questioned for the next ten days about his association with Canaris and a contact of Canaris called Countess Theotoki but was not accused of any direct part in the 20 July plot against Hitler's life. He was also charged with being Italophile, pro-Jewish and with being under the influence of the Catholic church, in particular because of his Vatican con-

169

nections. The proceedings were broken off after ten days because of pre-occupation with the latest Russian Army advances, and Helfferich, who had freedom of movement, simply left Berlin on 22 January for Italy, without notifying the RSHA. Once back in Verona, he calmly resumed his duties as Liaison Officer with SID, apparently with the blessing of Harster.

On the Allied side there was an increase in security measures on two specific fronts: particular attention was paid to the tightening up of coastal security, in view of the enemy's apparent increased interest in landing agents by small boat; and check points close to the front line were increased in number. In the 5th Army area there were now between 150-200 such posts, manned by Carabinieri and Allied Military Police, plus roving patrols. On the 8th Army front, 200 check points were manned by 350 Carabinieri and 200 men from the Italian Guard Battalion. On average, an enemy agent seeking to cross an Army area would probably have to negotiate four lines of control, as well as variable 'snap checks'. The size of the problem is shown by the figure of over 6,000 people, crossing from north to south, handled by the 5th Army Refugee Interrogation Points in the month of March 1945, of which 14 were unmasked as GIS agents.

FEBRUARY 1945

February proved to be a comparatively uneventful month in the field of counter-espionage, with a marked drop in the number of enemy agents captured. The full moon periods do not seem to have been exploited: only two parachute agents were known to have been dropped, and they were both captured. Little serious sabotage activity was reported and only in one case did this seem to have been German-inspired. It was considered that this drop in activity might to some extent be accounted for by the progressive reorganisation of the GIS under SD management, and the possibility of preparations being in hand for a wholesale evacuation north-wards to the 'Mountain Redoubt'. The number of agents known to be in training was obviously in excess of the Wehrmacht's needs for purely tactical intelligence, and it seemed probable that the major part of this sur-plus would be given post-occupational missions, with sabotage operations predominating.

Total arrests during the month numbered 42, of whom 27 were line-crossers. Of the seven parachutists known to be at large at the beginning of the month, five were rounded up, while two new ones were dropped; one of these was as far forward as Fano (just south of Pesaro, some 50 miles behind the front line), with instructions to return at once through the lines with tactical intelligence. This was the first instance recorded of airborne entry by a short-range tactical spy. With the exception of one free-lance Fascist, who was making for the enemy lines (where he intended to hand in such information as he had collected) the remainder were all stay-behinds; two of them were women. The most remarkable feature was that only 17 had actually been despatched from EOT during the month, the balance having come over previously and had only now been arrested. One of the parachutists had had a W/T operator dropped with him at the same time, the latter still being at large. Both infiltration routes across the lines, and places of capture, were evenly spaced across the whole front, with pride of place again in the 13 Corps sector north of Florence.

Five of the saboteurs (out of 10 despatched) had been ordered to penetrate, in two groups, as far as Capua and Rome, and to obtain their sabotage materials from dumps previously hidden there by the GIS. The target for one of the groups was an airfield, which had in fact never been used by the Allies (a fact which underlines the Luftwaffe's complete failure to achieve any photo reconnaissance over AOT). The other group was to attack 'anything in the general area of Rome' which seemed to offer a favourable opportunity.

On the military front the period was one of intense preparation for an Allied operation by Commandos and Royal Marines, using DUKWs (amphibious trucks) to cross the wide Comacchio lagoon and thus outflank the German left wing on the Adriatic coast. Secrecy in these preparations was of vital importance, and given the absence of any defensive counter-measures by the Germans it would seem that none of the many GIS tactical agents launched in the Adriatic sector was able to avoid capture and report intelligence of any value about this operation.

Four of the agents captured during the month had previously completed successful missions. The despatching agencies were in the main the Trupps of FAK 150 (15 agents), FAK 212 (13) and the SD (6). One interesting arrest in Rome was an agent from ALST Paris, who had been left in the Vatican as a 'stay-behind' when Rome was evacuated. Only three of those arrested surrendered voluntarily; 21 were caught by controls (RIPs, forward troops and Carabinieri posts), 8 from checks on names in the Wanted list and seven as a result of information from other arrested agents.

A counter-intelliegence operation of a less orthodox, but highly effective, kind was employed during the month when a GIS agent school, at which there were reliably reported to be a large number of agents in training, was bombed by the RAF at the instance of GSI(b) Eighth Army and 2 SCI Unit. Eleven direct hits were reported on the school buildings, which were completely demolished.

An interesting report from KdM Munich to the RSHA Militärisches Amt at this time listed the 'current state of W/T agents of Munich KdM sent into action in Italy'. These comprised eight agents, working to six W/T sets and located as follows:

Berri (agent's code name):	Florence area, sent in 20 August
Tonio:	Cagliari, Sardinia, sent in 26 August
Castor and Pollux*:	Rome, sent in 22 November
Achill:	Brindisi, sent in 4 December
Tanto and Foto:	Messina, sent in 30 December
Mares:	Palermo, sent in 31 December

All the above had been dropped in by parachute.

The report went on:

Berri and Tonio must be considered overdue. Both were heard on schedule for the last time by Jakob (the GIS Base Station) when Tonio complained that he could not hear Jakob and therefore presumed that Jakob could not hear him either. At that time Jakob was of course working with an 80-Watt set, which since then has been exchanged for a more powerful one. This may be the reason for the failure to establish contact.

The W/T agents Castor and Pollux and Achill (when names are given in pairs, the first name is always the W/T operator) were supposed to stay off the air for the first three weeks of their mission. Like them, the W/T agents Foto/Tanto and Mares, who were supposed to stay off the air until 6 January, have not yet come up on the air.

Since in the case of all those named we are dealing with carefully tested agents, who in part have even links of friendship with their trainers, it is at the moment hard to explain why they have not so far established contact. Their W/T training was in every case supervised and assisted by Jakob's testing section, and the W/T sets were supplied by Jakob.

If this is not due to personal or technical failings, the possibilities which may have prevented the establishment of contact may be listed as follows:

1. Chance arrest by the enemy when they jumped or during the period up to their first W/T contact schedule,

---

* Castor and Pollux were in fact the brothers Enzio and Bruno Mei. They were quickly captured by the Allies. Achill was Giovanni De Marinis, who surrendered 5 December. Mares was Pietro Caravano, also arrested. Tanto was Luigi Maggio, arrested later in Sicily along with Foto (Domenico Fontana).

2. Injury when jumping, which made it impossible to conceal the W/T set etc carefully, or made it necessary to destroy it at once,
3. W/T set (or essential parts thereof) smashed on landing,
4. Arrest by the enemy when preparing to establish W/T contact,
5. Identification by the enemy as a result of poor cover or security during the period of their training,
6. Betrayal by elements infiltrated into the training or command staff at this end, or recruitment by the enemy of our own personnel (in this respect, attention is drawn to the not unfounded suspicions of Dr Cora of Kommando 190L).

A number of other chance or unforeseeable possibilities must also be taken into account. Nevertheless in general it seems disturbing that in all these air-drop operations, after careful training and precautions and cover as laid down, success up till now has been lacking. Without at this stage dropping the idea of further air-drop operations, which entail a vast amount of work and expense in their preparation and execution, we should appreciate your views on whether air-drop operations overall have proved cost-effective and on whether it appears advisable, in less promising cases, to devote ourselves to air-drop operations to the degree that has been undertaken hitherto.

It may be noted, however, that a KdM document shortly thereafter shows that W/T agent Mares did in fact establish W/T contact at some subsequent point, for on 19 February he reported from Sicily the presence of two British 'auxiliary aircraft carriers' in the harbour of Augusta, Sicily. Since he had already been arrested by the time Castor and Pollux were interrogated by CSDIC, it is clear, without seeking further confirmation from classified records, that his W/T link was now being brought into use by one of the SCI stations for deception purposes (either with or without his co-operation).

Apart from the various missions into AOT by Achill, Tanto and the others, the KdM document mentioned above also provided the RSHA with a list of 16 W/T operators, some of whom were women ('Funker bzw Funkerinnen'), again with cover names such as Micros, Pepo, Diogenes and Socrates, who had been installed over the period end October/end December in EOT (all but three of them in the last week of November), in San Remo, Bologna, Alassio, Genoa, Cuneo, Turin, Serravalle, Reggio Emilia, Milan, Venice and Como. It cannot be said that the GIS report seems particularly accurate, since a considerable sheaf of agent reports, sourced and dated through late November and December, shows that several of the agents concerned were already reporting information by W/T at dates prior to those on which they were alleged to have become operational.

By and large, except for one or two 'opportunist' reports, and one good sub-source covering Marseilles/Toulon, KdM Munich had little success in providing intelligence about events, military or otherwise, in AOT; on the other hand it did produce considerable information about the Italian Resistance and partisan movements in EOT. Given the number of young men volunteering for these, it would not in fact have been very difficult to infiltrate informants into such organisations.

MARCH 1945

The month of March broke all records for the arrest of enemy agents: no fewer than 91 were taken into custody* as compared with 56, 58 and 42 in the previous three months. Sixty of these were caught in the forward areas, the remainder further to the rear. The sixty were fairly evenly divided between the 5th and 8th Army areas. Approximately 48 of the total were line-crossers, 10 arrived by parachute and 15 – an unusually high figure – landed or attempted to land from the sea. Twelve of those arrested were already in situ on stay-behind missions. Seven out of those arrested were women. In only five cases were the agents provided with W/T communications; all the others were either to re-cross the lines themselves, or to use couriers to carry back their information.

The Abwehr II programme of sabotage was stepped up during March: they had hoped (vainly, as it transpired) to operate on a large scale. More than 28 saboteurs were arrested, all but four of them in the forward 5th and 8th Army areas. Several sabotage agents were dropped by parachute. Six of the ten parachuted agents had been dropped during the month, the balance having arrived at various times during the previous months. Two of the new arrivals landed in the Pesaro-Fano area, the remainder well outside the Army Group zone. Three men were dropped near Lake Bolsena, early in March, in one of the 'Personnel Drop Containers' described in Chapter 11. One of the parachuted saboteurs admitted to having sabotaged a petrol pipeline near Rome on two separate occasions previously.

Of the 15 agents who landed, or attempted to land, from the sea, four, who apparently had combined espionage and sabotage missions, were picked up at sea off Leghorn on 16 March. Three more landed near Cervia (on the east coast between Ravenna and Rimini) on 14 March with a boatload of four other, apparently genuine, refugees.

As recounted in Chapter 6, a big operation was mounted by the KdK on 15/16 March against Ancona, with the aim of sabotaging fuel and stores dumps, and to attack a bridge and an airfield, as well as using one-man

* They included a boy of 13 – the youngest spy so far encountered.

boats to sink shipping inside the harbour. While these raids were in progress, eight agents were to be landed by dinghy near Ancona. While the KdK attack had to be aborted due to thick fog round Ancona, the agents did succeed in getting ashore: their missions included the whole gamut of espionage, sabotage, propaganda and subversion. They were, however, all picked up within a short space of time.

One-third of those arrested were on sabotage or subversion missions, the remaining two-thirds on intelligence-collecting missions. There was a steady demand from the German army commanders for tactical intelligence on the forward areas – a demand which noticeably increased during the second half of the month – prompted by the anticipation of an Allied offensive in the immediate future. Sabotage targets included oil pipelines, vehicles, railways and, for the first time, signal lines.

Other briefs included the spreading of alarmist rumours, the distribution of propaganda leaflets and, in three cases, the organisation of guerrilla bands – all, it must be said, futile operations at this stage of the war. In two cases, agents had been told to ascertain what the reaction of the civilian population would be to an Allied victory. Some 10% of the missions were concerned with political intelligence, and in particular, relations between the different Allies. One agent had been briefed personally by Mussolini.

The US 92 Division, on the extreme west of the front i.e. the coastal sector below Spezia, achieved some sort of record by arresting ten enemy agents during this single month.

The despatching agencies for the 91 agents captured were, as far as they could be identified (agents were not, of course, usually aware of which specific unit they had been recruited by: Allied CI had to work this out from locations of training schools, cover names used by the German staffs etc) 32 agents from FAK 212 and its Trupps, 14 from FAK 150 and FAK 190, and 12 from the SD. In the case of the remaining 33 it had not been possible, by the time the monthly statistics were assembled, to allocate a definite controlling unit.

During the month, the discovery of a Fascist group in Naples provided an interesting variant from the usual stereotyped sabotage and espionage operations run by the GIS. The group grew out of the activities of one agent, who had originally been recruited by the SD in the summer of 1944 as a stay-behind agent in Rome. He and his partner, after the fall of Rome, went south to Naples in order to carry out acts of sabotage and espionage in the port, a task which they found extremely difficult, not least because of the lack of either sabotage materials or a W/T set. One of the two then made his way back successfully to EOT, where he told the SD about their problems, mentioning at the same time that he had been assisted in Naples by the head of an underground Fascist organisation in the town. The SD at once showed interest and told him to return to Naples to develop the organisation into a large-scale movement; they promised that a W/T operator would be sent in to provide the necessary communications link. The agent was then sent back to Naples by parachute, to await the arrival of the W/T operator.

On 6 March the promised agent was dropped in by parachute near Salerno, and immediately surrendered, giving details of his proposed mission. This resulted in the agent in Naples being arrested and, in turn, led to the arrest of the Fascist underground leader, who in the meantime had moved to the naval base at Taranto.

By the end of March 25 people involved had been arrested and a clandestine press seized. Of the 25, six could at once be classified as enemy agents; it was not clear by that stage how many of the remainder were aware of the GIS connections of their movement.

An improvement in security alertness against parachuted agents is well illustrated by the following incident, which as a result of good liaison between a Field Security Section, the Military Police and a nearby Radar Interception Station led to the capture of two enemy agents.

Immediately on receipt of a warning that unidentified enemy aircraft were flying in the area that night, a rough plot of their course was obtained from the radar station, and FS patrols were immediately sent out to comb the area. Shortly before 6am one of these patrols picked up an Italian, who at once came under suspicion for the following reaons:

(a) his appearance resembled one of two agents whose particulars had already been circulated, as those of agents expected to be sent in by parachute in the near future
(b) he claimed he lived in a neighbouring town and had come out to buy eggs
(c) his Identity Card showed him to be a resident of Turin
(d) his pockets contained articles, including a toothbrush, which did not bear out his story that he was a local inhabitant.

After being challenged with this conflicting evidence the man admitted that he had been dropped by parachute, and was on his way to a rendez-vous with his partner. Details of this second member of the team were immediately sent out to all the security units and police in the area. On the following day a Military Policeman, who had memorised the description of the wanted man, recognised him in the street and promptly arrested him.

One of the most unusual security cases during the month was that of a South African POW who had been captured in Tobruk in June 1942. After numerous escapes from POW camps in North Italy he was, on being recaptured after yet another escape, offered the opportunity of crossing into AOT on a short-range espionage mission for the GIS. He accepted, and surrendered immediately to Allied forward troops as soon as he was launched by the Germans. His story sounded so extraordinary that he was subjected to intensive interrogation, but in the end his account was accepted as being true. It could only be presumed that the GIS, who were well aware that he was an escaped POW, had reckoned that his bona fides would be accepted by the Allies and that he would be briefed to return to the GIS and act as a double agent for the Allies – whereas he would in fact be a triple agent for the GIS.

The complications would have been extreme: he was returned to South Africa instead.

In Germany, at this time, the Nazi radio was endeavouring to organise a 'Werewolf' campaign of guerrilla warfare, to be waged by teenage lads against the invading Allied armies. In North Italy 'Radio Repubblicana' also began a similar campaign, under the more prosaic title 'Movement for the Insurrection of Invaded Italy', broadcasting a series of bulletins addressed to sympathisers in Allied Occupied Italy. A typical example, directed in this case towards the inhabitants of Calabria, in the extreme south, ran (in translation) as follows:

Fascists in invaded Italy! Fascists of Calabria! This message is directed to you in particular, you Fascists and men of honour in most Italian Calabria, the homeland of Michele Bianchi, you who have already formed numerous and powerful bands, which seriously trouble the invaders and the traitors who are accomplices. The Lisbon press has already mentioned your deeds. We now tell you: strengthen your ranks and make them ever more solid; assemble the young; wrench the weapons from the hands of Bonomi's henchmen; whenever you meet an isolated enemy soldier, suppress him; whenever an enemy vehicle stops, attack it and set it on fire; capture the driver and the other passengers and, if they are enemies, kill them; set on fire all gasoline dumps; blow up ammunition dumps; react to enemy propaganda by stating that Germany's recovery will not fail to come soon and that it will be terrible. In Germany, the enemy armies will find their cemetery. The enemy commanders themselves state that their losses are very grave. Act as guerrillas by day and by night; be the first to bring about the mother country's insurrection! Italia!

The CI document which circulated this information commented blandly: 'It would be interesting to know just how many gasoline and ammunition dumps these Italian werewolves will be able to find in Calabria . . .'

At the end of March, GSI(b) at 15th Army Group HQ made the following assessment of future GIS intentions:

It is clear that the enemy is still making fairly intensive preparations for a post-occupational organisation in N Italy, which may to some extent be directed from Switzerland. Day-to-day interrogations of agents reveal additional information concerning stay-behind plans that embrace sabotage and subversive operations as well as sabotage.

If the enemy has been considering his position on the Italian front only, which has so far remained stable, he may well have thought it worth while to maintain his espionage and sabotage activities against Allied-occupied Italy on the same scale as hitherto, and to continue plans for a stay-behind network in the north; but he can hardly have failed to take notice of his overall military situation, and to realise that such results as he may hope to achieve in the limited Italian field are not likely to have any very appreciable effect on the outcome of the war, or indeed on the Allies' ability to maintain their control once the war has been won. It is somewhat surprising therefore to find that he is now actually extending his activities in Italy, and is at the same time still making extensive plans throughout South-east Europe. It seems probable that the explanation may lie partly in a real need for tactical information from the Italian front, in order to be able to delay, for however short a time, the day of defeat in the South, partly in the ineptitude and corruption of many members of his intelligence service, who, regardless of military realities, are anxious to justify their existence, and so to live as long as possible in the relative comfort and security which their work assures them.

APRIL 1945

The CI events of April, which without doubt will have been very interesting, would normally have been written up by GSI(b) at 15th Army Group over the first days of May. With the Wehrmacht surrendering on 3 May, however, such mundane work seems, perhaps understandably, to have gone by the board (unless pertinent documents turn up in some remote archive file in the future) since the officers concerned were fully preoccupied, both with plans for the rounding-up of all the GIS officers on their records, and for an impending rapid move to Verona, where it had been decided that 15th AG would establish itself. As a result, no arrest figures for GIS agents have so far come to light. All that can be done is to put on record the fact that the total of enemy agents arrested, from the time of the landings in Sicily in the summer of 1943 until the end of March 1945, will have been in the region of 500. A considerable number more remained to be arrested after the end of hostilities, but these were of course agents arrested inside EOT, in the main, and not those embarking on missions across the lines – although these include those who had been established in post-occupational rôles within EOT before the German surrender.

MAY 1945

Events in May divide readily into two different halves: the rounding-up of known agents, wherever they might be located (in GIS training schools, in their homes, or in their 'stay-behind' locations), and the locating of GIS officials – particularly in order to arrange an urgent intgerrogation of these latter. In both cases there was considerable security attention paid to the prospect of any further (post-surrender) resistance movements or covert activities.

GIS AGENTS

Approximately 210 enemy agents were arrested during the month of May. This figure included those who had been trained as agents by the GIS, but who claimed that the surrender had overtaken them before they had been given any mission; roughly two-thirds fell into this category, while of the remaining third, who had post-occupational missions, virtually all claimed that, in view of the military situation, they had no intention of going ahead with the tasks allotted to them – a claim which Allied CI officers were tolerantly prepared to accept at face value.

While various plans for post-occupational espionage, sabotage and subversive activity came to light during the interrogation of agents, all seem to have been based on the assumption of a German withdrawal, not of a German defeat, and all pre-supposed the continuance of some form of central direction or inspiration, if only from within the confines of a Nazi 'National Redoubt' in the mountain fastnesses of Austria and Southern Germany.

No sabotage of any significance was reported during the month. Three 'stay-behind' groups were of special interest. The first was the 'BALDO' network of post-occupational espionage and sabotage agents in Venezia Giulia; a number of agents from this group were arrested in May. The second had been installed by FAK 211 (the first identification of this unit in the Italian campaign, although the Wehrmacht 'Frontnachweiser' of 15 December 1944 shows that it had been in Verona from at least that date). The network had been set up under the cover of a cosmetics firm called GIBIM PRODOTTI Corporation; from documents recovered, it appeared that the agents of the group were taken on as sales representatives and employees of the firm, and even received letters setting out the terms of their employment and the sales commission to which they would nominally be entitled – an example of unusual GIS thoroughness which had not hitherto accompanied their 'stay-behind' planning. Of a probable 24 persons belonging to the group, 11 were arrested during the month.

The other group was organised by Prince Valerio Borghese of X Flotilla MAS: it consisted of upwards of 70 people. Its purpose seems to have been to help Borghese build himself up as the 'strong man' of N. Italy, with X Flotilla MAS operating as a strictly nationalist organisation, which would endeavour to save the North from total destruction by the Germans, and later perhaps to save Italy from Communism. The group was not briefed for any specific mission, but was to await orders from Borghese in due course. The organisation was penetrated by a Lieutenant Zanessi, who had been sent north on a mission by an Allied agency and was able to give complete details of the group to the Allied security authorities shortly after the German surrender. By the end of the month some 30 members of it had been rounded up, including Prince Borghese himself (who had, incidentally, become Chief of the Fascist Italian Naval General Staff in March 1945).

It is interesting to note that in the 1960s and '70s Borghese came to the fore in Rome as a leading neo-Fascist figure in Italian politics.

GIS OFFICIALS

At the time of the surrender Allied CI authorities were in possession of fairly complete information on the Order of Battle of the GIS units operating in the area under command of the German OBSW; it was possible therefore to proceed rapidly with the round-up and interrogation of key personalities. To assist this, the co-operation of both the SS HQ in Bolzano and of Army Group C was enlisted to locate and collect the heads or representatives of the various GIS departments and units; POWs passing through Allied 'cages' were also screened for suspects, while further investigations and searches were made in the areas not yet occupied at the time of surrender, especially in the Merano-Bolzano region to which so many of the units had previously withdrawn.

The combination of these methods produced good results and by the end of May most of the key officials of the RSHA had been identified and taken into custody; good headway had been made with their interrogation by CSDIC, who were able to extract a good deal of valuable and interesting information. There were still a large number of minor officials unaccounted for, but it seemed probable that many of these were in fact already in custody, but not so far identified, in the now vast POW cages. In all, 291 officials of the RSHA were accounted for during the period. Isolated cases occurred of GIS officials trying to conceal their identity by obtaining false documents and uniforms (particularly in the case of SS members, who abandoned their distinctive emblems and dressed themselves as ordinary Wehrmacht soldiers), but the practice does not seem to have been carried out on a widespread, let alone an organised, basis.

The following is a breakdown of the units to which the arrested officials belonged:

> BdS Italien: 26
> SD Aussenkommandos and Aussenposten: 49
> Führungsstelle and Funkstelle Italien: 88
> (i.e. the GIS HQ and radio base)
> FAK 150 and sub-units: 17
> FAK 190: 19
> Abwehr I(M): 7
> FAK 212 and sub-units: 23
> FAK 309: 12
> SID and RFIS: 5
> MEK 80 and X Flot. MAS NP Battalion: 45

A later G-2 report dated 15 September 1945 states that at that time 1118 enemy agents and suspected agents had been interned.

FASCISTS

Little trouble was caused by Fascist elements. Many hundreds of the more notorious and dangerous were simply eliminated by the Partisans immediately following the German withdrawal and surrender, and the main ambition of the remainder, somewhat understandably, was not to attract attention. Little remained for the Allied security authorities to do in this direction, and candidates for the Allied internment camps were found to be comparatively few.

14
Subversive Post-Occupation Movements

Intensive interrogation of captured GIS and Italian officers and agents, coupled with widespread investigations in N. Italy, failed to reveal any evidence that the RSHA had planned any post-surrender resistance movements or covert networks to carry on resistance. Various plans for post-occupational espionage, sabotage and subversion were indeed drawn up, but all of these were based on the assumption of a German withdrawal, not of a German defeat, and they all presupposed the continuance of some form of central direction from a 'National Redoubt' in the mountains of Austria and S. Germany.

One report, dated 1 January 1945, was received from an Allied agent in N. Italy referring to a circular, dated 1 November 1944, which (it was claimed) had been issued by Hitler to the SS in Italy. It ordered the immediate establishment in every Italian province of a 'Fifth Column' personnel centre, to be composed entirely of 'first-rate German officials' and to be responsible for a number of small groups in its area. These groups, who were to be composed of Italians from outside the Fascist Party or the GNR, with the clergy especially favoured as a suitable choice, were to start work as soon as the Germans had withdrawn from the area, organising sabotage and propaganda and operating an information service. The German garrison commander was to leave behind a list of persons to be liquidated by a bullet in the back of the head. Every centre was to be given sufficient Italian money to last three years. The SS Headquarters in Trieste was also to provide each centre with a 'specially trained female staff' for work of special secrecy, and this staff was to be lodged with 'the best families' in order to facilitate their work. Information was to be passed up to Centre HQs at frequent intervals by personal courier; at least four W/T stations were to be established in each provincial capital, and one in every town of more than 5000 inhabitants.

The Allied CI comment on the above plan ran: 'This ambitious plan . . . is unlikely to prove as formidable in practice as it sounds now in theory' – an assessment which could be rated as the under-statement of the year . . .

At around the same time a somewhat similar report was received from an OSS source: according to this, Pavolini, Secretary of the Fascist Party, had directed that extreme Fascist elements should make preparations for 'banditry and harassing activities' against the Allied forces after the occupation of North Italy. They were to prepare a knapsack and a civilian suit, and when the time came, were to escape to the mountains, from which a revolt would be organised. These Fascists were said to have been divided into units, provided with a cash reserve and six months' advance of pay per man. The HQ of the new organisation was thought likely to be in Monza, near Milan.

Another extremist Fascist 'post-occupational' organisation was mentioned briefly in Chapter VI. The plan provided for the setting up of an underground brigade, to be known as 'Brigata Nera Italia Invasa' in every department in AOT (excluding Sicily and Sardinia). These brigades were to be organised by specially selected personnel drawn by Pavolini from Black Brigades in Northern Italy and sent to the South for the purpose. The target figure for each brigade was to be between twelve and fifteen hundred members. As the Allied armies advanced, brigades already in existence in the territories overrun were to go to ground and become underground Fascist resistance groups. Their organisation, as drawn up on paper, was elaborate and thorough, and included an Elimination (i.e. Assassination) Squad and a Sabotage Squad (the HQ of the latter, located in Florence, was to be staffed by ten men from the Swimmer-Parachutist group of the X Flotilla MAS). Financial arrangements were lavish, with members given ample salaries, family allowances and life insurance of half a million lire.

The following is a CI comment made at the time on the above Black Brigades plan:

It is not known how much progress, if any, has been made in the implementation of this ambitious scheme for the re-establishment of Fascism in AOT. It is obvious that, in its present extravagant form, it stands little chance of success under existing conditions.

THE VEGA BATTALION POST-OCCUPATIONAL NETWORK

During April 1945 five small groups of X Flotilla MAS personnel, to a total strength of not more than 45 men, were sent to Milan, Genoa, Turin, Bologna and Venice to carry out P/O tasks in anticipation of the Allied advance. They were to carry out sabotage and espionage rôles on the direct instructions of Prince Valerio Borghese, Commander of X Flotilla MAS, and were commanded by Naval Lieutenant Mario Rossi.

Rossi had, according to his own account, been feeling for several months a growing reluctance to have any sabotage carried out and to destroy Italian industry in a futile attempt to delay the inevitable Allied advance. He communicated these sentiments to the officers under his command, who declared their agreement with his views. Now that defeat seemed imminent he decided also to spare his men, and at a meeting of all group commanders on 6 April he instructed them to refrain from all acts of sabotage and to establish themselves in their allotted towns as civilians; they were to keep in touch with the central organisation in Milan and to 'obtain the collaboration of that political party which appeared most likely to help them bring about the reconstruction of Italy'.

The despatch of the 'five stay-behind' groups followed shortly after this meeting – four officers and half a dozen ORs to Genoa, two officers and 56 ORs to Bologna, one officer and three ORs to Turin, two officers and seven ORs to Venice, and finally the HQ group for Milan, consisting of five officers (including the Battalion Paymaster) and twelve to fourteen men.

In addition to the above groups Rossi, on his own initiative, sent another group to Genoa, about 20 strong under 2/Lieut Mantini, with the specific mission of contacting the Committee of Liberation (CLN) and helping them to neutralise preparations made by the Germans to blow up the port.

On 17 April Rossi, who had obtained an introduction to the Socialist Party of Milan, approached the latter with an offer to place his stay-behind network at their disposal (presumably for political work). The Genoa group also contacted the local Socialist Party. The arrest of all the main VEGA members, however, brought all these activities to a grinding halt.

15

Trial and Execution

One aspect of counter-intelligence work, which does not immediately spring to mind as such, was the bringing to trial of captured agents and, where appropriate, their execution. This was, in fact, an important deterrent, which was regularly drawn attention to by leaflets, dropped by our aircraft over EOT, warning prospective agents of the fate which awaited them. Much time and effort was devoted to the preparation of cases for trial, and there was a feeling among some security personnel that such work, besides being onerous, was unproductive and should not properly fall within their province. There was no doubt, however, that time spent on trials contributed to a very positive degree to Allied security. Fear of a death sentence was the strongest possible deterrent to people considering whether to accept, or to carry out, espionage missions on behalf of the GIS, and the publication of details of executions was one of the most effective security measures which could be applied.

There were many examples of the actual effect which was created by this publicity. One agent smashed his W/T set as a direct result of reading an Allied leaflet, some gave themselves up, others abandoned their mission once they had reached AOT, and yet others merely walked out on the Germans after their recruitment and before their despatch to AOT.

The relevant paragraph of the Hague Convention (Rule 29) in 'Notes on the Collection of Evidence', is quite specific in its wording: 'A person can only be considered a spy when, acting clandestinely or on false pretences, he obtains or endeavours to obtain information in the zone of operations of a belligerent with the intention of communicating it to a hostile party.' To obtain a conviction the Prosecuting Officer had therefore to prove three separate propositions, the first two of which would not normally be difficult, but the third – that the accused intended to communicate information to a hostile party – usually needed circumstantial evidence concerning the situation in which the person was originally discovered or arrested.

Complete statistics for trials and execution have not been discovered in Allied records, but the following figures will give a fairly accurate picture:

From December 1943 until the end of June 1944 some 200 agents had been arrested. Over 40 had by then been brought to trial, of whom 35 were found guilty. Sixteen had been executed by the end of June.

From July 1944 until January 1945 a similar total of 200 agents had been arrested in the forward, Army-controlled, areas (i.e. excluding arrests in other parts of Italy, of which there were a number). The following is a breakdown of the outcome:

Trials held: 25
Death sentences: 21
Life imprisonment or 20 years: 3
Acquitted: 1
Death sentences commuted: 4
Death sentences awaiting confirmation: 10
Executions carried out: 7

There are also a number of month-by-month statistics available; it seems likely that these include figures for the whole of AOT:

January 1944:	4 death sentences.
March 1944:	10 death sentences, 2 given 20 years.
April 1944:	12 tried, 9 convicted, 6 executed.
June 1944:	5 brought to trial, one death sentence, 4 prison terms.
July 1944:	identical figures to those for June.
August 1944:	11 trials, all leading to convictions. 3 death sentences, 8 given long prison terms.
September 1944:	7 brought to trial, 3 death sentences.
October 1944:	3 death sentences carried out.
November 1944:	Eighth Army area: 3 tried, 3 death sentences, 2 executed. One agent hanged himself in his cell after refusing to talk under interrogation.
December 1944:	7 brought to trial, all convicted. 6 sentenced to death, one to 20 years. Two of the death sentences were imposed on female agents, but had not been confirmed at the time these statistics were compiled. There were 2 executions.
January 1945:	12 agents tried, 11 convicted. There were 9 death sentences and 3 executions.
February 1945:	8 agents brought to trial; 2 were sentenced to death, 4 to prison terms, 2 acquitted. One execution was carried out.
March 1945:	2 death sentences, 4 prison terms, 2 executions.

On the basis of the above monthly figures, therefore, a total of 53 sentences were handed down, although a few of these may have been commuted subsequently. The total does not include the results of any trials which may have taken place in April or May 1945.

16

The Wolf's Lair

The following is an account, made by an Allied liaison officer shortly after the German surrender in May 1945, of a visit he had made to Obergruppenführer Wolff at the Headquarters of the HSSuPF in Italy, in order to discuss administrative details of the surrender of SS and Sicherheitsdienst staffs:

To a generation of staffs brought upon on the severe and aesthetically displeasing austerity of the Table, 6-foot and the Chair, Folding Flat, the interior of the SS Headquarters in Italy is likely to come as a revelation of a staff system not wholly known to the Allied world. The unwary visitor may soften something of the initial shock by a preliminary visit to the relatively modestly-equipped Wehrmacht Headquarters adjoining General Wolff's headquarters. There the functioning electric lift (equals US elevator), the carpeted floors and the other adjuncts of material comfort may surprise him and indeed cause him a degree of wistful envy as he bethinks himself of the Tent 160-pounder or (be he of more senior status) the sparsely-furnished caravan in which he has been wont to pass his days and nights. None the less he will still be ill-equipped to face the degree of sinister opulence which will face him as he enters the portals of the SS headquarters.

The entrance combines the varying splendours of ancient Greek temples and the Paramount cinema. On either side of the massive doorway stands a bayoneted, steel-helmeted German SS guard, a figure which might have stepped out of a pre-war Nazi propaganda leaflet. One always experienced, on entering, the slightly disagreeable feeling that one might never come out alive. The feeling heightens as the visit proceeds. Within, one steps onto a priceless thick carpet and for a moment is blind, before one's eyes adapt themselves to the soft discreet lighting which characterises the whole building. A representative of the office one was visiting was invariably present to greet one in the entrance hall; visitors were not encouraged to wander around alone or even under the supervision of the reception clerk at the fantastically large desk in the hall. One follows the guide and steps off the rich carpet onto a highly polished marble floor, a process which presents the grave risk to the unwary of slipping and offering an undignified spectacle to the silent and unsmiling ranks of the SS standing around. There is little conversation

187

as one proceeds up the thickly-carpeted stairs. There is indeed little conversation anywhere in the corridors. The sensation that the big film is now in process seems to have affected staff and visitor alike. None the less there is much to attract the attention despite the silence of the building. On all sides, coming into and leaving various mysterious doors, are the feminine elements of the SS. None wear uniform; all are well-dressed; all are young; all are beautiful. Some view the Allied visitors with bitter resentful eyes; some with merely frank curiosity; and a few with the pleasant realisation that they still have new worlds to conquer.

The visitor to General Wolff is shown into a room reminiscent of the conference room at Hitler's Brown House. The soft lights are still there. The carpet is as opulent as ever. A cocktail cabinet in the corner is well stocked. In the centre of the rooms stands a small table around which are grouped a number of comfortable armchairs. Ashtrays are provided for all. The general atmosphere is of tasteful opulence; even the picture on the wall has been chosen by a connoisseur of good pictures. The visitor sits facing the light. There is a slightly embarrassed silence. Then a side door opens and SS Obergruppenführer Wolff, Himmler's plenipotentiary in Italy, enters.

The first impression is of a distinguished, rather heavily-built man of about fifty years. The hair is iron-grey, the face ruddy, the manner and pose gracious, as one doing a great favour to the visitor in receiving him. General Wolff sits down on the armchair with its back to the window and the interview begins. He offers you a cigaratte, asks your permission before lighting up himself, and views you through kindly, shrewd and guarded eyes. The interview is throughout a strain, for you have the impression that every word you utter is being noted down and will be carefully studied later for any information or implication it may contain. Wolff himself talks volubly in a soft husky voice. He is a beautiful speaker and the voice of itself has such charm that you may well not hear what he says simply through the suave persuasion of his voice. Your questions are answered smoothly, apparently readily; only occasionally does Wolff betray his own nervousness by running his tongue around his lips or by mopping his brow. The interview is throughout polite; both sides observe the conventions; rarely if ever does the mask drop, but throughout you know that this is a man who is very frightened, who realises that the game is up and who is banking everything on his own personality seeing him through. The interview ends and with short bows on either side the visitor leaves, escorted by an officer of the staff who does not let you out of his sight until your car is safely off the premises.

Not once in the whole visit has there been any indication that this is an operational headquarters. Never once in all his visits is the visitor likely to hear the sounds of a typewriter or see the paraphernalia of a military office. Whoever you visit, whether Wolff or a junior member of his staff, the interview is always held in a comfortably furnished room with its wireless set and cocktail cabinet and its soft lights. Always the soft lights; they probably constitute the most sinister feature of this incredible headquarters, behind whose luxurious trappings and cautious politeness there lurked such an air of sinister evil that it was always with a feeling of relief that one passed out, and the iron gates which block the entrance to the drive closed behind one.

17

German Assessment of their Intelligence Sources

Immediately after the German surrender in Italy in May 1945 an interesting examination was made by CSDIC to assess the efficiency of the German Army's operational intelligence organisation in Italy and to obtain an Ic view of the results achieved. To this end 13 Ic officers of the following formations were questioned* on similar lines, and their statements were collated together under various subject headings:

> HQ Army Group 'C'
> HQ 10 Army
> HQ 14 Army
> HQ 76 Panzer Corps
> HQ 1 Para Corps
> HQ 148 Infantry Division
> HQ 65 Infantry Division
> HQ 26 Panzer Division

Their comments under the various headings often included a wide range of examples to illustrate the points made. In the interests of brevity such examples have been limited to those of more particular interest.

INFORMATION OBTAINED FROM POWS

10 Army comment
The necessity of extracting everything possible from POWs was emphasised by Army HQ early in the campaign. It was possible from POW statements to keep an accurate record of unit organisations, strengths, armaments, personalities, reinforcements and morale. Because the (W/T) intercept unit frequently heard signals from units and installations in the rear that were not known to the German 'I' side, questions about these were latterly included in all POW questionnaires.

---

* It should be mentioned that, as experienced Ic officers, they were only prepared to respond positively to interrogation after they had been specifically authorised to do so by the German Army Group Commander in Italy, General-Oberst von Vietinghoff.

1 Para Corps comment

A measure of the importance of POW statements in the Corps 'I' side in the latter stages of the Italian campaign is given by the fact that, at all times when there was a lack of POWs on any sector of the Corps front, the enemy picture was uncertain and blurred. *British* POWs, when willing to talk, often showed a lack of knowledge of the situation, which detracted greatly from the value of the interrogation. *American* POWs were on the average better informed. All POWs of any importance were interrogated three times at least, at Division, Corps and Army.

CAPTURED DOCUMENTS

As the Italian campaign was for the German armies a protracted fighting retreat, the quantity of Allied documents falling into their hands was very small compared to the quantity of German documents captured by the Allies. Documents formed, nevertheless, the most reliable source of intelligence, a reliability put at 100%.

10 and 14th Army comment

Captured documents were first examined and evaluated at Division, and any important results telephoned to Corps and Army. At Army, documents were re-examined and any important ones translated by the interpreters.

Example: on the Adriatic sector, W/T traffic instructions were captured which gave the complete organisation, down to companies, of 1 Canadian Corps, together with all rear services.

1 Para Corps comment

Thorough and painstaking examination of all captured documents – even of seemingly unimportant ones – yielded information of tactical significance. At times, especially when the campaign took on the character of a war of movement, captured documents brought in information which not only corroborated and completed POW statements, but also betrayed enemy intentions and capabilities. For example, publications of the 'I' staff of 1 British Infantry Division, captured during the Anzio fighting, gave an account of the British appreciation of the German situation in Central Italy at that time, and following from it certain Allied operational intentions.

At the beginning of June 1944, orders and sketches of the 91st US Recce Battalion shed valuable light on the Allied pursuit then advancing west of the Tiber. At the end of July 1944, when a senior NZ officer was captured by the Germans, a valuable marked map was, not due to the fault of this officer, captured with him. This map showed the direction of a forthcoming attack by 1 NZ Division and had a direct effect on the operations which followed. In Autumn 1944 a code-list was captured, the distribution list of which furnished a complete Order of Battle of 6 South African Armoured Division and of certain other units attached to it at the time – including a battalion of the Indian Regiment FFR. This capture removed any possible misconceptions about the arrival of a new Indian division.

66 Infantry Division comment
In March 1945 the body of Brig-General Brown of the 34 US Infantry Division was recovered from a plane shot down over the German lines. Several documents were found on the corpse, including a report on patrols carried out by 34 Infantry Division, and a road map showing routes to the HQ of Corps and neighbouring divisions. These documents confirmed the presence of 34 Division in the line, and the identities of other neighbouring formations.

AGENTS

Intelligence from agents was at all times very unsatisfactory. The information which they could best provide – i.e. tactical and operational reserves, as well as troop movements and the arrival of convoys in the South Italian ports – percolated through to Army Group in a meagre trickle. Reliability: at most 50%.

14 Army comment
The line-crossers sent out by the FAT of 14 Army brought back useful results during the summer and autumn 1944 in respect of areas immediately behind the front line. For example, the impending sending into the line of 92 Infantry Division and of the Brazilian Division was anticipated by agents. After stabilisation of the front in the Appenines, returning line-crossers became fewer in number and finally almost ceased. Reports from agents further afiield often arrived too late to be of use, due to the lack of W/T sets.

1 Para Corps comment
Corps was forbidden to interrogate returning line-crossers; their information insofar as it was of interest, was communicated to Corps HQ by Army HQ. In view of their rarity, agents' reports had little value.

76 Panzer Corps comment
Information from agents was fragmentary, inaccurate and misleading. In Corps's opinion, results in no way justified the work and expenditure involved. Reliability: judged by Corps as not above 20%.

Apart from the identifications of enemy formations, patrol reports produced only tactical information of local interest.

1 Para Corps comment
Corps laid great store by patrol reports, and at least one recce or fighting patrol was as a rule carried out nightly by each company; in consequence Corps usually possessed a complete picture of the forward enemy positions.

The smoke-screens laid down in the Sillaro Valley by troops under US 5th Army during the positional warfare effectively neutralised the German OPs (Artillery Observation Posts) and made necessary the use of deep patrols by 1 Para Corps. These patrols took up a position in the enemy hinterland during the night, observed there for 1-3 days, and then returned to their own lines by night. A thorough interrogation of these deep patrols brought important information on the enemy defensive system, supply routes, immediate reserves etc.

76 Corps comment
Deep patrols, which penetrated the enemy lines to a depth of as much as 15 km, brought much important information of divisional level interest.

OP REPORTS

OP reports were a useful complement of Patrol reports. the comparing and collation of these two sources at divisional and Corps level seldom failed to provide points of interest. Reliability: 80-90%.

1 Para Corps comments
Intelligence OP reports formed a most essential part of information on the enemy, sent through from regiments to Division. They supplied pointers on enemy armament, traffic behind the enemy lines, and even in certain cases recognition of enemy formations. For example, British troops could always be distinguished from US troops by their steel helmets. The relief of parts of US II Corps in the sector west of Monte Grande by the Italian LEGNANO Group before the start of the 1945 Spring offensive first became known by an OP report: the OP had observed the characteristic Alpini hats with their feathers.

It was often possible, with the help of powerful glasses, to observe divisional or formation signs on the arm or helmet. A relief carried out by Indian or coloured troops could often by observed immediately.

Intelligence OP reports as a source of intelligence suffered from two grave drawbacks. The first (of enemy origin) was the successful use of smoke-screens, especially on the Anzio Beach-head, at Cassino and in the

Sillaro Valley south of Bologna. The second drawback was the laziness and lack of interest among the German forward troops themselves, which was only overcome in a small minority of units.

PRESS AND RADIO INDISCRETIONS

Because of the insufficiency of more orthodox sources of intelligence, press releases were occasionally of assistance to the German 'I' side. Reliability: very variable.

10 Army comment
Despatches by Allied War Correspondents (often intercepted by the German Intercept Service before they appeared in the Allied press) often contained useful material on the Allied Order of Battle, losses, morale and appreciations of German intentions which indicated Allied intentions.

Examples: 1. Press release that HM George VI had lunch at the HQ of 1 Canadian Corps after visiting the Cassino battlefield. The German 'I' side deduced from this that the Corps was resting in the Cassino area; 2. From the despatch of an American woman correspondent, who visited a US division in reserve near Florence, the location of divisions under US II Corps was clarified.

14 Army added the following
The Allied press gave information mostly of only historical interest, because papers arrived at Army too rarely for their indiscretions to be of operational interest. Intercepted War Correspondents' despatches were of greater value.

Examples: 1. Announcement in the press of the arrival of a Negro Division in Italy to join 5 US ARMY; 2. War Correspondents' despatches about a visit by General Mark Clark to this Negro Division, from which its prospective commitment on the Arno front could be deduced; 3. Press release on the composition, strength and history of one of the regiments (370?) of 92 Infantry Division; 4. Announcement of the commitment of a Jewish Brigade on the Italian front; 5. Arrival of the Brazilian Expeditionary Force in Naples, announced in the press and on the radio.

1 Para Corps added the following
A critical reading of 'Union Jack', 'Stars and Stripes' (British and US army newspapers in the Mediterranean theatre), and '8th Army News' was useful for filling in the enemy picture. With these papers, however, as well as with the radio station 'Stimme der Achten Armee', it was chiefly a question of piecing together mosaics of news, which provided next to nothing of operational interest.

194

The intercepted despatches of War Correspondents could sometimes be exploited operationally. Many ventured to forecast German intentions and in doing so nearly always gave a precious indication of Allied intentions in the sector concerned. The discussions by correspondents in January and February 1945 as to whether the Germans would withdraw across the River Po before the start of the Allied offensive were read very carefully by the German 'I' side. The impression was gained that a German withdrawal before the opening of the Allied attack would be highly unpalatable to 15th Army Group (the decision of the German High Command had, however, already neutralised all the efforts of the German 'I' side to influence a decision to withdraw). An intensive reading of 'The Times' newspaper, which was available to the Corps Ic until summer 1944, gave useful indications of the probable lay-out of Allied forces in the Spring offensive at Cassino. These indications were obtained from the very detailed War Correspondent despatches about the Cassino fighting during the second part of March 1944, which not only described the fighting, but also indulged in discussions of mistakes – and lessons to be drawn from them – which seemed to the Germans officially inspired.

76 Panzer Corps gave the following example
Move of 4 Indian Division from Italy to Greece publicised in the Press.

65 Infantry Division added the following
A solicitude for national susceptibilities on the part of the Allied press department was of assistance to the German 'I' side, because it was frequently stated soon after operations whether a certain height or village had been taken by Polish (or Brazilian or NZ or Indian) troops.

PROPORTIONATE VALUE OF DIFFERENT SOURCES OF INTELLIGENCE

The following estimates by Army and Corps of the proportion of intelligence supplied by the different sources to the known enemy picture are only approximate:

	Before the Senio offensive (9.4.45)	*After start of offensive*
10 Army		
POW statements	60%	20%
W/T intercept	25%	65%
Air Reconnaissance	10%	15%
Agents	5%	0%

	Before the Senio offensive (9.4.45)	After start of offensive
14 Army		
POW statements	50%	0%
W/T intercept	30%	50%
Agents	10%	5%
Press Indiscretions	10%	5%
76 Panzer Corps		
POW statements	50%	impossible
W/T intercept	35%	to
Ground Observations	15%	estimate

INTELLIGENCE AWARENESS OF GERMAN TROOPS

The Ic officers interrogated gave varying, and partly contradictory, accounts of the extent to which German front-line troops were conscious of the importance of collecting intelligence. A selection of their statements follows. It will be seen that the lower the formation, the greater the candour.

(a) The German troops were in the main 'I' conscious and were particularly good at bringing in for examination captured documents, arms and ammunition, badges, uniforms and sometimes enemy corpses complete with uniform and arms. Ic at Army HQ fostered their enthusiasm by prizes and grants of leave. (SOURCE: 10 ARMY)

(b) By and large the forward troops gave valuable help, especially in passing agents through the lines and routing them back when they returned. Prizes were frequently given to encourage forward troops, e.g. for the indentification of the unit of 20 tanks knocked out on the Cinquale. (SOURCE: 14 ARMY)

(c) Forward troops had little understanding for 'I' matters and less enthusiasm in giving the 'I' side assistance. Chief reason: the celebrated 'Starrheit' (inflexibility) of the German soldier. The Ic was not in a position to make his needs felt among the forward troops unless he was backed by the GOC himself. It was always at the best of times a formidable task to get detailed information on enemy activities. The correct handling of POWs and captured documents was a matter requiring constant instruction (given by the Ia). As a rule, captured weapons and pieces of equipment were only sent back when prizes had been offered for them. (SOURCE: 1PARA CORPS)

196

(d) Attempts to instruct the front line soldier in collaboration with the 'I' side were in the main weary and fruitless. In spite of constant instruction to the contrary, troops kept all items of enemy equipment that they could carry and failed to send the rest back. (SOURCE: 76 PANZER CORPS)

(e) The ordinary German soldiers were not 'I'-conscious. In addition, their security was bad. The Italian civilian population often knew of impending German reliefs before the neighbouring German HQs. The troops only cooperated in cases where it was obviously to their own advantage (warning of bombing attacks, indications of a coming enemy attack). (SOURCE: 26 PANZER DIVISION)

(f) Few soldiers had any ideas of the meaning or purpose of the 'I' side. It was unpopular because it frequently had to ask questions, the answering of which required extra work. In addition, the 'I' side was associated in the minds of German soldiers with Security, and in consequence a subject to be avoided. (SOURCE: 148 INFANTRY DIVISION.

(g) The German soldier was as little 'I'-conscious as the German High Command. Both were equally glad when they could steer clear of anything that smelled of 'I'. (SOURCE: 65 INFANTRY DIVISION)

18
CSDIC Assessment of German Intelligence Results

Following the Ic interrogations described in the previous chapter, CSDIC carried out an assessment of the German knowledge of Allied formations and troop movements. Their overall assessment ran as follows:

After taking into consideration the comparative inadequacy of the 'I' framework in the German Army and the ever-increasing denial to it of valuable sources of information, it must be admitted that the enemy's overall 'I' picture was at most periods fairly accurate. Serious gaps in the enemy's knowledge certainly existed, and it seems clear that he consistently overestimated Allied strength in Italy; this led, however, to less operational inefficiency than might have been expected.

Examples listed below of temporary uncertainties regarding troop movements and re-groupings can chiefly be attributed to the eventual almost total absence of air reconnaissance and the gross unreliability of the German espionage organisation.

The enemy's greatest single weakness was probably a failure to gauge accurately the strength of the units opposing him. This was mainly due to insufficient information on the state of reinforcements. The enemy tolerated a looseness and inaccuracy which inevitably prejudiced objective appreciation.

Whenever doubt existed as to the strength of a formation, the German 'I' side assumed on principle that it was up to strength. Of all the Ic's interrogated, only the Ic of 1 Para Corps seems to have made a positive attempt, on the basis of POW statements, captured documents and other sources, to present his Ia with a comparative factual estimate of the forces opposing the Corps. He states that whereas in the case of American formations it could safely be assumed that strengths would be kept up to establishment and that losses after major attacks would be replaced fairly promptly, the same could not be assumed for British formations. After many actions British units remained weak for a considerable period. When in March 1944 on the Anzio Beachhead 5 British Infantry Division dissolved the 4th company in its battalions, this was regarded by the Corps 'I' staff as a symptom of this weakness in reinforcements, and the subsequent amalgamation in other divisions of the HQ Company and 'S' Company was regarded with interest in this context.

Attempts were latterly made to accumulate more precise details on Allied methods of reinforcement, with POW statements offering the best material, but an accurate picture of the size and capacity of IRTDS etc was never possible due to the lack of other reliable sources, chiefly air recce.

The useful results of the deep patrols carried out winter 1944-45 in the Bologna area gave in the main information of local significance only. The last occasion in the Italian campaign when an almost complete picture of reserves and rest-areas, as well as ammunition and other dumps, was available was in the first three months of the Anzio Beachhead, when a comparison of POW statements and air photos yielded excellent results as far as strengths and reinforcements were concerned.

For reinforcements and material arriving by sea the German 'I' side had to depend almost entirely on the misleading and occasionally mendacious reports of agents, the single exception again being provided by the Anzio Beachhead, when a thorough daily recording of observed ship movements and port activities gave a clear picture of the arrival and departure of troops and material. Only towards the end of the Beachhead (May 1944) did the picture become blurred, and the real strength of the Allied forces for the break-out battle was not clearly assessed.

Since the Summer of 1944 the only really reliable source of intelligence on troop movements was W/T interception of traffic control wireless networks. OP Reports provided supplementary information. POW statements needed confirmation.

19

Conclusions

The Wehrmacht's urgent need for tactical intelligence, coupled with suitable terrain and a readily available pool of indigenous recruits for agent operations, and the simplicity of installing 'stay-behind' agents as the Germans retreated slowly up the length of Italy, all made the scale of the GIS's agent-running efforts in the Italian theatre hardly surprising. Such efforts were, of course, even larger on the Russian front; but there, such operations seem to have been predominately of the Ic type, using Russian POWs in uniform, and local inhabitants opposed to the Communist regime, in short-term, short-range missions. Moreover the vast size of the Russian front, with inevitable 'wide open spaces' through which agents could infiltrate, or into which they could be dropped by parachute without much risk of being discovered, simplified such operations; also, the acute shortage of accommodation, with towns and villages destroyed either by the fighting or by earlier 'scorched earth' policies, will have made the installation of 'stay-behind' agents with W/T sets a far more hazardous and difficult task. For all these reasons the Italian theatre represents a fairly unique, and highly active, intelligence battleground.

In any objective assessment of the results achieved by GIS operations in Italy, such results, when weighed against the manpower employed and the effort put in to the recruitment, training and despatch of agents, seem to come down heavily on the debit side. To be sure, such activities tied down a not inconsiderable number of counter-intelligence and security personnel on the Allied side; but the Germans were shorter of skilled manpower than the Allies and could less afford the investment. Certainly there were cases of GIS agents surviving two or even three trips into AOT: but it is difficult to find a record of even a single GIS agent who produced significant intelligence reports, over and above low-level 'tidbits' about divisional identities and movements. The very fact that, as related earlier, General Wolff boasted after the end of hostilities that he had had seven W/T agents reporting successfully from AOT, when in reality every one of these was working for the Allies and sending deception material, proves the point sufficiently.

The reasons for this overall lack of success could be analysed as follows:

(a) The unreliability of Italian agents working for the Germans. Few could be described as having a fervent belief in the Axis cause, or a passionate determination to carry through their mission whatever the odds. In many cases they were quick to surrender or to confess.

(b) Poor security by the GIS, in that groups of agents trained together were often in a position to betray, when caught, sufficient details to identify their fellow-trainees when these appeared in AOT. Poor operational security added to the problem – failure to provide water-tight cover stories backed up by appropriate documents, the issue of standardised equipment which, once identified from the arrest of one agent, provided 'signposts' betraying subsequent agents from the same organisation.

(c) Effective collaboration with the Allies by anti-German Italian intelli-gence officers and by resistance personnel in EOT, which provided an intelligence input on German intelligence premises, staffs etc.

(d) An increasingly efficient Allied CI organisation, especially in the con-tribution made by skilled interrogators.

(e) The preoccupation of a large sector of the German security and intelli-gence forces with the battle against the Italian partisan and resistance movements – a problem which hardly had any counterpart inside AOT.

(f) Probably some useful input on CI matters from Enigma material.

It is hard to escape the conclusion that, human nature being what it is, some GIS officers, especially in the later months, aimed at quantity rather than quality in their agents, in order to prove to their superiors how active they were being, and how numerous their agents, in order to avoid the ever-present threat of being 'combed out' and sent to fight on the Russian front.

On the sabotage side, which occupied a considerable percentage of GIS work, results were no better. All the damage done to the Allied war effort in Italy amounts to not much more than one minor railway bridge and a few vehicles blown up by members of X Flotilla MAS, a petrol pipeline or two put out of action for a few hours, and possibly a few telephone lines cut. If we exclude the X Flotilla MAS operations (carried out under the aegis of, or jointly with, the GIS) the launching of a total of over 200 sabotage agents seems to have produced no end-product of any significance what-ever. Yet there were plenty of targets available, especially in the shape of easily-damaged aircraft, often located close to the coast and thus accessible from the sea. Moreover, the destruction of aircraft, which were causing tremendous damage to German lines of communication and to front-line troops, would have provided a really positive contribution to the fighting. In the case of the X Flotilla MAS attack at Bellaria, for example, just four RAF lorries were destroyed; yet a hundred yards or so further inland, across deserted sand-dunes, four squadrons of Spitfire fighter-bombers were strung out over a wide area, virtually there for the taking with a little skill and daring. On the south-east coast of Corsica a very similar situation prevailed; a deserted, almost uninhabited coastline with, a couple of hundred yards inland, some dozen squadrons of Mitchell B-25 bombers of US 57 Bomb Wing, which day after day had been cutting the bridges of the River Po with great precision, causing the German supply services enormous problems. When one considers what British Commandos were able to achieve at St Nazaire and elsewhere, often in the face of huge odds, or the damage done to hundreds of targets in France by SOE and the Maquis, something was clearly lacking on the Axis side. Yet, as the Brandenburg Regiment and the X Flotilla MAS showed, there was no lack of courage and daring available among the Axis forces; what was so often missing, however, was the detailed intelligence necessary for the planning of coup-de-main and sabotage operations.

On the whole, it may be said that the collection of intelligence by the German fighting formations (including such aspects as POW interrogations and W/T intercept work) was generally effective; the main weakness lay in coverage of the Allied hinterland – ports, airfields, dumps, base camps, shipping etc – which could only be covered effectively by agents or by air reconnaissance. In both these fields they failed badly.

Given that the whole raison d'etre of the Abwehr and SD operations against the Allies was to assist the Wehrmacht, by intelligence and sabotage, in winning its battles, it is amply clear from the evidence in Chapter XVIII, that German Ic staffs had only a poor opinion of the results, summed up in the words of the Ic of 76 Panzer Corps: 'Results in no way justified the work and expenditure involved'.

An epitaph with which Allied Counter-Intelligence staffs would fully concur, certainly in respect of the military aspects of the Abwehr and SD operations. In fairness, some exception may be made in the case of air and, particularly, shipping intelligence coverage by agents of Abwehr I(M) and, to a lesser degree, of Kommando 190(L), whose operations were somewhat better organised and survived somewhat longer than the general run; it was their bad luck, however, that the German Navy and, more especially, the Luftwaffe, were by the final months of the campaign simply in no position to mount attacks on targets indicated by these agents, so that the acquisition of intelligence in such fields served, in reality, little purpose. The ultimate tragedy lay in the fact that a considerable number of young Italians sacrificed their lives to carry out missions which, in the last analysis, would contribute little of any positive value to the cause they were supporting.

OBSW Report of 3 Feb 1944

The following is a translation of the text of a German report dated 3 February 1944, from Wehrmacht Front HQ in Italy:

Questioned about the work of our own intelligence on the Nettuno [i.e. Anzio] landings, Oberbefehlshaber Südwest replied: 'We had no intelligence before or after the landings. The Abwehr had sent some Trupps into action in Southern Italy at the beginning of June [i.e. 1943] but no usable link was working by January 1944. OB Südwest had, in addition, ordered two agents with a W/T to be sent in to the Naples area shortly before the landings, and communication with them had been established. But they were not able to give any report about the landings themselves.

The employment of line-crossing agents is limited by and large to the front line areas, to a depth of some 30 kilometers behind the Front. A greater depth of mission is impossible for reasons of time and distance, since otherwise the intelligence arrives too late into our hands for it to be evaluated.

Air Reconnaissance: in the days preceding the landings this was very patchy. There was no reconnaissance of Naples since 11 December because of lack of aircraft and the strength of the defences.

Mussolini's Letter to the German Ambassador

The following is the translation of a letter from Mussolini to the German Ambassador to the Republican Government:

Dear Ambassador,

I have the duty to call your attention to a number of incidents which have occurred recently and which because of their special seriousness stand out from the complex of annoyances of a general character.

You will be aware that in many provinces of the Po Valley requisitions have assumed an all-embracing character, ranging from the peasants' livestock to each and every means of transport *without exception*, to sewing machines, typewriters, the furniture of houses, household linen, clocks etc. A large part of what is requisitioned is not paid for. Among the mass of reports the most serious is the following, which I am copying for you from a report by the Head of Bologna Province, dated 5 August. It runs:

> 'In the Commune of Goggio Montano the German troops have pro-ceeded to requisition all the cattle and have committed other abuses. A German warrant-officer, commanding the local garrison, is said to have detained the Prefectorial Commissioner without any justified reason, releasing him only after an undertaking by the latter that he would send his own wife to the warrant-officer, and is reported to have seized from the Commune a number of 14-16 year old girls. As you can well understand, the matter has caused great alarm among the local families, and has been reported to the local German headquarters.'

I do not know what steps have been taken by this headquarters, because I have no information on this, but I would hope that, if this unheard-of action by the warrant-officer is found to be true, he will receive the most severe punishment.

Also, indiscriminate reprisals on the mass of the populace do not obtain the desired effect. From a report by the Italian authorities in Vicenza it appears that the Communes of Crespadoro, S. Pietro and various hamlets of the Commune of Atlissimo have been almost completely destroyed, and numerous inhabitants of these communes have been killed.

These very severe reprisals have left a deep impression, especially in the valleys of Chiampo and Agno, and have badly shaken the feelings of sympathy of the population towards the Germans.

A report dated 11 August from the Fascist authorities of the Province of

Pesaro describes the situation in the following terms:

'1. The province, while not yet being occupied by the enemy, has fallen into chaos and the people lack any guidance, help and those elements essential to life.

2. The food situation, due to the total lack of such essential commodities and to the absence of grain threshing in many areas, is tragic. The health situation threatens to become equally tragic due to the lack of medicines.

   Requisitions have stripped the population of every single means of transport, from handcarts to bicycles and cars, of every kind of livestock, food resources and in some cases even of houses and furniture.

3. In many localities the German troops have carried out reprisals against the rebels (e.g. the partisans T.N.), reprisals which have been solely to the detriment of the local population and what is more make no discrimination between Fascist, anti-Fascist or uncommitted elements. It sometimes happens that families are affected by these reprisals which have members fighting alongside the Germans in the Republican forces. I quote the following examples:

   (a) Near Urbania, during a German reprisal operation, the father of National Republican Guard sergeant-major Monceri was shot – a man whose two brothers and two sisters had been shot a few days earlier by the rebels.

   (b) The family of militiaman Gabrielli Leopoldo, composed of seven people, at Tavolicci (Casteldelci Commune) was completely wiped out by the Germans in the course of reprisals.

   (c) The said hamlet of Tavolicci was completely destroyed by the German SS, who killed more than 70 people: women and children were burned with their homes, while the men were killed by shooting. From a reliable source we hear that the reprisals were due to the initiative of a German SS warrant-officer on the grounds that at some previous period rebel elements are supposed to have found asylum in the hamlet.

   d) The hamlet of Fonte Corniale (Commune of Monte Felcino) was burned by the Germans and the mother of Comrade Guido Marcucci was burned to death; he is a medical officer of the GNR and a relative of Comrade Giuseppe Lombrassa, Under-Secretary of State for Corporations and a member of the PFR.

Such incidents have created a state of mind which it is easy to imagine, and they contribute only to dig an abyss between the Italian people and the German armed forces, the more so because reprisals of this kind do not solve the problem of the rebels, who simply move off and continue their activities elsewhere, while the local populace pay, unjustly, for help given under duress and not voluntarily, due to the total absence of local forces of public order.'

Also the reprisals in Milan on 10 August, due to the way in which they were carried out, had a diametrically opposite result. An official report states that 'the execution took place in Piazzale Loreto in a feverish manner and without any of the proper formalities. The 15 individuals were set down by lorry at the corner of Piazzale Loreto and invited to line up, face to the wall, along a house under construction. It appears that the unfortunate men did not known they had been condemned to be shot and since they were in working overalls thought that they were being sent to work in Germany. When they realised that their last hour was come there were scenes of desperation and they tried to flee in all directions. The execution platoon, taken by surprise, began firing bursts of machine-gun fire which at once killed almost all of them, but with mortal wounds in various parts of their bodies. Thus some of the corpses looked horrifying. One of these unhappy men managed to escape, although badly wounded, and got up to the first floor of a house, but when he reached the landing he fell dead in a pool of blood and was dumped on the pile of the others.

At 8am SS General Tensfled [a misprint for Tensfeld, *T.N.*] living at Monza, (who had ordered the execution) was telephoned for permission to remove the bodies, but this was refused, so that only at 6pm it was possible to carry them to the mortuary. During the whole morning a large crowd was halted in front of the pile of corpses and there were many scenes of horror and fainting, especially on the part of the women.

The execution, and the circumstances in which it took place, have aroused in the whole population a highly unpleasant impression with reflexes of increased hostility towards the Germans, in spite of there being unanimous execration towards the cowardly attackers who massacred passers-by as in the Viale Abruzzi. Among the working classes excitement persisted and was manifest yesterday with temporary strikes in some industrial establishments. Last night leaflets from the so-called 'Committee of National Liberation for Upper Italy' were distributed in the streets of the city. I enclose an example.

And now allow me, dear Ambassador, to draw your attention to what is happening in Reiner's kingdom. The work of separation [i.e. of the Italian provinces along the Austrian border, *T.N.*] is going on systematically.

Here is the final proof, in the field of the administration of justice.

Recently the director of the Justice Department, Messiner, who has always been prominent in his desire to cut every link between the Government of the Republic and the Justice authorities of Venezia Giulia, has issued two decrees which confirm this direction.

In the first it is so laid down that all disciplinary proceedings against magistrates, Registrars and Justice officials that according to the judicial regulations should come under the Ministry of Justice, become the responsibility of the Supreme Commissioner and, thus of the Head of the Justice Department; in the second it is decreed that all correspondence between the Justice authorities of the Littoral and the Ministry of Justice must first be passed to the said Head for him to see. Conversely, he is to be at once informed by the Justice authorities of any orders or decrees coming from the Ministry.

Insurmountable difficulties are made to the very rare requests for some magistrate to be transferred out of the Littoral zone.

All this is now known in every corner of Italy, both north and south of the Appennines, and gives enormous support to Alexander's propaganda.

Did you know, dear Ambassador, that the Cappelli bookshop in Bolzano has been forbidden to sell Italian books? I have a report in front of me from which I am copying the following excerpt:

'The strange situation in the three frontier provinces lends itself to propaganda unfavourable to Germany, as has been shown during the transit of the Italian divisions returning from Germany and anxious for news of Italy. They have had a very bad impression on learning that Bolzano and Trento are no longer part of the Italian Social Republic, that here they are not allowed to wave the Italian flag, nor may portraits of the Duce be shown: that in short the three provinces are in practice cut off from the remainder of Italy.'

And all this is happening while the Bonomi Government [i.e. in AOT, T.N.] is obtaining the administrative autonomy of other provinces, including Rome – the Rome which we abandoned much too quickly in October 1943, a colosal mistake for which we are now suffering the consequences.

From all the facts which I have given you in this letter it follows that an end must be made to indiscriminate requisitioning, which has reduced entire provinces to misery, to make an end of indiscriminate reprisals and give a new direction to the policies of the two High Commissioners Hoffer and Reiner. In short, one must give to the 22 million Italians of the Po Valley the feeling that a Republic and a Government exist, and that the said Government is considered an ally and that its territory is not 'war

207

booty' twelve months after the official recognition of the said Government by the Reich.

Not the smallest satisfaction should be given to those who consider us, as your allies, to be traitors!

Please accept, my dear Ambassador, the expression of my warm friendship and highest consideration,

Signed

HQ 17 August 1944   Mussolini

P.S. Just before I sealed this letter a further document has reached me from Piacenza:

'All the German troops in Bettola and Ponte dell'Olio acted as though in conquered territory. Radios, bicycles, mattresses were carted out of houses, and the menfolk, who had been summoned to report to the German Command Post, were carried off to the Concentration Camp at Bobbiano di Parma. This operation provoked immediate panic in the whole province and I imagine it was the result of a mistake, because the men went voluntarily to the German Command Post, and they were certainly not rebels, but peaceful elements. If they had been rebels they certainly would not have complied with the summons from the Command Post. Operations carried out in this way will not only not allow us to wipe out rebellion, but we shall obtain three results:

1. Hatred of the German armed forces on the part of the populace.
2. Increase in the ranks of the rebels by many people who prefer to take to the mountains for fear of being seized and carried off to Germany.
3. Desertions by workers and employees from workplaces and offices in Piacanza. Many workmen evacuate the town in the evening and go to sleep in nearby villages. Republican Fascists have been taken to the concentration camp in Parma, as for example the brother of the Fascist Repetti, killed by the rebels, doctors, commune officials etc. Some Republican Fascists and some GNR militia-men have had their homes sacked while their sons are fighting in the Italian SS or the Republican National Guard.

It is necessary, therefore, that this system be changed, because in this way we shall not succeed in destroying the plague of rebellion, but make new clients for rebellion, and lose the sympathy of those who have remained faithful to us.'

HQ 15th Army Group
Interrogation of Suspected Enemy Agents

Part I – Characteristics of Suspects Encountered in ITALY

1.   All persons arriving from EOT and all suspects, regardless of their innocent appearance or background, are possible agents until evidence to the contrary is obtained during interrogation. Therefore, since all enemy agents are necessarily liars because they are concealing their true identity or purpose, the first process in the screening of refugees and suspects for the purpose of detecting the enemy agent and then securing his confession is to select the liars from the non-liars.

2.   The liars are many and their reasons for lying various; generally speaking, however, they fall into the following categories:

(a) The deserter from the Republican Fascist Army.

(b) The deserter from the Royal Italian Army.

(c) The Black Market operator.

(d) The criminal or escaped criminal.

(e) The camp follower who seeks sympathy by falsely relating that he has but recently escaped from the Germans.

(f) The enemy agent.

3.   Though it may be a comparatively simple matter to arrive at the conclusion that a suspect is lying, it is not so simple to decide into which category he falls. Experience has shown, however, that the stories told by suspects in each category tend to contain certain recognisable features. These are summarised below:

(a) *The deserter from the Republican Fascist Army*

   (i)   Does not have to conceal the fact that he has crossed the lines; can account in detail for his journey through EOT to the front.

   (ii) Explains away a long period of time by claiming employment by an organisation of which he cannot remember the manager, co-employees, policy, restrictions, etc.

   (iii) Claims to have returned from imprisonment or forced labour in countries other than ITALY since 8 Sep 43.

(iv)   Claims residence in towns in which units of the Republican Army are known to have been or to be in training or rest or to have Headquarters.

(v)   Carries remnants of uniform or equipment.

This individual usually lies because he desires his freedom, but knows that he may be made a prisoner of war if his true identity is known; perhaps, also, he thinks that a worse fate than being classified as a prisoner of war awaits him if the truth is known. Assurance that the worst he could get is to be classified as a PW, or that not all who have served with the Republican forces are necessarily made PW, or that he can still be useful to ITALY by being incorporated in the Italian forces fighting with the Allies, will usually bring out the truth. This individual's all-consuming desire is usually to go to his family.

(b) *The deserter from the Royal Italian Army*

(i)   May claim to have crossed the lines, but cannot substantiate his story. May not even know where the front lines are.

(ii)   Claims to have been repatriated from outside ITALY to Allied Occupied ITALY after the Armistice.

(iii)   Claims employment or residence in localities where units of the Royal Italian Army are known to be in training or to have HQs.

(iv)   Claims residence in towns recently liberated.

(v)   Carries remnants of uniform or equipment.

This individual has usually served a lengthy period with the Italian forces and is disgusted with the treatment he is receiving or merely desires to divorce himself from the Army and return to civilian life. He will continue to lie as long as possible because, if the truth is known, he fears court-martial or at least a return to his unit.

(c) *The Black Market operator*

(i)   Usually does not claim to have crossed the lines, but, if he does, can account in detail for his journey in EOT to the front.

(ii)   Has recently left his home in AOT, but cannot give sufficient reason for leaving it. His home is usually a large city.

(iii)   Is in possession of large sums of money, much of which is in Allied military currency.

(iv)   Carries price lists or notes with figures on them.

This type of individual usually knows that he has violated AMG regulations and that he is therefore subject to prosecution and a jail sentence. He is invariably bull-headed even though his identity is obvious.

(d) *The criminal or escaped criminal*

(i) Usually does not claim to have crossed the lines, but claims that he was in a town other than his town of residence when it was overrun by the Allies.

(ii) Claims long residence in a town in which a penitentiary is located, e.g. VOLTERRA.

(iii) Claims to have changed his residence from his home town many years ago, but cannot given an adequate reason.

(iv) Claims persecution by the Fascists.

(v) Professes disregard of what is to happen to him and lacks fear of internment.

(vi) Lacks identity documents.

This type of individual has in many instances been released by the Germans, Fascists or Partisans before the expiration of his term and realises that to disclose the truth may lead to his re-incarceration for the unexpired portion of his term.

(e) *The camp follower*

(i) No evidence that he has crossed the front lines and, if he claims to have done so, cannot minutely describe his journey in EOT.

(ii) Carries remnants of Allied military uniform or equipment or pictures and names of Allied soldiers.

(iii) Reacts to American slang.

(iv) Speaks Italian in the infinitive or occasionally uses an English word.

(v) Usually resides in AOT.

(vi) Is usually between the ages of 15 and 25.

(vii) Casually asks to be employed with some type of Allied military unit.

This type is usually an adventurer who has come up from Southern ITALY and on occasions will give a story of having come from EOT because he believes that this will attract sympathy. The story is usually exceedingly weak and easy to break.

(f) *The enemy agent*

(i) Evidence on his person or in his story definitely proving that he was recently in EOT.

211

(ii)   Does not minutely account for his journey in EOT to the front; relates that he has travelled in successive stages in vehicles to the front, but inconsistencies exist in his description of the load, driver, type of vehicle, halts, etc.

(iii)   Residence is in EOT.

(iv)   Residence is now in AOT, but he cannot give sufficient reason for being away from it.

4.   It should be noted that the enemy agent's story may contain any or all of the features listed above under other categories. However, of all the individuals who cross from EOT into AOT, *it is only the enemy agent who need lie about the manner in which he reached the front lines. It is only the enemy agent who is usually brought from the point of despatch to the front in a German vehicle or under German escort, and it is, therefore, only the enemy agent who must manufacture a cover story for this part of his narrative.*

5.   If the interrogator is certain that the suspect was in EOT and recently crossed into AOT, and if the story relating the manner in which he came to the front lines is full of inconsistencies, then he can be regarded as a probable enemy agent. The suspect in his cover story may relate a trip which takes him close to enemy spy centres, suggesting that he was despatched from such a centre; his bearing, education, money, clothing, military history, etc, may further reveal causes for suspicion and place him as one being sent from a particular spy centre; BUT, should a lie be detected in his account of the final stage of his journey to the front, then that lie brands him as an enemy agent.

6.   Consequently, a standard procedure can be followed in interrogating all such suspects. The interrogation should briefly cover subject's past schooling and military life and at least the naming of all cities in which he has been since the Armistice. The chronological account should bring the subject from the date of the Armistice on 8 Sep 43 to the date of the interrogation: however briefly the earlier stages are covered, the five or six days prior to his crossing the front lines should be covered in *minute detail, hour by hour,* including descriptions of people, houses, food eaten, etc. If subject is an enemy agent and has been brought to the front lines by the Germans, it will be virtually impossible for him to recount a convincing story for these days.

'A Day in the Life of a Field Security Officer'

Towards the end of 1943, Field Security Sections in Southern Italy were invited to submit to their Headquarters, for training purposes, a paper under the title 'A Day in the Life of a Field Security Officer'. Several of the resulting documents adopted a humorous approach to the subject which, while underplaying the serious nature of most of their work, gave a by no means exaggerated sample of the sort of emotional and confused situations with which the FSS could be (and usually were) faced whenever a fresh town or village was occupied by the Allied forces – situations for which their formal training had scarcely prepared them. The following is the text of one such paper:

0800 hours:
Breakfast: disturbed by Russian priest who wishes merely to kiss the 'noble' captain on the cheek and bless him for having liberated his aunt, mother, sister, uncle, etc. Priest finally induced to be content with kissing Company Sergeant-Major.

0810 hours:
Voluble gentleman insists on seeing FSO privately. FSO listens to voluble gentleman for five minutes but can make neither head nor tail of trend of conversation. Interpreter summoned: voluble gentleman requires a new glass eye.

0830 hours:
Irate woman arrives demanding immediate release of her gaoled husband. Husband shut up by section two days previously for 'anti-Allied sentiments'. Irate woman begins to scream and hurl oaths, but is suddenly quietened by –

0845 hours:
Pleasant woman who arrives with 50 eggs as a thank-offering to the FSO for having shut up her husband two days previously for 'anti-Allied sentiments'.

0900 hours:
Position in office serious. Pleasant woman denounces irate woman as her husband's mistress.

0905 hours:
Position saved by arrival of Capitano X of the Carabinieri to see FSO. Both women disappear.

0906 hours:
FSO and Capitano X shake hands and click heels.

0915 hours:
FSO and Capitano X still shaking hands and clicking heels.

0920 hours:
Capitano X departs. FSO has not the slightest idea why the Captain came. The Captain promises however to come every day at the same time, presumably to shake hands and click heels.

0930 hours to 1030 hours:
FSO visited by local 'Bread Commission'. Members denounce half the inhabitants of Italy. Members pleased the FSO Captain has come to restore the Bread situation and lock up half Italy (disturbing noise growing in volume in the waiting-room). Members beg permission to assemble twice a week in Captain's office to present their complaints. Meeting interrupted by request for FSO to handle delicate situation in waiting-room. Apparently FSO has locked up the German maid of her Royal Highness Princess Y. Her Royal Highness has appeared in person, stating that she will die within two hours if maid is not released, as maid is the only person who can deal with her cancer of the breast. Her Royal Highness threatens to prove she has cancer of the breast. Immediate decision made to release maid: Her Royal Highness passes out on chair.

1030 hours:
Complete bedlam reigns: 'Bread Commission' still sitting. Office now contains roughly forty people.

1030 hours:
FSO retires to visit his Formation HQ. Arrives there to find he is wanted urgently by Area HQ. Arrives at Area HQ to find matter is no longer urgent, but Sub-area must see FSO immediately. Arrives at Sub-area to find matter is so urgent that an officer has gone round to contact FSO at his office. FSO returns to office and meets officer.

1130-1145 hours:
Officer and FSO discuss vital problems.

214

1145-1215 hours:
FSO spends his time shaking hands and clicking heels with various important Italian personages who call presumably for the pleasure of shaking hands and clicking heels with FSO.

1215 hours:
Office now filled to capacity. Section dealing with situation magnificently. People requiring aeroplanes to take them to their sick relatives in Sicily being dealt with appropriately. Ditto, people requiring news of their sons on the Russian front, release of their lovers shut up in gaol, bombs to hurl at Fascist meetings. CSM having difficulty with woman who is convinced we can compel her daughter's lover to make the impending child legitimate.

1230 hours:
Arrival of best informer – a priest.

1230-1300 hours:
FSO listens to priest whisper in his ear confessions of the day previous.

1300-1400 hours:
Office filled with odd people eating odd meals in various corners. Census of people reveals 25 genuine refugees being fed by us; 6 mysterious hush-hush personages who were to report at 1200 hours for interview by 'Z' Force from Formation HQ (this is their sixth day of reporting); a grave-digger who has brought his own lunch; a prostitute whom some unit mistook for a spy; Her Royal Highness Princess Y being attended by her German maid, now released; and the Bread Commission, who have now produced some bread.

1400-1500 hours:
FSO calls on various high Italian personages with intention of shaking hands and clicking heels. Intention not fulfilled: FSO had forgotten the existence of the 'Siesta'.

1500 hours:
FSO visited by two veiled women, sent to him by Port Security Section. Women sent back to Port Security Officer, as it appears their request for permisison to hunt means permission to fish.

1505 hours:
Office invaded by two large Levantines, who declare they have seen a spy. If we can provide two men, they will lead us to the spy. Two men provided.

1507 hours:
Two more men despatched as temporary guard for a woman who alleges she has been threatened with murder by a person unknown.

1510 hours:
Return of two veiled women, bearing note from Port Security Officer, stating these women wish to hunt, NOT fish.

1515 hours:
Two veiled women sent back to Port Security Officer with note saying that these women wish to fish, NOT hunt.

1530-1600 hours:
Several alarming telephone calls, which, summed up, demand that six men should be sent to XX immediately as Germans are being sheltered in a house, another six men should be despatched to raid a shop where a W/T set is to be found, three men required forthwith as bodyguard to a suspect Russian who claims to have swum the Adriatic to join the Allies, and two men to be sent round to the Carabinieri to collect eggs which are being presented to the Captain. Action taken: two men sent to the Carabinieri.

1600 hours:
Return of two veiled women bearing note from Port Security Officer, stating he thinks the two females want to hunt seagulls in a fishing-boat. If FSO gives permission to shoot, he will give permission to 'boat'.

1603 hours:
Return of two large Levantines with two NCOs. Spy in question turned out to be one of the Port Security NCOs who was shadowing the two Levantines for reasons unknown.

1603-1630 hours:
Spent in explaining to the two large Levantines that we do NOT pay our informers.

1630 hours:
Departure of 'Bread Commission'.

1631 hours:
Two veiled women despatched to Port Security Office with permission to shoot.

1632 hours:
Deputation of photographers arrives, wishing to know why they have been compelled to close their shops.

1640 hours:
Deputation of hotel managers, wishing to know why their hotels have been requisitioned.

1642 hours:
Call from HQ, asking for the FSO to present himself immediately.

1643 hours:
Call from Area HQ, asking for the FSO to present himself immediately.

1644 hours:
Call from Sub-area HQ asking for FSO to present himself immediately.

1645 hours:
Call from Political Liaison Officer to say he is sending round under guard two suspicious females – veiled – who seem to require permission to hunt . . .

1650-1730 hours:
FSO attempts the impossible in trying to present himself at HQ, Area HQ and Sub-area HQ all at the same time. HQ Area and Sub-area somewhat displeased with FSO, who has apparently no realisation of the value of time.

1745 hours:
FSO returns to office. In office a meeting is being held to discuss fate of a pigeon, brought in by some Italian. Should bird be killed forthwith and eaten for dinner, or should enquiries be made as to where it had come from and was going to. Decision arrived at: enquiries to be made.

1746-1800 hours:
Confusion while efforts are made to catch pigeon, which has taken flight.

1806 hours:
Telephone call from Signals: have we a pigeon? If so, they require same immediately. Two men despatched to collect an informer's canary cage in which to put pigeon. Arrival of two veiled women who require permission to hunt. Arrival of several staff officers from Formation HQ: can the FSO fix up a party for them for the night?

217

1810 hours:
Arrival of Italian, breathless and collarless, stating that some drunken British sailors had removed his collar and tie: would we take immediate action.

1815 hours:
Two veiled women who wish to hunt despatched to Port Security Officer.

1820 hours:
Arrival of Italian Bishop who wishes to denounce somebody. Unfortunately, because of the position he holds, Bishop refuses to give names of those he denounces. Conversation therefore drifts into religious matters and it is gathered Italian Bishop has no hesitation in denouncing the Pope.

1900 hours:
Office closed. Preparations made for the Section's Saturday evening dance.

The writer of the above article followed it with an unsolicited, but equally comic, description of the dance that followed; as it verges at times on the indelicate it has not been reproduced here, but interested readers can find it in the Public Record Office, File WO 204/824/A.

Dulag Luft Interrogation Methods

While it is not the purpose of this book to study the question of POW interrogation in detail, the subject is of such importance to the obtaining of tactical intelligence that it is worth drawing on an Allied report towards the end of the war, compiled by G-2 Plans Branch of HQ 12 Army Group. This investigated the history of Dulag Luft in order to assess both its effectiveness and any security lessons that might be learned in respect of the briefing and training of air crew.

Great efforts were made at the Dulag to induce Allied air force prisoners to go beyond the 'name, ranks and number' formula; the main technique was to produce a form labelled 'Red Cross Form' (and bearing the Geneva Red Cross) which the prisoner was persuaded to believe was required by the Swiss in order to let his family know that he was safe and a POW. The crux of the form was that, besides name, rank and number, it called for details of the prisoner's home address and for his date of birth. Great pressure was brought to get this completed, the prisoner being told that these details were valid demands under the Geneva Convention.

Air crew were normally, on arrival, put in solitary confinement, in very cramped and unpleasant cells, for 2-3 days in order to 'soften them up'; they were given no facilities to wash or shave, and their cells were totally empty of anything except a bunk. As the Report criticised, such treatment violated the spirit of the Geneva Convention, even if it did not violate any specific paragraphs in it.

In addition, German interrogators had one especially strong card to play; one which was not available to Allied interrogators: the innate fear of every prisoner that he might be handed over to the GESTAPO if he behaved too stubbornly. This fear was exploited brazenly, particularly in the case of air crew who were not (as was all too often the case) dressed in regulation RAF uniform, with badges of rank etc. (heavy pullovers, sheepskin flying jackets etc. were almost standard wear, especially for bomber crews exposed to long hours in bitterly cold aircraft); they were told that 'Germany is full of spies and saboteurs: you could be one. You will have to *prove* you are genuine air crew, or we have to hand you over to the GESTAPO, and you will be executed'. The 'proof' required was of course details ('which we can check against our records') of his unit – the name of his squadron commander, of the station CO, the home base airfield, what time he took off and so on. In fact, the Dulag Luft staff never handed any POW over to the GESTAPO. In the latter part of the war the SS insisted on providing staff of their own at the Dulag, in the form of GESTAPO and Sicherheitsdienst officers, but they were poor interrogators and were cold-shouldered by the German military staff.

The Allied assessment of the Dulag Luft interrogation machine was that:

(a) There was a lack of any orderly format for the completed interrogation report. This left many loose ends, which were never co-ordinated or followed up.

(b) The material obtained by interrogation was relatively complete in so far as it covered operations and tactics; anything else, for example technical and scientific developments, radar etc. was very poorly covered – in fact 'lamentable' was the word used.

(c) Three senior figures at the Dulag only spoke English with difficulty and were of only average intelligence, and certainly not enough to control an organisation which was supposed to 'get round' some 2000 Allied POW a month.

Nevertheless, certainly until the time of the Normandy landings, the organisational talent of the Germans, together with a fairly noticeable indifference towards the spirit of the Geneva Convention was sufficient to 'mould' countless Allied air crew into 'collaboration' in their own interrogations.

SS Ranks, with their British-Army Equivalents

Oberstgruppenführer	=	General
Obergruppenführer	=	General
Gruppenführer	=	Major-General
Brigadeführer	=	Brigadier
Standartenführer	=	Colonel
Obersturmbannführer	=	Lieut-Colonel
Sturmbannführer	=	Major
Hauptsturmführer	=	Captain
Obersturmführer	=	Lieutenant
Untersturmführer	=	Second Lieutenant
Hauptscharführer	=	Sergeant-Major
Scharführer	=	Sergeant

Sources

Documentary evidence is available for virtually all the facts given in this book. In a few cases where this is not so, the material is based on personal recollections by British officers working in Italy at the time (including myself); in most cases their evidence is confirmed by the recollections of at least one other colleague.

The following are the references of the principal documents used in research for the book:

Public Record Office
WO 204/831, 836 and 822: These files cover 15th Army Group Monthly Security Summaries and periodic 'Notes on CI in Italy', all of which provided the main bulk of the material used.

WO 204/943 and 907: material on 'S' Force

WO 218/71: 30 Commando

WO 204/964: Enemy Intelligence Services in Italy

WO 204/6763: a mixed file containing a number of documents on CI interrogation procedures and security organisation, plus in particular a paper dated 16 July 44 entitled 'Enemy Intelligence Services and Activities'

WO 204/821: CI and Security 1944-45

WO 204/833: Security Intelligence Reports

WO 204/837: Allied Security and enemy Intelligence Memo 15/6/44

WO 208/4212: Meldekopf Zeno and CSDIC interrogation of Karl Stange (AST Munich)

WO 208/2947: Abwehr History and organisation

WO 204/7287: Partisan missions

WO 204/6754: Interview with SS General Wolff

WO 208/9534 and 4212: CSDIC interrogation reports

WO 203/1012: CSDIC organisation

HQ Intelligence Centre, Ashford
Documents from Army HQ, New Zealand Military Forces, Wellington, dated 22/6/42, on history and organisation of CSDIC

CSDIC/SIM/Zi 188 dated 8/11/44: Interrogation of Capitano Stroppa

CSDIC/IAI/AB 126: Reorganisation of X Flotilla MAS

Naval Staff Duties (Foreign Documents Section) MOD
FDS 65/54: German Small Battle Units Operations
TSD/FDS/325/50: KdK, Brandeburg Regt etc

Bundesarchiv, Koblenz

Band 22 Bestand R 58: RSHA
R 58/471: Vorbereitung von Sabotagemassnahmen gegen Anzio
R 58/413: Lage in Frankreich: Meldungen von Agenten des Meldekopf Zeno
R 58/109: Einsatz von Agenten in Italian-Einzelfälle

US National Archives, Washington
File 918554-Part 9, Handbook 15/3/44: The German and Italian Intelligence Services (detailed organisation and history)
NND 851510: CSDIC Interrogation of Ugo MEI (CSDIC/CMF/Z 134)
NND 851531: Detailed Interrogation Report on Thirteen German Intelligence Officers (CSDIC CMF/M 296)
NND 851513: CSDIC Interrogations of Herbert Kappler, Wilhelm Harster and Otto Helfferich (CSDIC/CMF/9)

List of Illustrations

Glossary

AAI: Allied Armies in Italy.

Abteilung: German designation for a subordinate department.

Abwehr: The Intelligence organisation of the Wehrmacht; less specifically, it means 'defensive security'.

Abwehrkommando: unit of the Abwehr operating in support of an Army in the field; later renamed Frontaufklärungskommando (FAK).

A-Force: A small specialised Allied unit providing deception material for Axis agents who had been 'turned'.

ALST: Abwehrleitstelle. A senior station of the Abwehr abroad, controlling several ASTs (qv).

AMG: Allied Military Government.

Amt: Functional department of the Sicherheitsdienst (Amt I, Amt II etc).

AOT: Allied Occupied Territory; that part of Italy already occupied by the Allied armies, i.e. all territory south of the front line.

AST: Abwehrstelle, an Abwehr out-station

Aufklärung: Reconnaissance (including by agents – regarded by the Allies as no different from espionage).

AUST: Aussenstelle, the second smallest Abwehr sub-station.

Bataillon: German and French spelling of 'battalion'.

Baulehrkompanie zbV 800: Construction and Training Companies 800, originally recruited for Special Duties in the planned attacks on France and the Low Countries.

BdS: Befehlshaber der Sicherheitspolizei, the senior officer under the HSSuPF (qv) controlling GESTAPO and SD operations in occupied countries.

Brandenburg Regiment: essentially an offshoot of the Abwehr; a constantly changing force, somewhat akin to the British Commandos and SOE.

Brigate Nere: Black Brigades, colloquial name for the Corpo delle Camicie Nere (Blackshirts) – see CCNN.

Carabanieri: Italian National Police, in fact part of the Army.

CCNN: Camicie Nere; Blackshirts, Mussolini's principal political/security organisation, roughly equivalent to the Nazi SS. The full title was Corpo delle Camici Nere (CCNN – doubling the initials is an Italian convention indicating that a word is in the plural).

C/E: Counter Espionage.

CFC: Centuria del Fascio Crociato, founded in October/November 1943 as a central reservoir of agents for the GIS (qv).

CI: Counter-Intelligence.

CIC: Counter-Intelligence Corps, the security organisation of the US Army.

CMF: Central Mediterranean Forces, the Allied overall regional command.

CNL (CLN Italian): Committee of National Liberation, the controlling body of the various Italian resistance organisations.

CS: Control-Spionaggio – Italian Counter-Intelligence.

CSDIC: Combined Services Detailed Interrogation Centre.

DELTA: Defensive Intelligence, the most important branch of SID (qv).

D/F: Direction-finding – location of a radio transmitter by taking a series of compass bearings of its transmisions.

DIA: Division Infanterie Algérienne, part of the FEC (qv).

DUKWs: US-manufactured amphibious trucks.

DULAG-LUFT: Luftwaffe Interrogation Centre, based near Frankfurt.

Einsatzkommando: mobile operational unit of the Sicherheitspolizei (SPO).

EOT: Enemy-Occupied Territory – that part of Italy north of the front line.

FAK: Frontaufklärungskommando, originally Abwehrkommando (qv) renamed after the RSHA (qv) took over the Abwehr from Admiral Canaris.

FATs: Frontaufklärungstrupps, see p.47.

FEC: French Expeditionary Corps – the Free French Army, based on French Army units originally stationed in N. Africa.

Frontläufer: German term for Line-crosser (qv).

FSS: Field Security Section, British Army units providing security and counter-intelligence service; its members normally belonged to the Intelligence Corps.

Gamma men: a frogman unit of the X Flotilla MAS (qv).

G-2: US Army staff branch dealing with security and CI matters.

GESTAPO: Geheime Staatspolizei, German Secret State Police, part of the Sicherheitspolizei.

GFP: Geheime Feldpolizei – the security section of the Wehrmacht.

GIS: German Intelligence Services – both Abwehr and Sicherheitsdienst.

GNE: Guardia Nazionale Repubblicana, the Fascist Police Force.

GSI(a): British Army staff branch dealing with straight military intelligence.

GSI(b): British Army staff branch dealing with counter-intelligence and security.

HSSuPF: Höherer SS und Polizeiführer: regional commander of all German security forces and SS.

Ia: Operations Officer in a German Army command.

IAI: Italian Army in Italy – on the Allied side.

Ic: Intelligence and security element of German formation staffs.

ICU: Intelligence Collecting Unit, an ad hoc specialist force formed to exploit the Intelligence and CI potential of newly-captured cities; also called 'S' Force.

IdO: Inspekteur der Orpo – German police commander under the HSSuPF (qv).

IdS: Inspekteur der Sipo und des SD, senior German police commander in home territory, under the HSSuPF (qv).

IRTDS: Infantry Replacement and Training Depôts.

KAPPA: department of SID that installed W/T equipment to enable Mussolini to keep in direct contact with SID HQ.

KdK: Kommando der Kleinkampfverbände, the Small Boat Assault Unit of the German Navy.

KdM: Kommando des Meldegebiets, an SD area command HQ, replacing the Abwehr AST (qv).

KdS: Kommandeur der SIPO und des SO, regional commander of the German security apparatus under the BdS (qv).

KG: Kampfgeschwader, Luftwaffe combat wing.

KO: Kriegsorganisation – Abwehr station in a neutral country, usually under diplomatic cover.

Koch Outfit: a squad of 67 people, formed by Pietro Koch in Rome, specialising in tracking down and torturing anti-Fascists and Allied Agents.

Kriegsmarine: the German Navy.

KRIPO: Kriminalpolizei, German Criminal Police, part of the Sicherheitspolizei.

LCS: London Controlling Station.

Line-crosser: an agent sent on foot through the front line into enemy territory.

MAS: See X Flotilla MAS.

MEA: Marine-Einsatz Abteilung – Special Operations Section of the German Naval Staff.

MGIR: Movimento dei Giovani Italiani Repubblicani – see p.64.

MEK: Marine-Einsatzkommando, German Small Boat Assault Unit.

MK: Meldckopf, the smallest Abwehr sub-station.

NEST: Nebenstelle, an Abwehr subordinate outstation.

OBSW: Oberbefehlshaber Südwest: Supreme Commander of all German Forces in the region.

OKH: Oberkommando des Heeres: the German Army General Staff.

OKW: Oberkommando der Wehrmacht: the German High Command controlling all three services.

OMEGA: department of SID supposed to run offensive intelligence operations abroad.

ORPO: Ordungspolizei: the normal 'law and order' police in Germany.

ORs: 'other ranks' ('enlisted men' in the US Army).

OSS: Office of Strategic Services: the US secret intelligence and special operations organisation.

OVRA: Opera Vigilanza per Repressione Anti-Fascismo, Mussolini's secret political police.

PAG: Personen-Abwurf-Gerat – Personnel Dropping Equipment. See p.154.

POW: Prisoner of War.

P/O: Post-occupational. See 'Stay-Behind'.

RASCL: Rear Army Security Control Line: a line defining the rear boundary of the area under the direct control, in respect of security measures, of the Allied armies.

Referat: Subordinate section of a German Abteilung or Amt (qv).

RFSS: Reichsführer SS = Heinrich Himmler.

RIP: Refugee Interrogation Point.

Razzia: an aggressive police or army sweep to round up Jews, suspects etc for forced labour in Germany. 'Ratissage' in France.

RSHA: Reichsicherheitshauptamt – the Central HQ, under Kaltenbrunner, controlling GESTAPO, Kripo and SD, and finally the Abwehr after the fall of Canaris.

RUDI Group: special Italian Naval sections employed in anti-Partisan operations under command of Abwehr Kdo 212.

SA: Sturmabteilung, the original Nazi 'Brownshirts'.

Sachgebeit: area of duties in Ic, part of a German Army command. See p.50.

S/B: 'Stay Behind': agents installed to operate in towns about to be captured by the Allies, in order to send back intelligence in due course – usually by radio.

SCHUPO: Schutzpolizei – the ordinary German policeman on the beat.

SCI: Special Counter-Intelligence – specialist Allied CI units.

SD: Sicherheitsdienst – the Nazi Party's intelligence and counter-espionage service.

S Force: see ICU.

SIA: Air Intelligence organisation within the SID (qv).

SID: Servizio Informazion Difesa – the Italian Intelligence Service, run by the Armed Forces.

SID/CS: the half of SID that joined the Allies after the Italian armistice.

SIGMA: the Internal Political Intelligence department of SID from March 1944.

SILO: Security Liaison Office – a branch of CSDIC (qv) specialising on Yugoslavia and the Balkans.

SIM: Servizio Informazione Militare – the Italian Military Intelligence Branch.

SIM/CS: Italian CI units on the side of the Allies.

SIPO: Sicherheitspolizei: the Nazi Security Police.

SIS: Naval Intelligence organisation within the SID (qv).

SKL/S: section of the German Naval War Staff in control of the Small Battle Units Command (KdK).

Sonderführer: 'Specialist', an honorary rank given to civilians working in GIS units.

SOE: Special Operations Executive, the British sabotage organisation operating in German-occupied countries.

UPI: Uffizio Politico Informativo: secret intelligence branch of the Fascist Republican Party.

VEGA: a battalion of swimmer-demolition troops – a special Italian formation linked with GIS operations; part of X Flotilla MAS (qv).

VI/S: sabotage unit commanded by Otto Skorzeny.

V-Mann: Vertrauensmann – the standard GIS term for an agent or informant.

VO: Verbindungsoffizier: Liaison Officer.

Wehrmacht: the German Armed Forces as a whole – Army, Navy and Air Force.

W/T set: standard contemporary British Army terminology for a radio transmitter.

X Flotilla MAS: crack Italian naval unit comparable to the Special Boat Section of the Royal Marines; see p.67 et seq.

Y Service: Branch of the British Intelligence Service responsible for intercepting enemy tactical radio signals.

Z Officer: officer in the administrative section of the Abwehr (Abteilung Z) – usually a civilian (Sonderführer).

ZETA: postal censorship department of SID (qv).

Index

231